DATE DUE

JA 3 1 '01		
SE 3 0 '05		
OC 21 '05		

The United States
and
Post-Cold War Interventions

GUIDES TO CONTEMPORARY ISSUES

Richard Dean Burns, Editor

This series is devoted to exploring contemporary social, political, economic, diplomatic and military issues. Each volume contains an extended narrative that introduces opinions and interpretations relating to the issue under discussion and concludes with a bibliographical survey of essential writings on the topic.

THE UNITED STATES AND POST-COLD WAR INTERVENTIONS

Bush and Clinton in Somalia, Haiti and Bosnia, 1992-1998

Lester H. Brune

Regina Books
Claremont, California

10 9 8 7 6 5 4 3 2 1

Library of Congress Cataloging-in-Publication Data

Brune, Lester H.
    The United States and post-cold war interventions : Bush and Clinton in Somalia, Haiti, and Bosnia, 1992-1998 / Lester H. Brune.
      p.   cm. — (Guides to contemporary issues ; #11)
    Includes bibliographical references and indexc.
    ISBN 0941690-86-5 (cloth : alk. Paper). – ISBN 0-941690-90-3 (pbk. : alk. paper)
      1.United States—Foreign relations—1989-1993. 2. United States--Foreign relations—1993- 3. United States—Foreign relations-Somalia. 4. Intervention (International law) 5. Somalia—Foreign relations—United States. 6. United States—Foreign relations—Haiti. 7. Haiti—Foreign relations—United States. 8. United States—Foreign relations—Bosnia. 9. Bosnia—Foreign relations—United States. I. Title. II. Series
E881.B77 1999
327.73—dc21   98-52432
                                               CIP

Regina Books

Post Office Box 280
Claremont, California 91711
Tele (909) 624-8466 / Fax (909) 626-1345

Manufactured in the United States of America.

CONTENTS

SELECTED CHRONOLOGY

SOMALIA, HAITI & BOSNIA

1990

21 Jan.	Yugoslav League of Communists dissolves
3 July	Republic of Slovenia declares its Sovereignty
1 Oct.	Referendum in Croatia Republic approves Autonomy
16 Dec.	Haiti elects Aristide as President

1991

16 Jan.	Somalian President Barre exiled; civil war begins
7 Feb.	Haiti's Aristide inaugurated after Duvalerist coup fails
25 June	Slovenia and Croatia Declare Independence; Serb-Croat War begins; first "ethnic cleansings"
8 Sept.	Macedonia proclaims independence
25 Sept.	UNSC embargoes military arms to Yugoslavia
30 Sept.	Raoul Cedras' Junta overthrow Aristide in Haiti
27 Nov.	Cease-fire by Croatia, Serbia and Yugoslavia
16 Dec.	European Union recognizes independence of Slovenia and Croatia

1992

2 Jan.	Vance plans for an effective cease-fire for Croatia, Serbia; Carrington's peace plan fails
1 Feb.	President Bush for forcible return of Haiti's refugees
21 Feb.	UNSC approves UN protective force for Yugoslavia
1 Mar.	Election favors Bosnian independence; Serbs boycott
18 Mar.	Haiti's parliament rejects plan for Aristide's return
4 April	1,200 UNPROFOR to Croatia; Serbs bombard Sarajevo
7 April	U.S. and European Union accept Bosnian independence
30 April	UNSC approves mission for Somalia (UNSOM I)
8 June	UNSC has UNPROFOR protect Sarajevo airport
14 Sept.	UNPROFOR to protect all Bosnian humanitarian aid
9 Oct.	UNSC decrees "no-fly" zones over Bosnia
3 Dec.	UNSC has U.S.-led force protect aid for Somalia
11 Dec.	UNSC Preventive Force for Macedonia includes U.S.
12 Dec.	U.S. Marines begin UNITAF mission in Somalia

1993

2 Jan.	Vance-Owen plan to divide Bosnia into 10 provinces
14 Jan.	Clinton adopts Bush's policy to repatriate Haiti's refugees
28 Feb.	U.S. begins air-drop of supplies to besieged Bosnians
27 Mar.	Somalia militants agree to transitional government
3 April	Bosnian Serbs reject Vance-Owen plan
16 April	UNSC makes Srebrenica a "safe-haven" zone; six more "safe-havens" named May 6
1 May	Clinton's "lift and strike" policy aborted
5 May	In Somalia, UNOSOM II replaces U.S.-led UNITAF
25 May	UNSC establishes Yugoslav War Crimes Tribunal
7 June	UNOSOM II begins hunt for Aideed
16 June	UNSC Levies oil, arms, banking sanctions on Haiti
3 July	Aristide and Haiti Junta sign Governor's Island Pact
26 Aug.	U.S. sends 400 Rangers/Delta Forces to Somalia
3 Oct.	12 American killed in Mogadishu; Clinton explains plan to exit Somalia by 3/31/94
12 Oct.	Haiti's militants prevent landing of U.S.-Canada non-combat forces; Aristide is not restored
12 Dec.	Somalian humanitarian aid talks fail

1994

28 Feb.	First NATO aircraft down 4 Serb planes in "no-fly" zone
1 Mar.	Bosnian Muslims & Bosnian Croats accept Washington pact to unite
10 April	NATO air strike when Serbs violate "safe haven" zone;
8 May	Clinton permits asylum interviews for Haiti refugees
10 June	Clinton broadens UN embargo on Haiti
31 July	UNSC approves U.S.-led invasion of Haiti, if needed
4 Aug.	Bosnian Serbs reject contact group peace plan; Milosevic cuts Yugoslav aid to Bosnian Serbs
15 Sept.	After Clinton ultimatum to Haiti; Carter Negotiates Cedras' exile, Aristide's return for Oct. 15
4 Nov.	UNSC to withdraw Somalian troops by 3/31/95

1995

1 May	Croatia attacks Croatian Serbs in Slavonia
24 May	After NATO air strikes, Serbs kidnap UN troops as "human shields" to protect armaments

27 May	French President Chirac for redeploying UN troops
11 July	Bosnian Serbs capture Srebrenic; massacre Muslims
4 Aug.	Croatia begins major offensive against Croat Serbs
8 Aug.	Clinton takes lead in Bosnia, sends Anthony Lake to EU talks; Richard Holbrooke to Balkans
5 Sept.	NATO's intensive air strikes on Bosnian Serbs until Sept. 21 when peace process accepted
26 Sept.	Bosnian factions accept single state with two entities: Serb Republic and Croat-Muslim Federation
12 Oct.	Cease-Fire in Bosnia
21 Nov.	Dayton Peace Accords by three Balkan presidents; Bosnian Serb leaders accept on Nov. 23
13 Dec.	U.S. Congress barely approves U.S. troops to Bosnia
14 Dec.	Formal signing of Dayton Accords in Paris
17 Dec.	Haitians elect Rene Preval as president
20 Dec.	NATO forces arrive in Bosnia

1996

27 Feb.	UNSC suspends sanctions on Bosnian Serbs who complied with demands of NATO forces
1 Mar.	Siege of Sarajevo ends, most Serbs leave city
3 April	U.S. Commerce Secretary Ron Brown; 34 others die in plane crash; publicizes slow Bosnian civilian rebuilding program
14 June	Balkan leaders sign arms control agreement
12 Aug.	Somalia's Hussein Mohammad Aideed replaces his father
14 Sept.	Bosnia national election begins process for new government of Bosnia-Herzegovinia
20 Dec.	NATO extends Bosnian Mission for eighteen months

1997

3 Jan.	New "Two-entity" Bosnian Parliament meets for first time
11 Jan.	Bosian Croats and Muslims merge their armed forces.
4 Feb.	Protests since November persuade Milsoevic to permit the opposition coalition's elected mayor of Belgrade, Zoran Djindjic, to take office.
16 June	Tudjman reelected Pesident of Croatian Republic
14 Sept.	Municipal elections in Bosnia confirm ethnic divisions

23 Nov.	Bosnian Serb elections enable moderates to take power in Parliament.
27 Nov.	UN withdraws the last of its forces from Haiti whose economic problems remain serious.
18 Dec.	President Clinton announces the U.S. and NATO's S-FOR will remain in Bosnia indefinitly after June 1998.

1998

17 Jan.	As radicals protest, moderate majority in Bosnian Serb Parliament elects Milorad Dodik as Prime Minister.
2 Feb.	Leaders from Somalia's factions meet in Cairo to begin a reconciliation process; it soon fails.
5 Mar.	U.S. reimposes sanctions on Yugoslavia after Milosevic sends his army to destroy Albanian rebels in Kosovo
31 Mar.	UNSC imposes arms embargo on Yugoslavia, seeking Milosevic's concessions on the Kosovo conflict.
15 Sept.	Bosnian Serb elections keep moderates as parliamentary majority but radical Nikola Poplasen replaces moderate Plavsic as president.
13 Oct.	Under threat of NATO air attacks, Milosevic agrees to withdraw most Serb forces from Kosovo, to permit international monitors to enter, and to negotiate peace terms with Albanians.

PREFACE

During sixty years of the twentieth century, Americans endured a struggle, sometimes "hot" and other times "cold", against the totalitarian forces of nazi-fascism and communism before the collapse of the Soviet Union. Although in 1990, some Americans joined Francis Fukayama in celebrating the "end of history" with liberal democracy's victory, world events quickly disclosed a new set of uncertainties that needed to be confronted in the Post-Cold War era. Americans discovered that these new domestic and foreign problems were more difficult to solve because, in part, the Cold War's political consensus had disappeared.

The Post-Cold War era raised new questions about the United States' domestic and foreign policies. How could the national debt of over five trillion dollars be cut back or eliminated? Could the national defense budget be cut? If so, by how much? Could the U.S. dispose of its international political responsibilities and simple focus on global free trade as it did in the 1920s? Should the U.S. be the world's policeman who stops or prevents distant conflicts in small countries that do not directly threaten the security of the United States? Should the U.S. assume a moral obligation to respond to the humanitarian needs of desperate peoples?

The present study examines three Post-Cold War episodes in which the U.S. responded, if hesitantly, to internal crises with military intervention and assistance—Somalia, Haiti, and Bosnia. It describes the problems that precipitated the local crisis; the initial U.S. failure to respond; why and how the U.S. eventually intervened; and the results of each intervention. The three cases represent a fascinating diversity of interventions because each of the three involved more differences than similarities.

There was, however, one overarching Post-Cold War political and economic issue which related to each of the three interventions. This issue is the contrast between the Post-Cold War era's growing global interdependence in economics and communications while at the same time that political debates in the United States and Europe sought the return of political power to local communities. This was evident not only in Somalia, Haiti, and the former Yugoslavia, but in the United States where politicians sought to reduce the federal government's responsibilities for an individual's well being and return this role to the states. This controversial American political debate is not argued in the present study but it was evident in the parameters of Post-Cold War political environment.

My gratitude must be expressed to several people. Important contributions to this study were made by Richard D. Burns, who suggested the topic of U.S. intervention policy and assisted me at all stages of the book's production, and by my wife, Joan, who has been more valuable than she realizes in providing patient and critical input. In addition, Bradley University's library staff must be commended for their kind consideration and efficiency in serving my requests for research materials.

Lester H. Brune
Professor Emeritus of History
Bradley University

CHAPTER ONE

INTRODUCTION

The demise of the Soviet Union (USSR) and its Warsaw Pact alliance between 1988 and 1991 brought a satisfaction of victory in the United States as well as concerns about the nation's role in the Post-Cold War world. For forty years the ideological clash between the "tyrannical communist world" and the "democratic capitalist free world" had provided Americans with a reason to respond whenever the communists sought to extend their influence. By 1991, however, United States' security planners found they needed to devise new strategies for dealing with future crises around the world. The costs of future responses to foreign crises, moreover, had to be reconciled with the U.S. national debt that had increased from one trillion dollars in 1981 to over five trillion dollars by 1992.

Although the end of the Cold War surprised President George Bush and America's foreign policy establishment, there had been several signs of the impending Soviet collapse when Bush was inaugurated on January 20, 1989. In December 1987, Premier Mikhail Gorbachev and President Ronald Reagan had signed a treaty limiting intermediate range nuclear weapons and, five days before Bush was sworn-in, Gorbachev had removed all Soviet troops from Afghanistan, ending a Cold War crisis that began in 1979. At a Vienna meeting the day before Bush's inaugural thirty-five communist and democratic nations, including the USSR, approved a significant follow-up to the 1975 Helsinki agreements. These accords committed these nations to respect an individual's freedom of information, religion, travel, and privacy; to reduce the conventional armed forces of the Warsaw Pact and North Atlantic Treaty Organization; and to plan the institutionalization of the Conference on Security and Cooperation in Europe.

One event, seen as insignificant in January 1989, actually started the process that would cause the collapse of the Soviet Empire. From January

15 to 21, army units in Prague suppressed crowds demonstrating against communism and arrested over 400 protesters. The repression was temporary, however, as protests grew in size until Czech leaders agreed to hold multiparty elections which, on December 29, 1989, resulted in the election of Vaclav Havel as president—a dissident who had been imprisoned in January.

Throughout 1989, the Czech experience was duplicated in different ways in other Warsaw Pact nations. East Germany protests led to the fall of the Berlin Wall on November 9 and the reunification of the two Germanys in 1991. Polish protests succeeded when the communists yielded power to the anti-communist Solidarity Party on August 24. Hungary's communists permitted multiparty elections leading to non-communist victories; Romanian protests led to the overthrow and execution of their communist leader; the Bulgarians forced their president to resign after approving multiparty elections but he renamed his party and kept control of parliament.

In Moscow, Gorbachev discovered that his reforms—involving economic changes and a public openness (*glasnost*)—and dissent in East Europe's communist states prompted the individual Soviet republics to seek their independence. Gorbachev survived a coup by hard-line communists in August 1991, but could only watch as various Soviet republics seceded from Soviet Union. The Russian Republic joined the Ukraine, Byelorussia and eight other Soviet republics to form the Commonwealth of Independent States (CIS) in December 1991 and, on December 25, 1991, Gorbachev resigned as Soviet president. The red hammer and sickle flag was lowered for the last time from the Kremlin wall.

THE U.S. ROLE IN THE POST-COLD WAR ERA

From 1989 to 1991, President Bush's national security team watched approvingly but passively as bloodless revolutionary events demolished the Soviet empire and new independent states emerged in the former Soviet Union. Although Bush's passive policy toward the Soviets may have been wise and "admirably suited to the moment," Michael Mandlebaum also believes this passiveness resulted in his failure to offer sufficient economic aid to assist democracy's growth in the countries liberated from communism. Bush kept the Atlantic alliance together but expected Europeans to solve problems arising in East Europe.[1]

Overall, of course, Bush faced the daunting task of defining Post-Cold War policy for the United States. The lack of a definite U.S. Post-Cold War policy became apparent after Bush called for a new "world order" at the end of the Iraqi war in March 1991. Problems in Somalia, Haiti, Yugoslavia and other regions quickly appeared, but neither Bush nor William Clinton was able to immediately devise strategies to meet these crises.

As the U.S. media, the public, and politicians focused attention on domestic affairs, the evolving Post-Cold War world became a critical issue for those concerned with international developments. Among individuals who dealt with world politics and economics, discussions regarding international policies for a world order congenial to the United States focused on four basic questions: Is isolationism possible? What polarity of power relations would evolve between nations? What type of future conflict is most likely? And, when, where, and how should the U.S. intervene?

RETURN TO ISOLATIONISM?

As early as 1990, Republican Patrick Buchanan proposed that with the Cold War ended, the nation could revive its earlier isolationist policies and he campaigned on that platform in 1992 and 1996. Buchanan's ideas on isolationism first appeared in a 1990 article in which he declared that communist losses in East Europe indicated the Soviet Union was no longer a military threat. The U.S. should now withdraw its armed forces from Europe and stop all foreign economic assistance. "Let us go back," he wrote, "to a time when the establishment wanted war but the American people did not want to fight"; that is, to the 1930s when the American First organization opposed U.S. intervention in Britain's war against Nazi Germany. Although Japan's attack on Pearl Harbor rallied the nation to war, most American boys were "brought home" by 1946 and remained there until the onset of the Cold War. Under Dwight Eisenhower, the Republican's adopted an internationalist policy against communism but with that battle won, Buchanan criticized Republicans who continued to advocate internationalism. He wanted to abolish foreign alliances such as NATO, adopt protectionist tariffs, and end illegal immigration. Despite these explicated proposals, Buchanan floundered at the polls in both campaigns.[2]

In 1992 and 1996 domestic issues dominated the elections because, with the Soviet enemy gone, there was no serious international crisis. As pollster John Mueller explains, Americans held basic "common sense" concerns about international policy but paid attention only if a crisis impacted their lives or a conflict caused American deaths or casualties.[3] Yet, the world of 1992 was not the world of 1941 as perceived by Buchanan. New communication technology linked continents together as never before in history. Therefore, unlike Buchanan, most commentators on foreign policy could not accept isolationism.

WORLD POWER POLARITY

Aside from isolationism, the major issue for the Post-Cold War world was what would replace the Cold War's bipolar balance of power? The two general options most cited were (1) the U.S. should retain its present Post-Cold War role as the "unipolar" global power, or (2) the U.S. should become part of a future tripolar or multipolar system.

Charles Krauthammer defined the "unipolar" concept in which the United States should act alone in deciding most international questions. Desiring an active U.S. foreign policy, Krauthammer rejected Buchanan's retreat to "fortress America" but admitted the U.S. has lost the dominant economic position it had held until the 1960s. Nevertheless, he asserted, the U.S. remained the principal center of the world's economic production, and could dominate world politics because it had the world's greatest military capability. Recognizing that in future generations the U.S. might simply be the largest partner in a multipolar world, he wanted Washington to act as the superpower directing the world during the transitory era toward those future relationships. U.S. leadership could include intervention under collective security, as happened in the 1991 Iraq war that he calls an instance of "pseudo-multilateralism", because the U.S. controlled United Nations activity. In the Post-Cold War interim, Krauthammer feared that the U.S. government might spend too much on social welfare programs and too little on the military. He concluded that "Our best hope for safety is in American strength and will—the strength and will to lead a unipolar world, unashamedly laying down the rules of world order and being prepared to enforce them."[4]

Senator Jesse Helms and other Republicans favored Krauthammer's unipolar concepts although Helms also wanted to restrict presidential prerogatives as commander-in-chief by foreclosing effective U.S. participation in UN peacekeeping operations. After the Republican congressional victory in 1994, Helms became Chairman of the Senator Foreign Relations Committee and a constant irritant to Clinton's foreign policies. A staunch advocate of limiting or ending U.S. involvement in any UN peacekeeping operations, Helms wanted the United States to leave the UN unless it was "radically overhauled". He wanted to stop the UN's "encroachment" on state sovereignty, cut fifty percent of its bureaucracy, overhaul the UN budget process, and limit its peacekeeping activities.[5]

A MULTIPOLAR WORLD?

Extensive literature about a multipolar world appeared after 1989, with two prominent authors represent different aspects of this perspective: Harvard Professor Joseph Nye, and University of London Professor Lawrence Freedman. These authors envision a world power structure of three or more power centers in which the United States would be the strongest. Nye indicated the unilateral hegemony of the U.S. was "unlikely because of the diffusion of power through transnational interdependence." Preferring the term "multilevels of power", Nye wanted to have a strong U.S. military but recognized that the U.S. would not be able to control the economic and political centers in an interdependent world. Thus, the U.S. should work with like-minded nations to resolve such international problems as relations between world markets, small nations having unconventional but destructive weapons, the international drug trade, environmental dangers of technological society, and diseases which can spread across continents.[6]

Similar to Nye's multipolarity, Freedman emphsizes how America's successful strengthening of democracy in Asia and Western Europe after 1945 created valuable political-military allies to rebuild the world's economic foundations, promote political democracy, and play the crucial role in stopping communist expansion. As a matter of course, U.S. allies also became able to compete with U.S. business for world trade and investments because these alliances encouraged European economic unity and a prosperous Pacific rimland. Freedman believes these European and Asian allies expect to have a greater role Post-Cold War role in international affairs and, if the U.S. accommodates their expectations, all parties will benefit by resolving economic and trade issues which could otherwise result in increased tensions or conflict.[7]

Both Freedman and Nye believe the areas peripheral to the U.S.-European-Japanese core blocs are the most likely ones of future warfare and threats to the core countries stability. Most Cold War conflicts occurred in Third World regions and controlling such conflicts would require cooperation between the multipolar powers. In fact, the break-up of the Soviet empire added to the number of peripheral underdeveloped nations where trouble broke out after 1989 and would continue to fester.

CONDITIONS JUSTIFYING INTERVENTION

The consensus of recent literature is that the Post-Cold War era significantly changed previous criteria for interventions, especially in the underdeveloped world. One important change is that which permits intervention in a nation's internal affairs if *world security* requires it. During the Cold War, international groups such as the UN would not intervene in a nation's *internal affairs* because national sovereignty was sacrosanct. The UN perceived itself as an impartial group excluded from intervention without an explicit request of a nation's government or of each nation involved in a dispute. Since 1989, this concept of sovereignty has been challenged because many small ethnic or cultural groups have claimed a right to secede from an existing government. These claims raised dormant questions about sovereignty because conflicts within some states called for external intervention without permission from an existing government or governments. Ted Robert Gurr's 1994 article listed fifty internal conflicts, thirteen of which had already resulted in the deaths of over 100,000 people each and caused the flight of thousands of refugees to neighboring states. This data seemed to justify some interventions, but it also indicates the difficulty in deciding which of fifty cases required intervention by the U.S. or other organizations.[8]

The existence of so many potential trouble spots led Robert D. Blackwell to propose that human rights violations would justify U.S. intervention *only if* the violations met certain criteria. They must 1) become public knowledge, 2) involve large numbers of people, 3) take place over a long period of time, and 4) affect a disproportionate number of helpless people, especially children. Blackwell's qualifications appear to require extensive suffering preceding any intervention, whereas other observers, including UN Secretary General Boutros Boutros-Ghali, searched for a means of "preventive intervention" that would forestall such human suffering.[9]

Although a variety of qualifications have been proposed to justify intervention in the Post-Cold War era, the present study focuses on the four criteria for intervention suggested by Josef Joffe:

1. There is a moral imperative for action.

2. There is a national interest involved, especially if military action is included.

3. There is a reasonable chance of success.

4. The intervening state has full domestic support.[10]

1. The moral imperative assumes that world security requires concerned nations to regulate the behavior of existing or evolving states when conflict erupts within or among them. Intervention may be necessary if the conflict violates human decency or affects the security of neighboring regions. To encourage democracy, Joffe believes the U.S. and other nations must protect human rights and civilized standards of moral behavior. Nevertheless, Joffe says "purely humanitarian" reasons for *military* intervention are insufficient unless the conflict threatens the perceived national interests of the U.S. or other states.

2. A challenge to a state's national interests is probably the most critical reason determining an intervention. Broadly viewed, national interest may be involved if conflicts spill across borders into neighboring states, disrupts international order or endangers the supply of a natural resource such as oil. "Spill-over" problems occur most often and they include the neighboring states becoming a sanctuary for refugees and a base of military operations by political exiles that endanger the host state's economic stability or its security.

Because America's geographic location separates it from the European, Asian, and African continents, concepts of the U.S. national interest have depended on a broad or restricted view of the nation's place in the world. An isolationist's view of the national interest is usually limited to defending U.S. borders or the Western Hemisphere. Internationalists, however, divide into at least two groups in interpreting the national interest. One restricts the U.S. action in the Post-Cold War world by expecting Europeans, Asians or Africans to be the principal actors in their region unless there is a clearly defined U.S. interest involved. A second wants the U.S. to be the world leader by asserting extensive U.S. influence and activity in all dangerous parts of the world. These three categories indicate the range of basic perceptions influencing national interest. In the final analysis, the president and his national security advisors (or congressional leaders) must relate their perceptions of the nation's foreign interests to its domestic interests when considering intervention. If the moral imperative and the national interest are positively ascertained, intervening should outweigh the consequences of *not* acting.

3. Estimating the chances of an intervention's success involves risky claims but the prospects may be evaluated by weighing three major

factors: the type of intervention to be undertaken, the target country's geographic location and military capabilities, and the intervention's objective.

The type of intervention may be a limited action such as an embargo or embargo enforcement, a more difficult act such an air strikes or naval bombardments, or a large-scale employment of combat forces. Obviously, the more complex and involved the intervention, the greater the risk.

Second, the geography of the region and the opposition's anticipated military strength must be compared to the intervening force's capacity. In the 1991 Iraqi war, the region's geography and Iraq's conventional war capacity favored a military response. Under different conditions, however, intervention may face geographic obstacles ranging from jungles or deserts to vast plains or mountains, and the opposition's military capability may range from well trained and well supplied conventional or guerrilla forces to demoralized paramilitary factions with an incompetent, low-technology military units.

Third and most vital, a mission's success depends on the political and/or military objectives expected to be fulfilled. General Colin Powell's description of the 1991 Iraqi campaign illustrates the connection between military and political objectives. Powell justified the president's decision to stop the war after 100 hours of ground combat without overthrowing Saddam Hussein by insisting that the U.S.'s objective was simply to liberate Kuwait. However, critics of this decision argue Bush's wartime rhetoric had enlarged the objective by demonizing Hussein and calling for a "new world order." The gap between Bush's political-oriented world order, presumably including a passive, cooperative Iraq, and Powell's limited military objectives raised expectations of what the mission would accomplish and, therefore, has resulted in continued post-war frustrations.

Stating objectives clearly is important in evaluating the chances for success but, as Lawrence Freedman observes, determining an objective is especially difficult when conflicts concern politics within the target state, a situation that recurred in Somalia, Haiti, and Bosnia. During a power struggle among competing groups, the intervening forces usually favor one group because they will be perceived to be victims and they are willing to cooperate with their new "protectors". If the fundamental political issues of a conflict are not settled during the intervention, the original power struggle will probably be renewed when the intervening force pulls out.

With these difficulties in mind, the possible objectives for a political-military intervention may be defined as: 1) peacemaking to "persuade" all parties to agree to a cease-fire; 2) peacekeeping to maintain a cease-fire that all parties accept and to punish violators if necessary; 3) peace prevention to act before a conflict erupts; 4) coercion to change behavior of a government or group violating international behavior standards; 5) coercion to unseat an unacceptable government and help establish a new government; and 6) providing protection to humanitarian aid providers while a conflict persists.

4. Democratic governments require domestic support for interventions to be undertaken and to be sustained. On the positive side, Joseph Nye finds it axiomatic that democratic governments never war against each other because their leaders must first exhaust all means to find solutions to their differences short of war. On the negative side, a democratic leader's need for domestic support may make military intervention difficult unless there is clear-cut threat to a vital national interest.

An important addendum to domestic backing is whether democratic leaders must have backing *before* intervening or may use their persuasive powers to *gain backing after* intervening. The timing of support is an American political concern because the "Vietnam syndrome" has blamed U.S. "losses" on the news media and public opinion. In 1983, President Reagan's Secretary of Defense, Caspar Weinberger, listed the need for "a reasonable assurance of public support" prior to any military intervention. Less attention was given to Secretary of State George Shultz who responded that Weinberger's requirement of public support *prior to a presidential decision* was "hiding behind the skirts of public opinion." Shultz argued the president should make decisions and then articulate reasons to win and maintain public support.[11]

Two factors influencing U.S. policymaker's and public's perceptions of foreign events are mass media reports and public opinion polls. Although the influence of transnational television reports, such as CNN, is controversial, the public's perception of world events are instantaneously updated because satellites quickly transmit pictures of human catastrophes. This capability can provide daily pictures of the hazards of intervening, but media "sound-bites" can seldom explain the complex causes involved in a conflict or the various reasons for presidential decisions.

Most polls after 1989 show that the U.S. public usually favors an active role in international affairs. Detailed annual polls by the Chicago Council of Foreign Relations have concluded that the public's distaste for foreign activity reached a low point of 54 percent in 1982, but reversed in 1992 when 62 percent approved an active U.S. role abroad.[12] In an extensive 1996 survey of the public's perceptions of foreign relations, Steven Kull and I. M. Destler found that most Americans lack accurate knowledge about international affairs. They report 74 percent of the public want the U.S. to promote peace cooperation and human welfare in the international arena, yet believe the country should "not be the single world leader." However, in-depth questioning on foreign affairs indicates the public lacked basic information. Poll respondents thought the U.S. provided 40 percent of costs for all UN peacekeeping whereas the U.S. contribution was two percent and in terms of gross national product of industrial nations, "the U.S. gives the lowest percentage of all."[13]

SUMMARY

There is little possibility that America will return to isolationism in the Post-Cold War years because the transnational nature of the world's economic and political features require U.S. involvement abroad. Less certain is whether United States policy will try to be unipolar or will accept a leading role in a multipolar world. Future conflicts will most probably be in peripheral Third World states where competing ethnic or political groups seek dominance while their troubles spill into surrounding regions.

Given these present circumstances, the present study analyzes interventions in Somalia, Haiti, and Bosnia using Joffe's four criteria which may justify intervention. These are: 1) moral imperative, 2) national interest, 3) chance of success, and 4) domestic support.

NOTES

1. Michael Mandelbaum, "The Bush Foreign Policy," *Foreign Affairs* 7 (Winter 1990/91): 5-22.
2. Patrick Buchanan, "America First, and Second, and Third." *National Interest* No.19 (Spring 1990): 77-82; William F. Gavin, "At the Roots of Pat Buchanan's Rhetoric," WPNW (Mar. 4-10, 1996): 24; and Owen Harries, "Pat's World," *The National Interest* No.43 (Spring 1996): 108-111.
3. John Mueller, "The Common Sense," *National Interest* No. 47 (Spring 1997): 81-88. On Bush and Clinton's lack of consensus see Barry Posen and Andrew Ross, "Contemporary Visions for U.S. Grand Strategy, "*International Security* 21 (Winter 1996/97): 5-53. For the polls and Republican's opposition to the UN and U.S. world

concerns, see Jessica Mathews "The U.N.—Are the Republicans Wrong Again?" WPNW (Mar.11-17, 1996): 28.

4. Charles Krauthammer, "The Unipolar Movement," *Foreign Affairs* 70 (Winter 1990/91): 23-33.

5. Jesse Helms, "Fixing the U.N.," *Foreign Affairs* 75 (Sept./Oct. 1996): 2-7. For reactions to Helms: *Foreign Affairs* 75 (Nov./Dec. 1996): 172-179.

6. Joseph S. Nye, Jr. "What New World Order?" *Foreign Affairs* 71 (Spring 1992): 83-96 and Nye, "The Case for Deep Support," *Foreign Affairs* 74 (July 1995): 90-102.

7. Lawrence Freedman, "Introduction," in L. Freedman, ed.,*Military Intervention in European Conflicts* (London: Blackwell, 1994): 1-13.

8. Ted Robert Gurr, "Peoples Against States: Ethnopolitical Conflict and the Changing World System," *International Studies Quarterly* 38 (Sept. 1994): 347-377.

9. Robert D. Blackwell, "A Taxonomy for Defining US National Security Interests in the 1990s and Beyond," in Werner Weidenfeld and Josef Janning, eds. *Europe in Global Change*. (Gutersloh, Germany: Bertelsmann Foundation, 1993): 108; also, Boutros Boutros-Ghali, "Empowering the United Nations," *Foreign Affairs* 71 (Winter 1992/93): 89-102.

10. Josef Joffe, "The New Europe, Yesterday's Ghosts," *Foreign Affairs* 72 (Winter 1992/93): 33. For other criteria see Chapter Nine's bibliography on "Intervention Theory."

11. Kurt Anderson. "The Watchword is Wariness: Weinberger Outlines Six Criteria for Sending Troops into Combat," *Time* 129 (Dec. 10, 1984): 1. For Shultz, see Fareed Zakaria," A Framework for Intervention in the Post-Cold War World," in Arnold Kanter, et.al., eds. *U.S. Intervention Policy for the Post-Cold War World* (New York: Norton, 1994): 185-86. For a discussion of democracy and peace, see Henry Farber and Joanne Gowa, "Politics and Peace," *International Security* 20 (Fall 1995): 123-146 and "Correspondence" 20 (Winter 1996/97): 177-187; and Edward Mansfield and Jack Snyder, "Democratization and the Danger of War, "*International Security* 20 (Summer1995): 5-38 and "Correspondence" 20 (Spring 1996): 176-207.

12. Steven Kull And I.M. Destler. *An Emerging Consensus: A Study of American Public Attitudes on America's Role in the World* (College Park, MD: Center For International And Security Studies, University of Maryland, July 10, 1996.

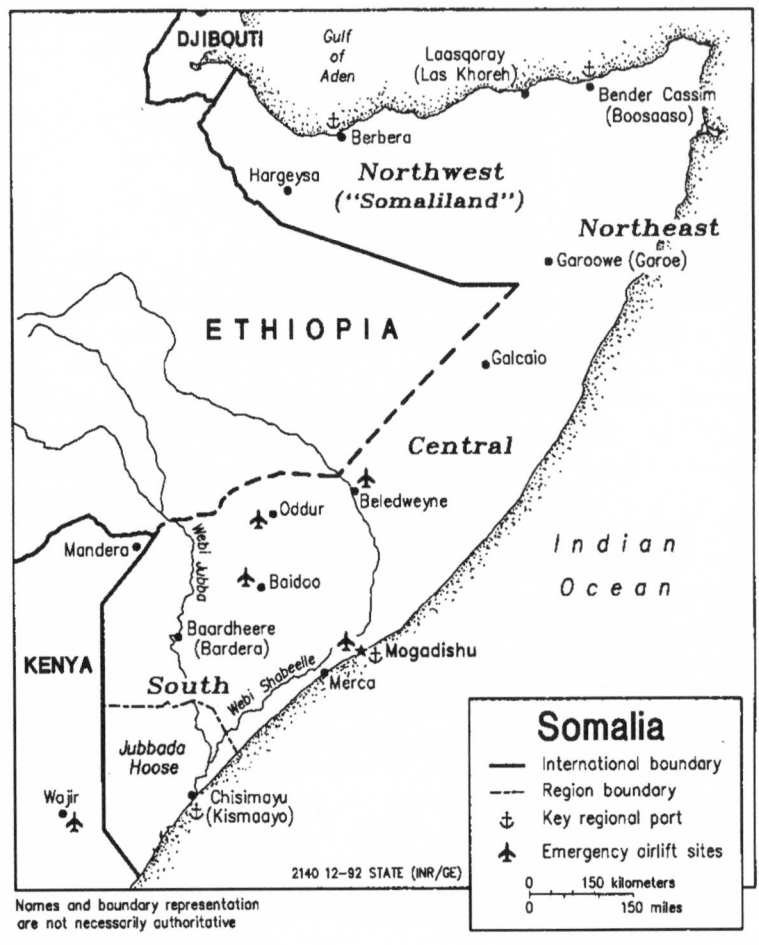

CHAPTER TWO

THE SOMALIA INTERVENTION

President George Bush's decision to intervene in Somalia in December 1992 may have been his final attempt to demonstrate U.S. support for a new world order. The method he chose, however, raises serious questions about his administration's criteria for intervention. Indeed, critics have denounced it as a formula for failure.

The disintegration of Somalia's government began with civil strife in 1988 and had reduced the state to political chaos by January 1991. For two years the United Nations tried, but failed, to obtain an effective cease-fire among the warring factions because starvation was causing the deaths of many children, women, and elderly men. A moral imperative acceptable to the American public had become evident by November 1992 but because the administration perceived no national interest at stake in Somalia, President Bush seriously qualified the role of the U.S.'s mission. His adoption of a strictly humanitarian mission resulted in the proverbial wrong intervention, in the wrong place, at the wrong time. After the U.S. withdrew in October 1993, the UN mission would continue until March 1995. Although the combined UN-U.S. intervention may have temporarily saved many lives, fighting among Somalian warring factions continued to cause food shortages and deaths long after they left.

SOMALIA'S IMPERIAL LEGACY

Throughout the 19th century, the European race for control of African territory created states with boundaries that ignored clan, family, and tribal dominions, including Somalian clans in northeast Africa. Although Ethiopia often exerted political control over northeast Africa, the pastoral regions along the Red Sea and Indian Ocean contained Somalian clans that had converted to Islam in the eighth century and shared a language and culture based on complex clan and sub-clan relations. After 1850, France, Great Britain, and Italy sought seaports on the Red Sea to control a waterway whose value greatly increased after the

Suez Canal opened in 1869. When they resolved colonial claims, French Somaliland contained the port of Djibouti, British Somaliland comprised the northeast triangle of the "horn" of Africa, and Italian Somaliland lay to the south including Mogadishu's port. These divisions ignored Somalian clan holdings as well as the Somalians in Kenya and the Ogaden province of Ethiopia.

In the 1950s, an African wave of rebellion did not effect the French in Djibouti but British and Italian colonies were united in 1960 as an independent state. On gaining independence, Somalia set up a republic with a president, prime minister and legislature in Mogadishu, although the British and Italians had done little to prepare them for nationhood. The state's pastoral economy had a subsistence level of living and clans and sub-clans were not ready for rule by a central government. Somalia's inter-clan relations had local ethical rules but lacked an overarching concept of law essential to a modern centralized nation.[1]

During the 1960s, the government misspent tax revenue and failed to build a transportation and communication infrastructure that would have united the entire country. Amid complaints about the government, military officers led by General Mohammed Siad Barre overthrew Somalia's president in 1969 and established a regime based on communist slogans adopted from the Soviet Union's agents who backed the rebellion.

General Barre's rule from 1969 to 1991 paralleled the Cold War. First the Soviets, and later the United States, extended him economic and military aid. After 1969, Moscow sought to expand its sphere-of-influence in the northeast Africa by moving into Ethiopia but their plans went awry. The Soviets armed Ethiopian rebel Haile Mariam Mengistu, who subsequently ousted American ally Haile Selassie, but they ignored the fact that Somalia was at war with Ethiopia to "liberate" Somalia clans in Ogaden—a province which Ethiopia had controlled since the 19th century. Barre's war, which had began against the U.S.-supported Selassie, was now waged against the Moscow-aided Mengistu. When Barre rejected Soviet orders to leave Ogaden the Soviets sent additional military equipment to Mengistu and had Fidel Castro send 18,000 Cuban troops to expel the Somalia troops. When Barre's forces reluctantly withdrew some 300,000 Ogaden refugees followed.

After this setback, Barre received aid from the United States, the UN and non-governmental (NGO) humanitarian groups. Washington replaced Soviet influence in Somalia in 1980, opening a naval base on the Red Sea.

President Ronald Reagan decreased U.S. economic aid from \$36 million in 1983 to \$8.7 million before canceling it in 1989; but the Pentagon's military aid continued until 1990 when rebel attacks weakened Barre's regime. Journalist Jonathan Stevenson, believes that the U.S.-UN food relief to Somalia over ten years had made the clans and refugees dependent on food imports and that the rebellion completely disrupted the food supply after 1988.[2]

UPRISINGS BRING ANARCHY

General Barre diverted vast funds to his war against Ethiopia and thus did not develop a sound economy for Somalia. Moreover, while the northern Somalian clans' livestock provided the nation's principal export income, Barre passed these funds to corrupt "friends". Governmental corruption, plus the miserable conditions of Ogaden refugees, prompted the uprisings against Barre in the spring of 1988.

Mohamed Sahnoun, a former official of the Organization of African Unity (OAU), identifies three "missed opportunities" between 1988 and 1992 when preventive intervention by the UN, the OAU, the League of Arab States or the U.S. might have deterred Somalia's descent into political anarchy. The first occurred in 1988 when the UN and the OAU gave only relief assistance despite reports by Amnesty International and Africa Watch of large-scale killing and human rights violations in Somalia. Led by the Issaq clan, the Somalia National Movement (SNM) attacked northern towns located near the U.S. naval base at Berera before Barre ordered a full-scale military assault on the Issaq. Using aircraft and heavy artillery bombardments, the attack destroyed 70 percent of Hargeysa and other Issaq towns, killing 5,000 men, women, and children.

Although the UN and NGO sent humanitarian relief to north Somalia, Washington suspended U.S. aid, an action that hurt Barre's regime but did not help his opponents. The Issaq's SNM continued its opposition and sought the backing of other dissatisfied Somalian clans.

With sporadic fighting disrupting Somalia, a second chance was missed in May 1990 when 144 prominent Somalia physicians, scholars, and other intellectuals promoted peace negotiations by signing a manifesto. Although the Manifesto's signatories risked their lives by defying Barre, neither the UN, the OAU, the U.S. nor others helped them. Although Italy and Egypt sought a meeting of Somalia opposition groups, clan leaders refused to attend.

The third and most critical "missed chance" to avoid wider fighting occurred on January 26, 1991 after rebels overthrew Barre. Unfortunately, the rebels' "success" occurred precisely at the same time Washington's attention was diverted elsewhere—to an U.S.-led UN coalition attack on Iraq to liberate Kuwait. U.S. naval units on duty in the Red Sea rescued American, Soviet, and other diplomatic personnel from Mogadishu. The UN also evacuated its Mogadishu relief headquarters and did not return until August 1991.[3]

Key Figures

Aideed, Mohamed Farah: leader of a strong military faction in Somalia, claiming to have overthrown Barre in 1991

Aideed, Husein Mohamed: former U.S. Marine and son of Mohamed Farah who replaces his father in 1996

Barre, Mohammed Siad: Military dictator of Somalia to 1991

Bir, General Cervik: Muslim Turkish general and commander of UNOSOM II forces: worked with UN envoy U.S. Admiral Jonathan Howe from May to October 1993

Hersi, Mohamed Siad ("Morgan"): an ally of Siad Barre and his clan

Jess, Ahmad Omar: an ally of Aideed in southern Somalia

Kittani, Ismat: UN envoy to Somalia who replaces Sahnoun in October 1992.

Mohamed, Ali Mahdi: chief opponent of Aideed in Mogadishu, he has support of the Organization of African Unity.

Sahnoun, Mohamed: first UN envoy of UNOSOM I in Somalia; fired by Boutros-Ghali in October 1992.

INEFFECTIVE UN INTERVENTION

Barre's overthrow in January 1991 brought chaos to Somalia that a UN humanitarian effort could not contain. Somalia clans that united against Barre had not developed plans for a new government and, consequently, at least thirteen clans and sub-clans subsequently fought for regional or national control. While humanitarian agencies tried to assist people, the UN finally obtained a cease-fire in 1992.

During 1991, the Somalia Salvation Democratic Front achieved political order in northeast Somalia near Boosaaso and the Issaq's SNM formed an independent Somalia Republic at Hargeysa. However, fierce combat erupted in southern and central Somalia where competing clans used "scorched earth" policies to destroy crops, homes, and cattle. As Barre's forces retreated toward Kenya or Ethiopia in January 1991, they devastated the country's best agricultural land as well as roads, bridges and hospitals. The most intense fighting was at Mogadishu where two generals involved in defeating Barre now led competing factions— Mohamed Farah Aideed and Mohamed Ali Mahdi.

The carnage following Barre's overthrow stimulated UN cease-fire efforts and additional humanitarian aid by the International Red Cross, the Physicians without Frontiers and other non-governmental groups (NGOs). Finally in December 1991, UN Secretary General Javier Perez de Cueller recommended that the UN Security Council (UNSC) sponsor a peacemaking venture if the two warlords would agree to a cease-fire. Together with Boutros Boutros-Ghali, who succeeded him on January 1, 1992, Perez asked the UNSC to assist in the search for Somalia's peace and security and UN officers negotiated a cease-fire on March 3 with Aideed and Ali Mahdi. Although fighting continued in parts of Somalia, a UN technical team in Mogadishu prepared for UN monitors to ensure UN aid.

After the warlords agreed, UNSC Resolution 751 of April 24, 1992, established the United Nations Operation in Somalia (UNOSOM I). The UNSC combined UN missions of humanitarian aid, peacemaking, peacekeeping, and state-building. It appealed for humanitarian assistance to be sent to Somalia, approved 50 unarmed UN officers to monitor the cease-fire, and instructed the secretary general to reconcile the combatants and enforce an arms embargo.

Between April and November 1992, UNOSOM I activity was handicapped by disagreement between UN bureaucrats in New York and Mohamed Sahnoun's UN staff in Mogadishu. Sahnoun was appointed by Boutros-Ghali, but the former OAU diplomat soon found that diverse UN relief groups failed to coordinate activities and delayed operations by bickering over distribution areas. Groups such as UNICEF did fairly well, he reported, but the UN High Commission on Refugees, the UN World Food Program, and the UN Department of Humanitarian Affairs worked at crossed purposes and refused to consult with Sahnoun. Moreover, UN humanitarian officers worked from comfortable lodgings in Nairobi, Djibouti and Mogadishu avoiding contact with Somalians in the county-side. In contrast to UN bureaucrats, most NGO personnel worked effectively under dangerous circumstances to distribute relief among the people. The NGOs had meager resources but quickly provided relief to the people; while in 8 months, the UN had distributed only one one-third of its relief supplies.

Equally seriously, Sahnoun disagreed with UN officials about negotiations with Somalian leaders. While UN officers only paid attention to Aideed and Ali Mahdi, Sahnoun met many clan and sub-clan elders around the country seeking their cooperation in the peace process. Sahnoun wanted the UN to involve clan leaders other than Aideed and Ali Mahdi in the forming of a government.

By October 1992, Sahnoun believed relief operations and peace talks were going well and he arranged meetings between Sweden's Peace Institute and Somalia intellectuals to discuss forming a government. Also, many clan leaders accepted his invitation to meet in January 1993 with representatives of Ethiopia, Eritrea, Djibouti, and Kenya for a "Horn of Africa" peace conference. Sahnoun believed the airlift of supplies which President Bush and various Europeans began in August had increased relief aid. Moreover, fighting had decreased in Somali except for problems between Aideed and Ali Mahdi. Sahnoun's evaluations were confirmed by Somalia experts from Africa Watch.

Late in October, however, Boutros-Ghali dismissed Sahnoun because he had by-passed the hierarchic channels of the UN bureaucracy. The breaking point between Sahnoun and Boutros-Ghali came after the Secretary General's New York office announced an additional 3,000 UNOSOM I troops would be sent to Somalia, a decision made without consulting Sahnoun or Somalian leaders.

Both Sahnoun and the Somalia leaders protested because UN officials tended to support Ali Mahdi, who wanted more UN soldiers, against Aideed who had the strongest following and did not want more UN troops. When the UN had sent 500 Pakistani soldiers to Somalia in September, Sahnoun had difficulty in persuading Aideed to accept them. Thus, Boutros-Ghali's October decision to deploy another 3,000 soldiers enraged Aideed and alarmed Sahnoun.

Prompted by the troop announcement, Sahnoun criticized the UN bureaucrats to reporters and on CBS-TV's popular "60 Minutes" program. For going public, Boutros-Ghali castigated Sahnoun, replacing him with a loyal bureaucrat, Ismat Kittani. Subsequently, Sahnoun's achievements broke down and turned many Somalians against Boutros-Ghali and the UN. Indeed, Aideed's followers charged that the UN was Somalia's real enemy—a claim that endangered all relief groups in Somalia.

Aideed's accusations against the UN prompted intense fighting in Mogadishu as he refused to deal with Kittani. On November 12, his forces shelled a Pakistani encampment at the airport and armed gangs looted warehouses containing relief supplies and obstructed relief convoys distributing food and medicine. On November 23, Mahdi's clan joined the action against the UN by shelling a UN ship unloading at Mogadishu port.

The UN's New York organization never admitted its shortcomings, of course, and the reasons for UNOSOM I's failures were not apparent to persons unfamiliar with past events in Somalia. More evident to Americans were the reports of warlord attacks on food supplies and the scenes of starving Somalians that followed Boutros-Ghali's ill-fated decision to send more UN troops to Somalia. UNOSOM I's intervention had failed, but President Bush apparently believed he could rescue it.[4]

BUSH'S INTERVENTION, 1992

Until more documentation is available, President Bush's decision to intervene in Somalia will be clouded by controversy. Either he lacked satisfactory information about Sahnoun's endeavors and the UN's policies or he ignored that data because he desired to show that his new world order could be implemented by U.S. forces; perhaps, before Clinton took office on January 20, 1993. In August 1992, Bush and especially General Colin Powell had been reluctant to act militarily in Bosnia when reports of ethnic cleansing appeared and in Somalia, they had opted only for an airlift of relief supplies to Somalia. In November, however, Bush adopted the risky option of sending 28,000 U.S. troops to Somalia on a "humanitarian" mission because, as Powell wrote in his memoirs, Somalia "wrenched our hearts." Bush indicated it would be a "difficult and dangerous job" and Powell's "best guess" was that it would take "two to three months". Neither men, however, appeared to understand the true nature of UNOSOM I's troubles, nor the vital connection between Somalia's political anarchy and the attainment of success for their "humanitarian" mission.

Perhaps like the American public, Bush, Powell, and Secretary of Defense Richard Cheney simply judged Somalia by the television pictures reaching their homes. These instant photographs depicted the horrendous suffering of starving women and children but never captured the savage reality of the young gangs. These thugs were riding about in Land Cruisers equipped with heavy machine guns and grenade or rocket launchers and killing or threatening the humanitarian workers and Somalian people. The gangs had robbed relief agencies and terrorized the population since the breakdown of government in 1991 and remained active in 1993. The full range of Somalia's political, social, and economic anarchy and UNOSOM I's inability to deliver relief supplies were not adequately conveyed by the brief TV clips shown the American public.[5]

Television supplied a moral imperative and the public support for Bush's decision to intervene, but the U.S.'s national interest was not directly involved because stabilizing Somalia's political order was not critical to America's economic or political well being. Lacking a commitment to repair Somalia's political order, Bush proposed to open the food supply routes and quickly withdraw the U.S. military, a concept which seriously qualified the chances for the UN to succeed in restraining Somalia's warlords and achieving a peace settlement.

More is known about how than about why President Bush's national security team believed a quick "military fix" was possible in Somalia. Soon after losing the 1992 election to William Clinton, Bush ordered a study about Somalia's relief requirements and the options for U.S. intervention. Apparently, Bush believed that Somalia's humanitarian relief had failed because UN experts alleged that 50 to 80 percent of Somalia's relief supplies were stolen or extorted from relief groups by armed gangs. Moreover, because it could not be distributed to the needy, as much as 12,000 metric tons of food rotted in Mogadishu's warehouses. The airlift Bush adopted in August achieved some benefits in bringing food, medicine, and supplies but conditions in Somalia had become less secure in November. Notably, the U.S. air lift commander, Brigadier General Frank Libutti warned Secretary of Defense Richard Cheney and General Powell that "If the United States [was] not careful, it could be in Somalia for ten or fifteen years."

Although Libutti's cautionary words may have influenced Powell's demand for a quick U.S. exit from Somalia, the Joint Chiefs reasons for discarding their previous reluctance to become involved in Somalia is unknown. On November 21, Admiral David Jeremiah, the Vice-Chairman of the Joint Chiefs, reported that the Pentagon's analysis of the situation indicated U.S. troops could deploy in Somalia, end the violence, and make certain that "the people were fed *within a short period*" (italics added). Journalist Don Oberdorfer believes Jeremiah's report marked a "sea-change" in Joint Chiefs thinking because Colin Powell accepted its conclusions provided an overwhelming U.S. force was deployed to secure the relief supply routes and quickly withdrawn.

Bush met with the Joint Chiefs on November 25 where he found that Secretary of State Lawrence Eagleburger and National Security Advisor Brent Scowcroft also favored aid for Somalia. Oberdorfer does not explain whether these officials considered the national interest or the chances for a peace settlement between Somalia's warlords. The Joint Chiefs gave Bush three options. Bush refused the first, to augment UN funds, and the second, to simply provide U.S. air and sea power—off-shore—to support UNOSOM I relief operations. Bush chose to have an U.S.-led multinational force intervene in Somalia, secure the area for relief distributions, withdraw in a short time, and give responsibility back to the UN. Bush instructed Eagleburger to discuss this offer with Secretary General Boutros-Ghali and prepare a UNSC resolution requesting the U.S.-led mission.

The UNSC passed the appropriate resolution on December 3 and the next day, Bush announced the U.S. would command a multinational United Task Force (UNITAF) commanded by U.S. General Joseph P. Hoar to establish protective conditions for humanitarian aid to reach Somalia's starving people. Bush did not refer to any U.S. national interest in Somalia but said the U.S. role was "humanitarian" and that he expected other nations would add to the 28,000 U.S. contingent. The final UNITAF force consisted of 37,000 military personnel, including 8,000 logistical troops.[6]

Immediately after the November 25 meeting, when Bush had chosen his option, journalists raised important questions about the objectives of the "humanitarian mission". They were joined by Secretary General Boutros-Ghali in asking the Bush team what "a secure environment for humanitarian relief" required and what connection was there between the U.S. operation and a political settlement among Somalia's warring groups. The journalists accepted the Pentagon's explanation that, unlike Bosnia, the Somalian intervention was "doable" because the northeast African terrain was neither mountainous nor tree covered and the disorganized warlords could not seriously threaten U.S. forces. But they did question the "quick exit" strategy under which the overwhelming U.S. force withdrew and left a much weaker UN force to sustain those routes against hostile warlords who had not accepted an effective political agreement. Generally, these reporters asked: What would happen after UNITAF ended? Former Secretary of State Henry Kissinger commented that if the warlords listened to the explanations of Bush and Powell, they would lay low and cooperate until the U.S. forces withdrew before renewing their struggle for power.

Among other critical reports, *U.S. News and World Report* disclosed doubts about the mission expressed in a note to the State Department by Ambassador to· Kenya Smith Hempstone. Indicating that Somalia's difficulties involved the strife of militant factions as well as food relief, Hempstone referred to the 241 U.S. Marines killed in Lebanon in 1983 on President Ronald Reagan's uncertain mission, and commented that if you liked Beirut, you will "love Mogadishu."[7]

Secretary General Boutros-Ghali addressed these concerns in a letter to President Bush after UNSC resolution 794 was approved. On December 8, Boutros-Ghali informed Bush that his talks with U.S. representatives had continuously raised questions about the security standards necessary to provide safety for humanitarian aid after UNITAF's mission ended. Boutros-Ghali's three points of "cardinal importance" in order to maintain aid distribution were: 1) UNITAF should place Somalia's heavy weapons under international control and disarm the irregular forces and gangs threatening the aid organizations; 2) UNITAF should establish a secure environment throughout Somalia, not just in UNITAF's designated supply route near Mogadishu; and 3) there should be assurances of close cooperation between the UN and UNITAF commands to retain compatible political and humanitarian conditions *before* the U.S. transferred responsibility to UN peacekeepers. The Secretary General said UNSC 794 stated "a secure environment" should mean peaceful conditions for future aid as well as temporary protection.

In December 1992, the Bush administration and Boutros-Ghali obviously held quite different interpretations of "a secure environment" and the meaning of Resolution 794. Former Bush official James R. Bolton indicates Bush's reply to the Secretary General stated "...the mission of the coalition is limited and specific: to create security conditions which will permit the feeding of starving Somali people and the transfer of this security function to the U.N. peacekeeping force." Bolton's words fall short of clarity about "security" and seem to contrast with Bush's December 4 speech which said he opposed Somalia's "armed gangs ripping off their own people, condemning them to death by starvation."

Whatever Bush intended, the divergent views reappeared in Boutros-Ghali's December 19 report to the UNSC. Except for the probable close cooperation between the U.S. and the UN, Boutros-Ghali indicates the Bush team rejected the important task of disarming Somalia's warring groups, which had been the major obstacle to UNOSOM I's success. The U.S. also refused to extend protection to all parts of Somalia, limiting UNITAF work to Mogadishu's central aid distribution region. In contrast to Bush's December 4th rhetoric, the actual U.S. mission was best represented by General Powell's comment when the first U.S. Marines landed near Mogadishu: "It's sort of like the cavalry coming to the rescue, straightening things out for a while and then letting the marshal's come back to keep things under control." The problem with Powell's analogy was that Somalia had no marshals to "come back" to control Somalia's warlords. Bush's refusal to disarm the warring factions and make all of Somalia safe meant UNITAF was a quick police raid that provided no effective aid after the police left.[8]

UNITAF'S LIMITED SECURITY

By May 1993, UNITAF's limited military mission had created security areas around Mogadishu's airport and seaport and along convoy routes linking eight cities in central and southern Somalia. The awesome display of U.S. military power provided temporary safety for aid workers to distribute food, which saved the lives of about 100,000 starving Somalians. But UNITAF also created an illusion of security from the warlords, which evaporated when the weaker UNOSOM II force took over in May 1993. The Somalians who were rescued for five months in 1993 again experienced a precarious existence after May 1993.

President Bush seemed to realize there was a connection between controlling Somalia's militant groups and having a successful military venture because in December he sent Robert B. Oakley to Somalia to obtain the cooperation of Somalia's warlords before Lieutenant General Robert B. Johnston's UNITAF forces landed. In retrospect, Oakley's political tactics as head of the U.S. Liaison Office in Mogadishu probably handicapped the UNSC Resolution 794's long-term peacemaking objectives in Somalia. Oakley arrived two days before the first 1,800 U.S. Marine force landed on December 9. Outside the glare of TV cameras, Oakley easily convinced Aideed and Ali Mahdi to restrain their guerrilla forces because the U.S. forces would destroy them if necessary and both warlords knew the power of the U.S. forces which had swept away Iraq's army in 1991.

Oakley's initial goal was simple—he did not have to make strong demands on the warlords such as requiring them to disarm or to sign a peace agreement recognizing one government for the country. Thus, he secured the warlords temporary cooperation. When the U.S. Marines landed on December 9, their only challenge was a beach full of rabid reporters and brightly-lighted TV cameras. Oakley's cease-fire agreement, finalized on December 11, was generally, but not completely, effective until May 4. During the next four months UNITAF confiscated some of the militants arms and ordered the heavy weapons of Aideed and Ali Mahdi to be stored in areas outside the UNITAF "security zones". However, this disarming was coincidental to protecting the humanitarian convoy routes.

More serious, perhaps, Oakley's dealings with Aideed and Ali Mahdi gave them the appearance of being Somalia's legitimate rulers because he concentrated on the domains of these two Mogadishu leaders. UNITAF seldom moved into the rural areas of central and northern Somalia where gangs operated or local clans had some control despite frequent fighting. UNITAF authority extended from Mogadishu along convoy routes to the cities of Kismaayo, Baioda, Bardera, and Beletweyne. UNITAF also took over the Soviet built airport at Baledogle, located 160 kilometers from Mogadishu, but paid little or no attention to the northern regions of Somalia.

UNITAF's worst problems were at the southern port of Kismaayo where extensive conflict revived. In December, fighting had taken place at Kismaayo between one group, allied with Aideed, led by Ahmad Omar Jess and comprised of refugee Ogadan clans, and a second faction led by General Mohamed Siad Hersi (known as General Morgan) which included members of Siad Barre's national army and the Marehan clan that ruled Somalia before 1991. The fighting at Kismaayo stopped in mid-December but was renewed again in February and spread toward Mogadishu in March 1993.

In February, Belgian troops repelled Jess' men who fled Kismaayo after looting the warehouses of the International Red Cross and other humanitarian relief groups. The fighting continued, however, and spread toward Mogadishu in violation of Oakley's cease-fire. To end the uprising, an American quick reaction force of 500 men and helicopters reinforced the Belgians and restored order. As a result, Jess' men remained at a village near Kismaayo while U.S. soldiers moved Morgan's warriors to a village near the Kenyan border.

Because Jess' forces suffered the greatest losses, Aideed complained that UNITAF had interfered against Jess rather than Morgan. Consequently, his followers staged demonstrations that avoided U.S. forces but sacked the Egyptian embassy and attacked Nigerian troops. There were six days of disorder before U.S Marines assisted the Nigerians and restored order in Mogadishu.

During January and February, Oakley and General Johnston took several ineffective measures to provide order in Somalia. They held a few meetings with regional and district clans and inaugurated a local police and judicial system in UNITAF's security zones. But as Oakley's deputy, Walter R. Clarke concludes, these attempts were ineffective because Aideed and Mahdi appointed the judges and police officials none of whom were properly supervised. UNITAF expected the Somalians to convict and punish gang violations, which they never did. UNITAF officers asked the remnants of UNOSOM I troops to control the militants, however, the UN troops lacked sufficient military power to carry out these requests. Under UNITAF, Aideed, Ali Mahdi and other warlords retained local authority and military capabilities which neither UNOSOM I, nor UNOSOM II, were strong enough to challenge. For the UN, the hopeful sign for future peace were two meetings at Addis Ababa that various Somalian leaders attended.[9]

UN Conferences At Addis Ababa

The United Nations sponsored two conferences designed to establish political order before UNITAF withdrew. While as many as fifteen Somalian groups were represented at these conferences, the UN experienced two major problems. First, UN and UNITAF officials disagreed over whether to deal solely with Aideed, Ali Mahdi and other militant leaders or to encourage Somali civilian elders to replace the military warlords. Secondly, many Somali warlords resented previous UNOSOM I interference and, in particular, Aideed disagreed with Secretary General Boutros-Ghali who wanted UNITAF to disarm all existing militias. Justified or not, Aideed, who personally disliked Boutros-Ghali, believed the UN favored Ali Mahdi because the Organization of African Unity had recognized him as Somalia's ruler.

At Addis Ababa I, from January 4 to 15, 1993, the UN hoped to begin Somalia's process of reconciliation but General Aideed sabotaged these sessions by rejecting the UN agenda for a reconciliation conference. Later, at Addis Ababa II, from March 13 to 26, there were two separate meetings: a Humanitarian Conference of delegates from public and private relief agencies and representatives of non-military Somalia groups; and a National Reconciliation Conference of fifteen military factions. The Humanitarian meetings were led by UN Undersecretary General Jan Eliasson and UN coordinator of humanitarian aid, Philip Johnston. The reconciliation meeting was supervised by retired U.S. Admiral Jonathan Howe, a former Bush administration official who replaced Kittani as Boutros-Ghali's Special Representative to Somalia and Lansana Kouyate of Guinea who, as Howe's deputy, chaired the conference.

The Humanitarian Conference brought donor representatives together with Somalian civilian groups that the UN wanted to replace the militant groups in reconstructing Somalia's political and economic society. These civilian delegates included signatories of the 1990 Manifesto, traditional clan elders, Somalian women's groups, and Islamic religious leaders. The UN hoped these groups would revive Somalia's traditional clan customs and prepare for a peaceful society by trying to restore regional councils, organize national political groups, education, job opportunities, and the agricultural and medical rehabilitation of the country. At the end of the Humanitarian sessions, donor groups pledged $130 million in aid although the amount fell short of Eliasson's plans for $160 million. However, these pledges became irrelevant after UNITAF forces withdrew because the breakdown of Somalia's internal security repelled the donors.

The critical sessions at Addis Ababa II were primarily talks between the fifteen military groups, which had to be reconciled and disarmed to bring peace to Somalia. The reconciliation meetings began on a sour note because secessionists, who wanted a decentralized Somalia government, filibustered against most resolutions and Aideed delayed sessions to protest UNITAF's favorable attitude toward General Morgan after fighting broke out again in Kismaayo on March 16. Once Aideed came to the reconciliation table, the UN achieved a political agreement on March 27. The military leaders reaffirmed their January cease-fire and approved a Transitional National Council (TNC) for Somalia. The TNC was a 57-member council with representation for each of the fifteen warlords, plus other non-military groups attending the Humanitarian sessions such as the women's group which gained one-third of the TNC representation. Unfortunately, the documents did not spell out the details for selecting regional councils, for drawing boundaries, and for enforcing the promises made by the signatories. After UNITAF forces withdrew on

May 4, the Addis Ababa II promises were quickly forgotten by the warlords.[10]

TRANSITION FROM UNITAF TO UNOSOM II

By early March 1993, Robert Oakley and other UNITAF officials claimed "a secure environment" existed for humanitarian relief distributions. With great exaggeration, Oakley supported a quick U. S. withdrawal by asserting "the problem of clan warfare which has taken Somalian lives is virtually gone," and urged a hasty transition from UNITAF to the UN. Before UNITAF withdrew, Boutros-Ghali wanted assurances about the Somalian warlord's cease-fire and a new UNSC mandate. To satisfy the Secretary General, the Clinton administration delayed UNITAF's final withdrawal until May 4.

The first steps toward UNOSOM II began in March with a change in U.S. and UN officials in Somalia. Robert Gosende replaced Oakley and Boutros-Ghali appointed Admiral Howe to replace Kittani and Turkish General Cevik Bir to become the UN military commander when UNITAF forces withdrew. On March 3, Boutros-Ghali reported on conditions in Somalia and requested a mandate for UNOSOM II. His report contained the warlords January promises to disarm and indicated that the turning over of heavy weapons had barely begun and the UN would require constant support to complete the task. UNITAF had disarmed few warring factions and accepted responsibility for only 40 percent of Somalia's territory, moreover, it had cleared few land mines outside its security routes. The UN had just started to form an independent police constabulary. Boutros-Ghali called UNITAF's military response a "police action" which separated the essential political-military mission from the "purely humanitarian" one and gave security to limited areas. UNOSOM II would require at least the 37,000 troops used by UNITAF and the U.S. had agreed to provide a tactical quick reaction force to supplement the U.S. task force staying in Somalia. Boutros-Ghali's report asked the UNSC to expand UNOSOM I's mission to meet the unexpected dimensions of peacemaking and monitoring as well as peacekeeping and protecting humanitarian supplies.

Before UNITAF left, the Security Council's Resolution 814 established the UNOSOM II mission by adding peacemaking and nation-building missions to that of humanitarian assistance and "peacekeeping" after the parties agreed to a political settlement.[11]

UNOSOM II's FAULTS—
WARLORDS' CHALLENGE

Following UNITAF's withdrawal on May 4, UNOSOM II officials faced two major difficulties: first, they lacked specific plans to change Somalia's transitional government into a permanent regime; second, UNOSOM II's much less powerful military capability made it difficult to coerce the Somalian warlords to accept peace. Consequently, within a month after UNITAF's withdrawal, UNOSOM II's peacemaking mission became a warlord hunting venture.

Although UNITAF's General Johnston had discussed a possible warlord challenge with Admiral Howe and General Bir in April, they developed no plans to deal with a military threat or to negotiate with the warlords. The lack of UNOSOM II's preparations resulted from many errors of judgment, such as Boutros-Ghali's depending on the cease-fire to hold, the U.S. and UN officials underestimating the will and fighting ability of Somalia's clans, and disagreement about dealing with warlords or civilian clan leaders.

After UNITAF withdrew on May 4, UNOSOM II faced its new challenges with reduced military personnel and less heavy equipment. From UNITAF's total of 37,000 troops, which were mostly American to cover 40 percent of Somalia, UNOSOM II now had 14,000 troops for all of Somalia. New contingents raised the UN total to 28,000 in August, but these included many inexperienced and poorly equipped troops from small nations such as Botswana and Bangladesh. The new personnel also included "nation-building" units such as 1,500 German engineers and technicians who were not trained for combat. The Canadians withdrew their troops when UNITAF ended but France, Italy, and Pakistan kept most of their forces in Somalia. The U.S. retained a task force of about 4,000 members under Major General Thomas Montgomery including 1,167 members of an elite Quick Response Force (QRF) stationed on U.S. navy ships offshore and under the independent command of U.S. Major General William Garrison. The QRF would respond to emergency threats to UNOSOM II provided the U.S. Central Command in Florida approved. Since the U.S. withdrew most of its heavy equipment and helicopters, except for those in Garrison's QRF, UNOSOM II forces had few armored vehicles and helicopters as well as fewer army personnel trained for combat.[12]

General Bir was also troubled by the breakdown of his central command authority which UNITAF forces had under U.S. General

Johnston. This collapse began in June when French officers learned that Garrison's Quick Reaction Force took orders from General Bir only after first checking with Washington via Florida. France was always contentious about the American's peculiar unwillingness to operate under allied commanders and, on learning about the U.S. command structure, the French and Italians reported the situation to their home governments. Thereafter, French officers accepted orders for their 1,130 forces only if Paris approved and, after July, the Italians' 2,538 soldiers sought Rome's approval before taking directions from General Bir. When difficulties began in Mogadishu, the French rejected Bir's orders to stay in their assigned locations and moved to safer and more comfortable quarters in Baidoa to protect relief supply lines. Following Rome's instructions, the Italians initially accepted Bir's orders to search for Aideed but in July their officers refused to continue that mission.

The confrontation of UNOSOM II with the warlords began soon after UNITAF's departure. On May 4, UNOSOM II commander Admiral Howe started a process to empower Somalia's transitional government by declaring that the penal law code for Somalia would be the code devised by Somalia's democratic assembly in 1960 and abolishing the 1969 code of Siad Barre's authoritarian regime. Howe intended to promote Somalia's police and judicial system, initiated by the UN in March 1993, and to allow UNOSOM II to enforce the cease-fire provisions of Addis Ababa II. The new law code favored a civil government of local councils under the TNC.

Initially, Aideed cooperated by asking Admiral Howe's support for a reconciliation conference between southern Somalia and the nearby province of Galcayo which had not been under UNITAF control. Howe approved the meeting but insisted the UN, not Aideed, must sponsor it. Believing Howe's decision was evidence that the UN subverted his leadership, Aideed rejected the UN sponsorship and renewed his verbal attacks against the UN. Using Radio Mogadishu to broadcast charges that UN officials were asserting colonial authority, Aideed urged Somalians to boycott the UN conference on Galcayo by attending his alterative meeting.

Under these circumstances, Howe's conference on Galcayo reached no agreements and after the conference, UNOSOM II officials decided to challenge Aideed by using coercive methods to assert UN strength. When U.S. intelligence reports indicated hostile forces were preparing attacks on UNOSOM II, Howe ordered troops to inspect the warlords' depots for heavy military equipment that UNITAF had ordered kept outside its security zones.

The clash with Aideed began on June 4 after Admiral Howe announced that UNOSOM II would enforce the March 26 Addis Ababa disarmament agreement and close down Radio Mogadishu because of its UN criticism. UN troops would inspect and inventory the weapons storage facilities in southern Mogadishu, an area dominated by Aideed. Although an official in Aideed's group warned UNOSOM II not to launch the inspection without consulting Aideed, Howe and Bir ignored the warning.

According to a UN investigation of the June 5 incident, Admiral Howe had sent Pakistani forces in armored personnel carriers on loan from the U.S. to carry out the UN weapons inspection. When the Pakistanis arrived at the buildings where the weapons and Radio Mogadishu were located, they faced protestors angered by UN policies. As the Pakistanis later left the buildings, Aideed's militia ambushed them and, simultaneously, his forces attacked a UN food distribution center elsewhere in the city. When Aideed's militia pinned down Pakistani troops, General Montgomery called in the U.S. Quick Reaction force to join Italian armored vehicles in dispersing Aideed's men. The fire-fight killed 24 Pakistanis and wounded 56 other UNOSOM troops. Aideed's followers celebrated by mutilating the Pakistani's dead bodies and displaying them in public.

Because of attacks in two parts of Mogadishu, UN officials concluded the attacks were planned and strongly condemned Aideed. In New York, UNSC Resolution 837 of June 6, identified the attacks as "calculated and premeditated" and authorized all necessary measures against those responsible plus the disarmament of all Somalian parties as agreed at Addis Ababa. Admiral Howe and Boutros-Ghali perceived Aideed as the number one enemy and demonized him as the obstacle preventing peace. Although some investigators said the UNOSOM II inspection provoked the June 5 incident, the UN insisted the Addis Ababa agreements permitted such inspections to control the warring factions' armaments.

UN peacemaking efforts now focused on the hunt for Aideed to punish the most powerful group in Mogadishu. Initially, Admiral Howe and General Montgomery minimized American participation in the hunt by using Pakistani, Nigerian, Moroccan, Italian, and Malaysian units. These UNOSOM II units employed air attacks, ground sweeps, and arms searches into Aideed's enclaves. On June 17, after Moroccan forces suffered heavy casualties during their search, Howe offered a $25,000

reward for information leading to Aideed's arrest but found no
informants. Many Somalians, however, accepted Radio Mogadishu's
complaints about the UN and sympathized with Aideed. As a result,
neither Howe's reward for Aideed's capture, coercion by UNSOM II
forces, nor a four-month search by an additional 400 U.S. Army Rangers
and Delta-force Commandos, revealed Aideed's hiding place.

In Washington, Clinton became more closely involved in Somalia
policy, telling a press conference Aideed's forces were responsible "for
the worst attack on U.N. peacekeepers in three decades. We could not let
it go unpunished." A 1994 U.S. Senate Armed Forces Committee
investigation indicated the president began a series of actions which he
later admitted made the U.S. responsible for the October 3 disaster that
ended U.S. intervention. In June, Clinton's advisors were divided about
the proper policy to adopt. Admiral Howe wanted Aideed punished but
General Powell and Defense Secretary Les Aspin favored negotiating with
Aideed. Talks with Aideed never occurred but the White House sent CIA
agents to Somalia to track down Aideed.

The CIA never found Aideed but an unsuccessful raid to find him in
July and two incidents in August led to joint CIA-Delta Forces efforts to
capture Aideed. A July 12 raid on "Aideed's headquarters" by the U.S.
Quick Reaction Force seized documents, communications equipment, and
armaments but not Aideed or his military officers. The QRF helicopter
gunships killed 54 Somalians and wounded many more, although the UN
claimed only 24 Somalians died. Most of the Somalian casualties were not
Aideed militants but clan leaders meeting in the building. There were no
U.S. casualties, but angry Somalian mobs attacked and killed four
Western journalists, whose bodies were displayed before international
television cameras. The journalists were Hansi Krauss of *Associated Press*
and Dan Eldon, Hos Maina and Anthony Macharia, all of *Reuters*.

Following the July raid, Aideed told his men to "kill all Americans"
and General Montgomery asked President Clinton to dispatch additional
special forces and heavy military equipment to Somalia. The State
Department favored the additional U.S. fire-power, but members of the
U.S. congress objected. Secretary of Defense Aspin and General Powell
also opposed additional U.S. forces but after a remote control device
exploded under a U.S. vehicle and killed four American soldiers on
August 21, General Powell obtained Aspin's consent to send 400 U.S.
Ranger and Delta forces, a proposal Clinton approved. Nevertheless, Aspin
refused to deploy the heavy tanks, Bradley Fighting Vehicles, and

additional AC-130 Specter gunships which Generals Montgomery and Garrison had requested.

As these additional troops left, Aspin voiced his fears that even greater military efforts would be needed to secure Somalia and urged the UN to undertake a more realistic program to create political groups that could bring peace to the region. Former President James Carter and many congressional critics urged a reevaluation of U.S. policy, while the Italians and French opposed the search for Aideed. UN Secretary General Boutros-Ghali resisted changes in UN policy because he claimed all future UN peacekeeping efforts would be endangered if Aideed was not arrested.

The arrival of 400 Delta and Ranger forces increased UNOSOM II military raids between September 5 and 15, and casualties escalated in Mogadishu, including the killing of Somalian women and children. Although four American were killed in an August ambush, Aideed usually attacked Nigerian, Moroccan, Pakistani, and Italian forces, which suffered 21 killed and 46 wounded before October 3. Although the U.S. Delta-Army Ranger forces arrested many Somalians and rounded up a few of Aideed's officers, innocent Somalians, and some relief workers, they never captured Aideed.

On September 25 after the downing of a U.S. helicopter killed three Americans, Congress quickly passed a non-binding resolution asking the president to obtain congressional approval if U.S. forces remained in Somalia after November 15, 1993.

Clinton wavered, however, until October 3 when U.S. Rangers experienced a disastrous episode. The Rangers raided the Olympic Hotel in Mogadishu where they captured 24 Aideed militants. On leaving the hotel with their prisoners, the Rangers met a contingent of Aideed's militia who shot down two U.S. helicopters and surrounded the Rangers. For four hours, the U.S. Quick Reaction Force and UNOSOM II units engaged Aideed's troops in battle. UNSOM II suffered its worst casualties in a single battle, including the death of eighteen Americans and one Malaysian and wounding of seventy-eight Americans, nine Malaysian and three Pakistanis. Somalians also captured U.S. Chief Warrant Officer Michael Durant and dragged his injured body through Mogadishu streets while TV cameras relayed the event to world-wide audiences. Durant survived, but the TV reporters seldom noted the Somalians had sustained an estimated 312 deaths and 814 wounded.

Aideed's tactic of "killing Americans" achieved its goal. A previously apathetic US public focused their anger on U.S. policy in Somalia. Under pressure, Clinton reviewed his options in Somalia and consulted with congressional leaders. On October 7, he announced U.S. withdrawal plans. He ordered U.S. commanders to stop hunting Aideed and said all U.S. troops would withdraw by March 31, 1994. Clinton admitted the UN erred in seeking Aideed's capture, but the U.S. would try to negotiate Somalia's political reconciliation. Until the U.S. withdrew in 1994, Clinton helped UNOSOM II peace efforts in Somalia, appointing Robert Oakley to begin conciliation talks with the factions.[13]

Following the tragedy of October 3, Oakley returned to Somalia but could not persuade the warlords to end Somalia's political disorder. He did convince the militants to avoid interference with the U.S. troop departures and on March 3, 1994, the last American soldiers left Somalia.[14]

Boutros-Ghali asked the UNSC to reduce its Somalia mission in order to facilitate political reconciliation. On March 25, UNOSOM II forces were reduced to 1,900 troops and ordered to avoid conflict. The smaller UNOSOM II troops were units from nations such as Pakistan, Egypt, Zimbabwe or Morocco. But UN "peacemaking" efforts failed and on November 4, the UNSC voted unanimously to withdraw entirely from Somalia. In March 1995, U.S. ships off the coast of Somalia assisted UNOSOM II's safe departure that ended UNOSOM II's mandate.[15]

The UN failed to achieve peace but humanitarian agencies continued to provide relief and rehabilitation assistance to the clans while civil strife continued throughout 1996 and 1997 as new contenders competed for power. Aideed's claim to be president of Somalia was contested by Ali Mahdi and by Osman Hassan Ali (Atto) who led five Mogadishu sub-clans to attack Aideed in July 1996. Atto failed to capture Mogadishu's airport but Aideed was wounded and died during surgery.

Aideed's death intensified the fighting after his son Hussein Mohamed Aideed was chosen SNA president. Hussein's mother had taken him to America during the 1980s where he became a U.S. citizen and served with the U.S. Marines during Operation Restore Hope in 1993. In 1996, he returned to Somalia to replace his father as president of the SNA and continue the fight against Atto and Ali Mahdi. Hussein Aideed also had to contend with Islamic fundamentalist radicals who organized projects to "clean up" Mogadishu while converting Somalians to the

Shiite Islamic concepts advanced by Iran's government since 1979 and by their disciples in the Sudan and Egypt.[16]

A ray of hope came from Cairo in December 1997 when, after four months of talks, Hussein Aideed and Ali Mahdi signed a "Declaration of Principles". They promised to launch reconciliation conferences beginning in February 1998 and to prepare a transitional government charter.

SOMALIA LESSONS

Somalia became a classic Post-Cold War case of how, why and when an intervention should not be conducted. Analysts have found a host of military and diplomatic mistakes committed by the UN, the U.S., and others.

The five most significant of these mistakes, for the present study of U.S. intervention, are:

1. interventions undertaken with time limits are almost always futile because they indicate the criteria of moral imperative, national interest, chance of success, and public support have not been met;

2. advance notice of a quick exit is a mistake because the success of an intervention involves a mixture of circumstances;

3. interventions where local groups are fighting for control should be avoided because political mediation without intervention may be impartial, but military intervention cannot be neutral;

4. humanitarian aid by non-government volunteers are a mechanism for relieving human suffering, thus, if these groups need protection, the problems are not simply humanitarian, but also political and military; and

5. viable, long-term political objectives for the target area must be projected before military intervention.

NOTES

1. I.M. Lewis is recommended for studies about Somalia's history and culture; see especially his *A Modern History of Somalia: Nation and State in the Horn of Africa* (Boulder, CO: Westview, 1988) and Lewis' listings in Chapter Nine.

2. Terrence Lyon and Ahmed Y. Samatar, *Somalia: State Collapse, Multilateral Intervention and Strategies for Political Reconstruction* (Washington, DC: Brookings Institution, 1995); Jonathan Stevenson, *Losing Mogadishu* (Annapolis, MD: Naval Institute Press, 1995): 7-11. On U.S. aid see Jeffrey A. Lefebvre, *Arms for the Horn: U.S. Policy in Ethiopia and Somalia, 1953-91* (Pittsburg, PA: University of Pittsburgh Press, 1993); Donald Rothschild and John Ravenhill, "Subordinating African Issues to Global Logic," in Kenneth A. Oye, Robert J. Lieber and Donald Rothschild, eds., *Eagle Resurgent? The Reagan Era in American Foreign Policy* (Boston: Little, Brown, 1987): 408-409. Declassified documents from communist files in Russia and East German provide details about Soviet policy: James G. Hershberg, and others, "New East-Bloc Evidence on the Horn of Africa, 1977-1978," *Cold War International History Project Bulletin* 8/9 (Winter 1996-97): 18-102.

3. Mohamed Sahnoun, *The Somalia Challenge: The Missed Opportunities.* (Washington, DC: Institute for Peace Press, 1994): 3-11; Jane Perlez, "Somalia Abandoned to Its Own Civil War," NYT (Jan. 6, 1991): E-2.

4. Sahnoun, ibid., 25-37; Jonathan Stevenson, "Hope Restored in Somalia?" *Foreign Policy* No.91 (Summer 1993): 138-154; Jane Perlez, "A Diplomat Matches Wits with Chaos in Somalia," (Sept. 26, 1992): E-4; and Perlez, "Aid's Departure Another Blow to UN in Somalia," NYT (Oct. 31, 1992): A-2. The Africa Watch experts were Alex DeWaal and Rakiya Omaar, "Doing Harm by Doing Good?" *Current History* 92 (May 1993): 198-202; and De Waal and Omaar, "Somalia's Uninvited Saviors," *Washington Post* (Dec. 13, 1992): C1,4. Another account of the UN problems in Somalia is Jeffrey Clark, "Debacle in Somalia," in Lori Damrosh, ed., *Enforcing Restraint* (New York: Council on Foreign Relations, 1993): 218-225.

5. On the TV imperative see Clifford Orwin, "Distant Compassion (Somalia)," *The National Interest* No.43 (Spring 1996): 42-49: Peter Applebaum, "Scared by Faces of Need, Americans Say, 'How Could We Not Do This?'" NYT (Dec. 13, 1992): A-16. For a thorough discussion of estimated victims see Steven Hansh, et.al., *Excess Morality and the Impact of Health Intervention in the Somalian Humanitarian Emergency* (Washington, DC: Refugee Policy Group, 1994).

6. Oakley, Robert B. and John L. Hirsh, *Somalia and Operation Restore Hope* (Washington, DC: Institute of Peace, 1995): 35-46; Don Oberdorfer," The Road to Somalia," WPNW (Dec. 14-20, 1992): 6-7. Colin Powell's memoir seems to indicate he approved the mission without clearly considering the national interest and ignored Brent Scowcroft's question "when do we get out?" until after the mission began, see *My American Journey* (New York: Random House, 1995): 524.

7. Keith Richberg, "Aid Workers Watching Country Favor Toughness toward Warlords," *Washington Post* (Nov. 27, 1992): A-1, 36; Henry Kissinger, "Somalia: Reservations," ibid (Dec. 13, 1992): C-7. The Somalia experts for Africa Watch opposed the intervention, contending a political settlement was the crucial issue because humanitarian aid was available if political authorities could stop the looting by warring factions, see Alex De Waal and Rakiya Omaar, "Doing Harm by Doing Good? *Current History* 92 (May 1993): 198-202. This point seems to be conceded by Colin Powell, *American Journey,* 565-66 where he writes the famine was not a whim of nature but due to internal feuding. For other journalistic critics see Bruce W. Nelan, "Taking on the Thugs," *Time* 140 (Dec. 14, 1992): 26-35; Elaine Sciolino, "Getting in is the Easy Part of the Mission," *NYT* (Dec. 6, 1992): E-1,3; Smith Hempstone, "Think Three Times before You Embrace the Somalia Tarbaby," *U.S. News and World Report* 113 (Dec. 14, 1992): 30; Editorial, "But Who'll Disarm the Thugs?" *NYT* (Dec 13, 1992): 16.

8. Boutros-Ghali letter in UN Blue Book Series, Vol. VIII, *The United Nations and Somalia, 1992-1996* (New York: UN Department of Public Information, 1996): Document 36 of Dec 8, 1992, pp. 216-217; Powell quote in Sidney Blumenthal, "Why Are We in Somalia?" *New Yorker* 69 (Oct. 25, 1993): 48-71; John R. Bolton, "Wrong Turn in Somalia," *Foreign Affairs* 73 (Jan./Feb. 1994): 56- 67 blames Clinton for changing the mission, while Walter Clark and Jeffrey Herbst, "Somalia and the Future of Humanitarian Intervention," *Foreign Affairs* 75 (Mar./April 1996): 70-85 emphasize that Bush was to blame for leaving Clinton with a strange mission. For official U.S. statements see *U.S. State Department,* "Intervention in Somalia," *Foreign Policy Bulletin* 3 (Jan./Apr. 1993): 18-29.

9. Oakley and Hirsh, *Somalia and Operation Restore Hope*, 47-76; Lyons and Samatar, *Somalia: State Collapse,* 31-43; Diana Jean Schemo, "The World Moves on Somalia: The Warlords Move Faster," *NYT* (Feb. 21, 1993): E-6.

10. Ethiopia was selected for the conferences because the demise of Soviet power resulted in the overthrow of Mengistu in the spring of 1994 and the new President Meles Zenawi was friendly to the U.S., Jane Perlez, "Rebels Take Control," *NYT* (June 6, 1991): E-3; Lyons and Samatar, *Somalia: State Collapse,* 44-52.

11. Oakley and Hirsh, *Somalia and Operation Restore Hope*, 47-76; a more critical account is Stevenson, *Losing Mogadishu*, 54-70. UN Blue Book, *Somalia,* Document 49, pp. 244-257 has the Boutros-Ghali report of March 3; Document 51, pp.261-263 is on establishing UNSOM II.

12. Lyons and Samatar, *Somalia: State Collapse*, 53-57; Oakley and Hirsh, *Somalia and Operation Restore Hope*, 93-97; UN Blue Book, *Somalia*, Document 61, pp. 279-295 is Boutros-Ghali's report of August 16 on UNOSOM forces and problems

13. Thomas W. Lippman and Barton Gellman, "How Somalia Started Biting the Hand that Fed It, "*WPNW* (Oct. 18-24, 1993): 14-15. Excerpted statements by congressional leaders and Clinton are in U.S. State Department, "Walk, Don't Run to the Nearest Exit," *Foreign Policy Bulletin* 4 (Nov./Dec.1993): 19-27; Powell, *American Journey*, 588-604; UN Blue Book, *Somalia*, Document 75, pp. 323-336 is Boutros-Ghali's report of Nov. 12, 1993.

14. Oakley and Hirsh, *Somalia and Operation Restore Hope*, 124-160; UN Blue Book, *Somalia*, Document 91, pp. 426-429 is Boutros-Ghali's report on UNOSOM II of Aug. 14, 1994; Barton Gellman, "Pursuing Aideed into the   Shifting Sands of U.S. Purpose," *WPNW* (Oct. 11-17, 1993): 7 and Gellman, "A Deadly Round of Mixed Signals Over Somalia," *WPNW* (Nov. 8-14, 1993): 31; Keith Richburg,"The Warlord's War," *WPNW* (Oct. 11-17, 1993): 6. Richburg was greatly dismayed by his experiences in Somalia, see Richburg *Out of Africa*, (New York: Basic Books, 1996).

15. UN Blue Book, *Somalia,* Document 116 is the final report of Boutros-Ghali on Sept. 19, 1995 before the UN left Somalia and only keeps political offices in Kenya available for negotiations. For an account favorable to Aideed, see Alex Shoumatoff, "The 'Warlord' Speaks," *Nation* 258 (Apr. 4, 1994): 442-450.

16. Assoc. Press, "Militia Says it Captured Somalia's Airport," NYT (July 7, 1996): A-3; Donald G. McNeil, Jr., "Somalia Clan Leader Who Opposed U.S. is Dead," NYT (Aug. 3, 1996): A-1, 4; and McNeil, "Aideed's Son Sworn In," NYT (Aug 5, 1996); James McKinley Jr.," How a U.S. Marine Became Leader of Somalia," NYT (Aug.12, 1996): A-3; McKinley, "Islamic Movement's Niche," NYT (Aug. 23, 1996): A-1, 6; and McKinley, "As Talks Stall, Somalia Strife Kills 300 Over 5 Days," NYT (Dec. 19, 1996): A-6. For a report on better conditions in northern Somalia, see Stephen Buckley, "A Port in a Storm Amid Anarchy in Somalia," WPNW (Mar. 11-17, 1996): 18.

CHAPTER THREE

U. S. INTERVENTION IN HAITI

Historically, the U.S. had often intervened in Caribbean affairs to maintain order, insure payment of debts or encourage democracy. In 1991, however, American officials differed over policy objectives after Haiti's military overthrew the democratically elected president, Jean-Bertrand Aristide. The sharp differences among Washington's factions centered on whether the U.S. should encourage democracy in Haiti or support Haiti's authoritarian regime to protect U.S. investments.

Officials in the State Department wanted to promote democracy by returning the democratically elected president to power. A group of senior agents in the Central Intelligence Agency (CIA) and the Department of Defense's Intelligence Agency (DIA), however, staunchly supported Haiti's authoritarian regime which accommodated U.S.-controlled, low-wage, corporate factories by producing low-cost goods for the "competitive" world market. Both factions claimed their plans would benefit U.S. investors, but the hard-liners in the CIA and DIA chose existing benefits rather than risk the uncertainty Aristide's democratic regime might bring. In assessing Haiti's situation, the U.S. public possessed little or no knowledge about these U.S. bureaucratic differences until 1993 when investigative reporters discovered these contradictory divisions seeking to influence policies in Washington and the U.S. embassy in Haiti.

Whatever subordinate's differences were, from 1991 to 1993 the White House remained passive toward Haiti's political problems, allowing negotiators from the Organization of American State (OAS) and the UN to seek Aristide's return. Presidents Bush and Clinton were primarily concerned about Haitian refugees fleeing to the U.S., but neither immediately linked the refugee issue with Aristide's return. By May 1993, however, the refugee question, the terrorist tactics of Haiti's junta which raised moral questions with human rights groups, and the failure of OAS-UN talks convinced Clinton that the U.S. had moral and national interests that required intervention.

Following a year of delays, Clinton took decisive action in 1994, when the U.S. developed a UN-approved mission to restore Aristide and encourage Haiti's democracy. Unlike Somalia, however, U.S. intervention in Haiti had important precedents.

HAITI AND THE UNITED STATES TO 1986

If the Somalian intervention was exceptional, the use of U.S. forces in Caribbean nations like Haiti was normal. In 1823, James Monroe's "doctrine" had warned Europeans not to intervene in the Western Hemisphere. Fortified after 1901 by Theodore Roosevelt's "corollary" to the Monroe Doctrine, presidents intervened at various times in Cuba, Panama, Nicaragua, the Dominican Republic, Columbia, Mexico, Venezuela, and Haiti.

In 1915, Woodrow Wilson sent the U.S. Marines to restore order in Haiti but, when they left in 1934, Haiti was no better off than before. The Marine occupation did not build democracy because U.S. Marine officers from southern U.S. states carried their anti-Black baggage with them, launching attacks on Haitians which historian Hans Schmidt describes as "tantamount to genocide."

The U.S. occupation helped Haiti repay its $24 million debt to European bankers but democracy fell by the wayside. President Herbert Hoover adopted a program that led to the withdrawal of U.S. forces in 1934, although until 1941, U.S. officials continued to supervise Haiti's political and economic affairs. Haiti adopted a constitution granting Haiti's president great authority and, by 1941, Haiti had funded its debts. There was no improvement, however, in the economy or agricultural system where most of the profits went to the wealthy Haitian elite. Haiti's political-economic life centered in cities where a wealthy mulatto elite dominated the coffee export trade, siphoning off the small farm profits of Haiti's majority through heavy export-import taxes, and keeping Haiti's black majority poor, illiterate, and politically ignored.[1]

After the U.S. left, Haiti's political power returned to the mulatto elite and their military allies. A junta led by General Dumarsis Estimé ruled until 1950 when a coup made Colonel Paul Magloire president. Seven years later General Francois Duvalier set up an authoritarian regime that lasted until 1986. Known as "Papa Doc" because of his medical training, Duvalier terrorized his opponents and halted elections in 1963 to become president-for-life. He controlled Haiti's wealthy elite, the army, the police, and the Catholic Church. The elite and the military retained social status if they were "loyal", a loyalty Papa Doc insured through secret police recruited from Haiti's black populace and known as the "Tontons Macoutes". This group gave power to some of Haiti's black majority but it deteriorated into a terrorist faction that arbitrarily tortured and killed suspected opponents of Duvalier and intimidated the general populace whether black or mulatto. The Macoutes were rewarded by "Papa Doc" but were increasingly hated by the public.

Duvalier gained supervision of Haiti's Catholic Church in the 1966 Papal concordat that permitted him to name Haitian bishops. Duvalier appointed the first black, Haitian-born bishop in 1966, Francois Wolf Ligondé, but soon black Haitians despised Church leaders who tolerated Duvalier's terrorism and frequently returned to their native Voodoo cult. To insure family control, Francois made his son, Jean-Claude ("Baby Doc"), president in 1972; however, he lacked the strong personality required to hold power. After marrying an aristocratic mulatto, Baby Doc adopted policies that led to his overthrow in 1986.

Baby Doc's most critical decision was to accept President Richard Nixon's offer to aid Haiti against the Cuban communists by bringing U.S. investments to Haiti. Under the Agency for International Development (AID), Nixon and successive presidents provided funds to construct factories employing low-wage workers to make products for corporations such as General Motors. AID funds created a new Haitian business elite that opened the nation to foreign investors, including financial institutions such as the National City Bank of New York. AID's publications described the advantages of Haiti's factories, such as an electronic plant saving 20 to 60 percent of costs of similar U.S.-made items. Haiti had no labor unions, no laws interfering with hiring and firing workers, no worker fringe benefits, and women workers who adapted "easily to industrial discipline." By 1991, U.S. companies made 90 percent of Haiti's exported manufactured items.[2]

In contrast to AID claims, a U.S. scholar reported that the menial wages paid Haitian workers never raised Haiti's living standards. In one U.S.-operated textile mill, workers earned $1.48 a day but had to pay for company lunches and bus fare. In brief, AID money only helped U.S. corporate profits and the income of Haiti's wealthy elite.

Duvalier's regime grew dependent on U.S. aid, which precipitated new problems. Haitians complained about the low wage income and repressive government, while American officials faced two other difficulties—the flood of Haitian refugees seeking a better life in America and the involvement of Haiti's army in transshipping Columbia cocaine to the mainland.

The refugee problem began in 1979 when 70,000 Haitians arrived, presenting problems for Presidents Carter and Reagan. Although U.S. policy permitted all Cubans to enter Florida, immigration officials questioned the Haitians' right to asylum because Duvalier was anticommunist and, allegedly, black Haitians sought economic not political protection. But did Duvalier's terror differ from Castro's? The Immigration Service built detention camps for Haitians and made extensive checks to learn if individuals fled for political or economic reasons. These camps became overpopulated and, in 1981, President Reagan negotiated an agreement with "Baby Doc" to allow the U.S. Coast Guard to patrol Haitian waters, stop all refugee boats, and return them to Haiti.

Secondly, by 1980, Haitian army officers were involved in the cocaine traffic. The U.S. Drug Enforcement Agency (DEA), the State Department, and the CIA knew Panama's General Manuel Noriega and Haiti's "Baby Doc" profited from the transit of illegal drugs. To stop the traffic evidence was needed to indict persons in U.S. courts, an effort requiring Haiti's cooperation. The "war on drugs" program coincided with growing complaints by Haiti's army and militia against Duvalier's regime and by Tontons Macoutes members who saw Baby Doc as a traitor to black Haitians. Following protests and demonstrations against Jean-Claude, an army faction led by General Henri Namphy took over the presidential palace, permitting "Baby Doc" to flee to Spain.[3]

SEARCHING FOR DUVALIER'S SUCCESOR

Namphy's appointment of a national council to prepare a new constitution and his call for elections pleased State Department officers who desired democracy. But CIA-DIA operatives wanted a strong Haitian leader to maintain order and guarantee profits for U.S. investments. As Bob Shacochis explains, the divisiveness in Washington between diplomats and "spies" continued throughout the years after 1986.[4]

Duvalier's overthrow did not change Haiti's authoritarian structure. U.S. officials expected Namphy to keep Haiti stable for U.S. offshore investors, but DEA agents and State Department officials advised Namphy to establish democracy as the best long-term political policy. In contrast, as U.S. reporters later discovered, CIA-DIA agents funded two Haitian groups with ties to the army: the *Sécurité Intelligence Nationale* (SIN), an

army intelligence-gathering group committed to the military regime; and
the Front for the Advancement and Progress of Haiti (FRAPH), a political
party favoring an authoritarian regime. SIN and FRAPH opposed
Aristide's democratic program before and after he won the December
1990 election.

Key Figures

Abraham, Herard: army general who aids the March 1990 coup that
led to democratic elections in December 1990.

Aristide, Jean-Bertrand: Catholic priest to the poor who is elected
president in December 1990 becoming a central figure in Haiti.

Avril, Prosper: colonel of army gains power in a coup in 1998 but
his promises for "democracy" fails and he is overthrown in
March 1990.

Bazin, Marc: Haitian businessman and former World Bank official
preferred by technocrats in Haiti's elections.

Cédras, Ráoul: military officer who led overthrow of Aristide in
September 1991; was exiled in 1994.

Duvalier, Francois ("Papa Doc"): military dictator of Haiti from
1957 to 1971.

Duvalier, Jean-Claude ("Baby Doc"): named to succeed Papa Doc
as President, he lost popularity and was overthrown in 1986.

Pascal-Troillet, Ertha: after March 1990 coup overthrows General
Avril, she, as a Supreme Court judge, becomes provisional
president.

Preval, Rene: member of Lavalas Party, he is selected by Aristide to
run as president in 1995 and wins five year term.

The CIA-DIA spent about $400 million to assist SIN's political
operations and $1 million to train their officers in alleged drug-fighting
tactics. SIN provided no valid data on the drug traffic or Haiti's political
development; instead it became involved in terrorist activity supporting
Haiti's elite and one SIN leader, Lieutenant General Ráoul Cédras,
organized the September 1991 overthrow of Aristide. Other SIN members
engaged in Haiti's drug traffic and, to the dismay of the CIA-DIA, the
DEA secured evidence to indict three SIN officers in September 1992.
DEA officials also named 41 Haitians who participated in Haiti's violence,
most of whom were SIN or FRAPH members. Nevertheless, because CIA
and DIA operations are clandestine, their spokespersons in Washington
could contradict DEA and State Department reports about the terror,
violence, and drug traffic of Haiti's army. CIA spokesman Brian Latell

praised Cédras and his officers, telling the U.S. Congressional Oversight Committee and senators such as Jesse Helms (R-SC) that stories of terror and violence in Haiti were exaggerated and Aristide was "mentally unstable" and unable to rule.[5]

Meanwhile, after March 1987, Haiti's politics was dominated by army factions and the Tontons Macoutes. Haiti's army had four factions whose leaders used mercenaries to compete for power, while the Tontons Macoutes terrorized the people in support of a Duvalierist. Haiti's 1987 election had attracted 16 different parties but foreign journalists observing the election found only political disorder. On election day, Haiti's army and paramilitary units attacked citizens waiting to vote, killing several hundreds and wounding many more. Namphy said the army saved Haiti from foreigners, "communists", and the "Catholic Church." In new "elections" without foreign observers on January 17, 1988, Leslie Manigat was elected but lasted in office only until June, when Namphy removed him for refusing to extradite a Duvalierist cocaine dealer to America, a dealer Namphy opposed. But Namphy was overthrown on September 17, 1988 and General Prosper Avril gained power for two years before a junta led by General Hérard Abraham deposed him in May 1990. Three coups in three years!

Abraham tried to follow the advice of U.S. State Department officials who were discouraged by Haiti's frequent political changes. He appointed Supreme Court Justice Madame Ertha Pascal-Trouillot as provisional president, pending elections. In mid-1990, however, Haiti was near political anarchy because diverse military groups opposed Trouillot and her officials could not collect taxes to pay the civil bureaucrats and army personnel. At the same time, Haiti's wealthy wanted "law and order," assembly plant workers wanted better wages, and peasants desired better living conditions. Under difficulty circumstances in 1990, many Haitians saw Father Jean-Baptist Aristide as a savior.[6]

ARISTIDE'S RISE TO POPULARITY

Thirty-seven years old in 1990, Aristide was a Roman Catholic priest who, like many Latin American priests in the late twentieth century, found reasons to challenge the church hierarchy for neglecting the needs of parish members. Aristide became an advocate of "liberation theology," a Christian ministering to the poor but criticizing the elite classes that claimed to be Christian but oppressed the lower class.

Aristide became popular through a radio program where he demanded drastic changes in Haiti's social, economic, and political structure. He became priest for Saint Jean Bosco Church, a slum parish in Port-au-Prince where he saw the daily plight of the poor and believed the way to improve their life was to end the power of Haiti's elite, corrupt army officers, and the Tontons Macoutes.

The overthrow of Duvalier's regime and the competition between power blocs increased the despair of Haiti's lower classes, who found Aristide's preaching appealing. In contrast, Haiti's wealthy and the established Church feared Aristide's radical influence and tried to stop it by frightening his followers. On September 11, 1988, during worship services at Saint Jean Bosco church, armed thugs broke down the church doors and attacked the worshippers with guns and machetes, killing thirteen people and wounding seventy others. The thugs then poured gasoline over the pews and set the church on fire. Outside, observers claimed Haitian police and fire fighters watched from a block away, arriving after the church was destroyed.

The attack did not intimidate Aristide's followers; instead, his miraculous survival made him more popular among students and some middle-class Haitians as well as workers and peasants. Aristide formed a party named Lavalas, a term by which he urged Haitians to "wash away" corrupt leaders just as pure strong, mountain waters uprooted the filth it passed over coming down a mountain.[7]

Although Aristide's popularity posed a threat to Haiti's power brokers, he was a moderate reformer compared to other groups organized after 1986. The most notable "radical" leader in 1990 was Victor Benôit, the presidential candidate of the National Congress of Haitian Democracy, who desired to uproot Haiti's elite and eliminate the Macoutes and other militants. He went farther by wanting to end Haiti's dependence on foreign investments, to make Creole the official Haitian language, and to promote Voodoo as Haiti's religion. Benoit was never as popular as Aristide because he lacked the formers charismatic rhetoric and popular ideas.[8]

In contrast to parties advocating major changes in Haiti's social-political structure, the U.S. State Department's "unofficial" candidate in 1990 was Marc Bazin, a former World Bank official and member of Haiti's business community. Bazin, like Namphy, had opposed Duvalier's regime and wanted to increase U.S. investments in Haiti's manufacturing that employed Haiti's low-cost workers. To assist Bazin, the U.S. National

Endowment for Democracy (NED) provided $36 million to finance his campaign. Reagan had established NED to promote anticommunist governments, when the Cold War definition of "democracy" included authoritarian, but friendly anticommunist regimes.

Despite three coup d'etâts from 1987 to 1990, Haiti's need for U.S. economic assistance compelled its leaders to conduct an election which, hopefully, would stabilize Haiti. Thus, when General Abraham took over in 1990 and named Trouillot provisional president, he also promised elections by the end of 1990. Initially, Aristide refused to run for president until the power of the army, elite wealthy, and paramilitary groups ended. But later Aristide joined Lavalas with the National Front for Democracy and Change (FNCD), a coalition whose leaders said they would help achieve his objectives after he won election as their candidate. The FNCD coalition included Aristide's workers and peasants but also members from the old merchant class who disliked the new manufacturing interests.

Consequently, Aristide won the December 1990 election—with 68 percent of the votes cast—which was certified as fair and free by United Nations observers. Despite this victory, Aristide again experienced a "miraculous" escape from militants trying to prevent his inauguration. Led by Roger Lafontant, Macoutes thugs took over the presidential palace in early January 1991, but were forced to leave when masses of Aristide's followers surged through the palace gates, risking their lives, to regain control of the palace. Aroused, Aristide's backers took vengeance on the once dreaded Macoutes paramilitary that had intimidated them for years, killing dozens of Tontons Macoutes and other gang members during the next week. Some Americans were aghast by the horrors of Aristide's supporters, but those who knew the vile reputation of the Macoutes could understand, if not condone, the action of a populace against their long-time tormentors.

Aristide's Lavalas Party subsequently won a plurality in January elections for the National Assembly, gaining more votes than any party but without a majority of the seats. Lavalas had 13 of 27 seats in the Senate and 27 of 83 in the Chamber of Deputies. The showing of the Lavalas Party combined with Aristide's overwhelming vote in December gained international support for the new government.[9]

THE SEPTEMBER 1991 COUP D' ETAT

Haiti's constitutionally elected government lasted seven months before an army junta overthrew Aristide. Immediately after the coup, Aristide's enemies, including the CIA-DIA, propagated the notion that the president's personal mental failings and political shortcomings justified the army's action. Based on later examination, however, it appears that Aristide simply lacked the political manipulative talents used by Haiti's power brokers. The critical factor subverting Aristide was the fear of Haiti's traditional rulers that if Aristide remained in power, he would abolish their sources of power and wealth.

Aristide was unaccustomed to the need of compromise in politics and the tactics required of a parliamentary president. He did not build alliances with those who did not always agree with him, nor share decisions with the coalition members of the FNCD, nor did he forcefully condemn the violence of rabid followers who killed Macoutes or suspected Macoutes by placing burning tires around their necks. While the extent of this violence was exaggerated by Aristide's enemies, especially when compared to that committed by other Haitian groups since 1986, he should have condemned these acts.

More fearful to Haiti's ruling class was Aristide's effort to uproot the their power base. Two of Aristide's efforts were designed to "wash out" corrupt practices of the past. First, he purged many army officers, replacing them with personal appointees. In issuing his orders, Aristide acted unilaterally, as the Duvaliers had done, avoiding Assembly debate. Aristide also sought to separate the army and the police, but his newly appointed police chief was as corrupt as his predecessors.

Aristide's most tragic appointment was replacing Abraham with Lt. General Ráoul Cédras, who would engineer Aristide's overthrow in September. Cédras had kept militants quiet during the 1990 elections but he secretly was a member of SIN and, being on the CIA's payroll, gave U.S. intelligence agents negative reports about Aristide before and after the September coup. U.S. embassy officials did not tell Aristide about Cédras' connections, moreover, the CIA probably never told the State Department about SIN.

During Aristide's months in office, the U.S. embassy issued favorable reports about his presidency and, apparently, no one anticipated his overthrow. The U.S. renewed economic aid to Haiti and, in August, the World Bank examined Aristide's record before agreeing to loan Haiti $422 million. In mid-September, Aristide visited New York City where he received the keys to the city and spoke to the UN General Assembly before he returned to Haiti on September 29.

The next day, Ráoul Cédras led a well-planned army uprising that forced Aristide into exile. One army group took control of Haiti's state-owned stations and TV networks; another unit seized the presidential palace but allowed Aristide to escape to exile, a decision the CIA said its agent, Colonel Alex Silva, persuaded Cédras to accept. In Port-au-Prince and cities throughout the country, Haiti's army undertook an extensive campaign against Aristide's followers who were tracked down, arrested, and tortured or killed.

Cédras' terrorism continued for a year, with the most destructive attack occurring in December 1993, when the CIA-DIA backed right-wing FRAPH attacked Port-au-Prince's largest slum area, Cité Soleil, whose 200,000 residents included many Lavalas. The attack killed 70 residents, wounded many more, and burned 1,000 shanties, leaving 10,000 people homeless.[10]

INTERNATIONAL GROUPS SEEK ARISTIDE'S RETURN

The U.S., the OAS and the UN reacted harshly to Aristide's overthrow. On October 3, President Bush announced a freeze on Haiti's financial assets and the OAS refused to recognize Cédras' junta, called for Aristide's restoration, and approved a trade embargo against Haiti which the U.S. supported.

Negotiations for Aristide's return began when Latin American foreign ministers, led by Argentina's Guido de Tella, visited Port-au-Prince in November 1991 to talk with Cédras. The foreign ministers were fulfilling an OAS decision of June 1991 where the Western Hemisphere's 34 democratic nations unanimously agreed to call an emergency meeting if any member nation experienced a military coup. On arriving in Haiti, de Tella told reporters that Haiti's coup challenged the OAS whose members hoped to preserve democratic regimes. With the U.S.-OAS embargo in place, the foreign ministers persuaded Cédras to send a group of Haiti's assembly leaders to meet with Aristide in Venezuela and discuss terms for restoring democracy. The talks moved to Washington where an agreement was signed in February 1992. The pact was ineffective, however, because Haiti's assembly rejected it for not giving amnesty to those involved in the coup against Aristide. Although Cédras allowed the OAS to send eighteen human rights observers to view the "declining violence" in Haiti, little resulted from this initial effort.[11]

Throughout 1992, reports from Haiti indicated new violence had erupted because Colonel Michel Francois, the head of Haiti's police, broke with Cédras. Francois' rural officers, known as *chefs de section*, intimidated or killed peasants favoring Aristide. Refugee Haitians in Guantanamo detention camps told UN officials that Francois targeted them to be tortured or imprisoned.

President Bush would not meet with Aristide at the White House in 1992, indeed, only members of the Democratic Party's Black Caucus showed enthusiasm for Aristide. Throughout 1992, Aristide failed to obtain effective enforcement of the economic sanctions against Cédras' regime. Haiti's poorest people suffered most from the sanctions because the wealthy visited the U.S. mainland or Caribbean states to maintain their elegant lifestyle. More critically, the European Community's members did not recognize the sanctions and about 90 percent of Haiti's oil came from Europe while European goods in Port-au-Prince were available to the wealthy. Although some OAS officials wanted to prohibit European ships from using Latin American ports, the Bush administration rejected such action and, in fact, Bush did not enforce trade restrictions on Haiti because of pressure from the U.S. business community. A major "leak" in the sanctions was the $250 million that Haitians in the U.S. sent to relatives. The exiles said their money was needed to feed relatives in Haiti.[12]

THE REFUGEE ISSUE

Aristide's overthrow and the militant attacks on his followers precipitated the flight of more refugees. By December 1991, 6,000 refugees tried to reach Florida but, under existing policy, they were taken to detention camps at the U.S. naval base in Guantanamo to await interviews by U.S. immigration authorities. Bush's administration claimed most refugees fled for economic reasons and were not eligible for asylum, a policy which was challenged in 1991 because U.S. human-rights advocates contended that Haiti's refugees should receive the same rights as those fleeing Castro's communism. In December 1991, Federal Judge C. Clyde Atkins ruled in favor of equal treatment by issuing an injunction to prevent the repatriation of Haitians as economic refugees; however, upon appeal a higher court reversed his ruling.

The refugee issue did not die and, ultimately, was one of many issues in the 1992 presidential campaign. On January 31, 1992, President Bush began forcibly deporting Haitians who arrived after the 1991 coup, sending 381 repatriates to Port-au-Prince where Red Cross personnel gave each one $15 and food vouchers to go home. Although the U.S. State Department argued there were no "documented" cases of repatriated Haitians who were punished at home, United Nations observers in Haiti claimed that "dozens" of these repatriates were beaten, imprisoned, or received death threats. The UN reports prompted Democratic presidential nominee William Clinton to challenge Bush's policy by contending that better methods for treating the refugees could be found.

Bush, however, hardened his policy in 1992 because refugees overflowed Guantanamo. Another 12,000 had arrived by May 1992 and reports claimed more were preparing to leave. To stem the flow, Bush ordered the U.S. Coast Guard to stop all boats of refugees leaving Haiti and take them back—a policy that virtually stopped the refugee exodus.

After his election in November, Clinton reverted to Bush's repatriation program upon learning that 100,000 refugees were preparing to leave Haiti. On June 2, 1993, the U.S. Supreme Court upheld Bush's policy, based on U.S. immigration laws and international treaties that the U.S. Senate had ratified.

Clinton's only qualification of Bush's policy was to encourage Haitians to apply for asylum at the U.S. Embassy but few Haitians did so because they would not risk passing Haitian police to enter the embassy. After William Coracelan obtained a valid U.S. visa for asylum the Haitian police followed him to the Port-au-Prince airport where he was arrested. Although he U.S. protested, the Haitian government never released him.[13]

CLINTON'S OCTOBER 1993 HUMILIATION

As with the refugees, the Clinton administration initially followed Bush's basic policies of lax enforcement of the OAS economic sanctions and allowing the OAS and UN to negotiate Aristide's return. In January 1993, another round of OAS-UN negotiations led by the UN's Dante Caputo revived hope that Aristide's return was imminent because Cédras' offered to admit 350 more UN human rights observers. These expectations were stymied, however, after Cédras wanted the lifting of OAS-UN economic sanctions *before* the observers arrived. The dispute over observers was another of Cédras' delaying tactics because the important issues remained undecided—amnesty for the junta leaders and the disarming of Haiti's military factions.

After Caputo's talks failed, Clinton proposed tougher UN sanctions against Cédras and, on June 16, UN Ambassador Madeleine Albright strongly supported UNSC Resolution 841 that levied a worldwide oil and armaments embargo against Haiti. To make the oil embargo effective, the European nations agreed to stop oil shipments and the UNSC gave Cédras one week for "positive action" permitting Aristide's return. But Cédras ignored the deadline and the arms and oil sanctions became official.

Cédras offered to meet with Aristide and, with sanctions in place, Caputo convened talks at Governors Island, New York. With Secretary of State Warren Christopher's backing, Caputo mediated between Cédras and Aristide from June 28 to July 3, 1993, when they signed the Governors Island agreement consisting of eight principal parts: 1. the UN embargo would continue until Haiti's Assembly ratified the agreement; 2. Haiti's Assembly would legislate reforms of the police and armed forces under UN supervision; 3. Aristide's party and other parties would be free to prepare for the president's restoration; 4. foreign financial groups would help rebuild Haiti's economy; 5. amnesty would be granted for the 1991 coup leaders but Cédras would retire when Aristide returned; 6. Aristide would name a new prime minister before arriving; 7. a 1,200 member UN peacekeeping force, including army technicians and engineers from the U.S. and Canada, would help Haiti to rebuild its infrastructure; and 8. a deadline of October 30 was set for Aristide's return.[14]

Following the July 3 Governor's Island "success," there were hopes for Aristide's safe return. The encouraging signs were Cédras appearance on Haitian television to urge acceptance of the July accords; Aristide's appointment of Robert Malval as prime minister was approved by Haiti's Assembly; and a successful Florida conference of Haitian businessmen who planned economic recovery with the World Bank, the International Monetary Fund, the U.N. Development Agency, and the U.S. AID.

Ominously, however, were reports of new violence in Haiti. Militants who opposed the Governors Island accords escalated the violence, the main instigator being police chief Michel Francois who had gained command over several paramilitary groups and the rural *chefs de section*, including former Macoutes who wanted Duvalier's heir to rule. The militants disrupted a UN meeting with Haiti's Minister of Finance, holding the delegates hostage and threatening members of the ministry staff with death if they supported Aristide. Following this incident, Aristide urged UN officials to remove Cédras, Francois, and the plain-clothes "police" who terrorized people. The July accords, however, did not require the disarming of Haiti's militants and, as in the case of UNITAF in Somalia, the UN could not restrain the militants.

Despite the violence and demonstrations in Haiti, the UN and the Clinton administration moved to fulfill the July accords. Although peace was not secure on September 23, the UNSC approved the dispatch of 1,200 "peacekeeping" soldiers, police, and technicians to Haiti and U.S. Defense Secretary Aspin announced 600 U.S. military engineers, medical technicians, and civilian affairs experts would be part of the UN group. The U.S. media failed to emphasize that the U.S. and Canadian personnel were not combat troops because Cédras had promised to provide security for the UN and Aristide. The U.S. and Canadian engineers and technicians would train Haitians and help rebuild roads, bridges, communications systems, schools, and other essentials.

Before the U.S. and Canadian personnel left for Haiti, various indicators made the UN venture doubtful because the lightly armed UN forces would be "inviting targets" for Haiti's militants. In Washington, there were disputes between the Pentagon and State Department because U.S. troops in Somalia also experienced trouble in September 1993. Finally, there was no definite evidence that Cédras would or could restrain the militants. On October 6, after 26 American and five Canadian logistic officials reached Haiti to prepare for the arrival of UN peacekeepers, Port-au-Prince's streets filled with militants who organized a general strike to close the seaport where UN troops would land. On October 11, the *USS Harlan County* arrived off Port-au-Prince carrying 220 U.S. and Canadian engineers and technicians, Haitian mobs blocked the dock and armed militants threatened waiting diplomats and reporters. Also, Haitian police set up roadblocks to search all foreigners and intimidate individuals in the UN mission.

Although UNSC officials warned Haitian leaders that economic sanctions would be resumed if UN vessels were blocked, the militants refused to leave the dock area. U.S. reporters, meanwhile, discovered that anti-Aristide DIA-CIA agents aided in preventing the UN landing because they told Cédras the UN could be easily thwarted. One report alleged that U.S. Marine Major General John Sheehan told Cédras "One shot and we're out of there."

On October 12, after waiting nearly two days to decide, Clinton ordered the *Harlan County* and U.S.-Canadian technicians to return home. He also asked the UN to renew the tough economic sanctions that had been lifted.[15]

CLINTON DECIDES TO TAKE ACTION

From October 1993 to May 1994, Clinton and Secretary Christopher hoped economic sanctions and negotiations would persuade Haiti's elite to restore Aristide, but these wishes went unfulfilled. Finally in May 1994, after the Haitian refugee problem became serious, and Aristide and Cédras failed to reach a compromise, Clinton opted for strong economic sanctions and their strict enforcement, aimed at Haiti's ruling elite, while preparing to use a multinational invasion force if necessary.

In 1993-94, Clinton was handicapped because of divisions about Haitian policy within Washington's bureaucracy. When Clinton and Christopher moved toward a stronger U.S. role in behalf of Aristide, CIA and DIA agents and their counterparts in the U.S. Embassy at Port-au-Prince complicated the president's task. Aristide's election in 1990 had dismayed these U.S. bureaucrats as well as Haiti's SIN, FRAPH, and other groups who feared Aristide's populist-style democratic program would displace the elite power brokers who maintained order.

After Aristide's 1991 overthrow, the CIA spread rumors about Aristide's mental health problems because the CIA-DIA military attachés at the Port-au-Prince embassy, John Kambourian and Army Colonel Stephen Lovasz, were staunch Aristide opponents. Clinton's new ambassador, William Swing trusted his embassy staff would support, not detract from the president's decisions. Swing's faith was no match for the "realistic" convictions of Kambourian and Lovasz. Moreover, Clinton's special envoy to Haiti, Lawrence Pezzella, who was acquainted with Haiti's power brokers, never delivered on his plans for a compromise with Cédras and was replaced in April 1994.

Kambourian, Lovasz, and other Aristide opponents supported Cédras' authoritarian regime as the only way to keep Haiti's peasants and workers obedient and productive. As Kambourian allegedly remarked to a U.S. businessman, "repression works. It worked in Russia for forty years."

In contrast, Clinton advisors such as Secretary of State Christopher, National Security Advisor Anthony Lake and UN Ambassador Albright sought Aristide's return but hoped to avoid military intervention. The State Department returned to its June 1993 policies of negotiating with Cédras and anticipated that more effective economic sanctions would obtain a better compromise than the July 1993 Governor's Island pact. Adding to Clinton's difficulties, however, was the increase of Haitian refugees that again raised human rights questions.[16]

The number of refugees increased after October 1993 because of Haiti's renewed intimidation of Aristide's supporters. Some Haitians discovered a way to elude U.S. Coast Guard ships—if they crossed by boat from Haiti to the Bahaman Islands, they could then wait for an opportunity to cross over to Florida. As the numbers of refugees in the Bahamas had greatly increased by December 1993, the local government, fearful that the Haitians might overwhelm their small population of a quarter million, enacted laws restricting Haitian work visas, residence status, and the right to asylum. Bahamian police arrested Haitians, demolished their homes, and rejected work permits. Neither the Bahamas nor the other Caribbean nations wanted Haiti's refugees whom, given an opportunity, preferred to go to the United States. In early 1994, so many Haitians left the Bahamas for Florida that Clinton's refugee problems were revived. Initially, Florida authorities screened them for asylum, treating them differently from those turned back by the U.S. Coast Guard.

The Bahaman issue, Haiti's revived terrorist campaigns, and reports that economic sanctions impacted Haiti's poorest the most, persuaded human rights groups to demand changes in the refugee and economic sanction policies. On May 7, Clinton announced a new plan under which refugees picked up by the Coast Guard would receive on-board hearings to determine their eligibility for asylum. In June, the White House estimated an average of 2,000 Haitian refugees were picked up by the Coast Guard each week to have their asylum rights determined. For those given asylum, the U.S. requested "safe haven" assistance from Caribbean nations; subsequently, Antigua, Grenada, and Jamaica agreed to grant refugees temporary asylum. The new system had enforcement problems, however, because U.S. ships near Haiti could not quickly process all of the arriving refugees. With over 1,800 on board the Coast Guard ship and more arriving, the U.S. Navy again erected tent cities at Guantanamo to detain refugees awaiting processing.[17]

As the refugee problem mounted, the Clinton administration stepped up its efforts to persuade Haiti's military leaders to restore Aristide and halt the refugee flow. Since October 1993, Clinton's options regarding Haiti were limited not only by divisions in the executive branch but by congressional opposition to military intervention. Excepting the Black Caucus, most members of congress opposed sending U.S. forces to Haiti and were influenced by the CIA-DIA testimony to oppose or be indifferent to Aristide's return. Not only Republican Senator Robert Dole, but Democrats such as Senator John Glenn of Ohio, opposed invasion plans because, as Glenn said, "How do you get out?" after defeating Haiti's army. Although Dole's proposal to prevent an invasion failed because General Cédras publicly endorsed it, the Senate unanimously approved a non-binding resolution that the president needed congressional approval to invade. However in late August, as Clinton became inclined toward military intervention, congressional leaders were reluctant to interfere.[18]

Neither the UN's or Clinton's negotiations with Cédras succeeded between November 1993 and September 1994. Dante Caputo tried to revive talks with Cédras but failed just as had Clinton's special envoy Lawrence Pezzulo. Clinton replaced Pezzulo with William H. Gray, III as his personal envoy. Gray was president of the United Negro College Fund and a former U.S. congressman who Clinton chose to reduce tensions between Aristide and the White House in early 1994. Clinton did not want to remove Haiti's military from power before Aristide returned, while Aristide rejected another reconciliation conference with Cédras. Clinton's differences with Aristide did not alter his need to assist Haiti because the persistent refugee crisis obligated him to do something.

Early in May, Clinton not only changed his refugee policy, but also asked the UNSC to tighten the economic embargo of Haiti and warned Haiti's military junta that the U.S. was preparing to use force, if necessary, to return Aristide. At Ambassador Albright's request on May 6, the UN Security Council approved a world-wide embargo on all exports to Haiti, excepting essential food and medical supplies and called on the Dominican Republic to close its borders to Haiti. The Dominican Republic had experienced a rare economic boom following the Haitian coup of 1991 by becoming a supply route of products for Haiti's elite customers in violation of the UNSC sanctions. In May 1994, however, the Dominican government said it would respect the embargo and, after waiting two weeks to smuggle hundreds of gallons of gasoline to Haiti, it shut its borders on May 29.[19]

Cédras ignored the sanctions and the warning of an impending invasion and, on May 11, he openly defied Clinton by formally deposing the exiled Aristide and his exiled Haitian legislative supporters. He also instructed the legislators remaining in Haiti's to elect 80-year-old Emil Jonassaint as Haiti's provisional president pending elections in December 1994. Reports from Haiti indicated that Cédras believed the U.S. would never invade Haiti because there was extensive opposition among many OAS members and in the U.S. Congress.

Clinton responded by adopting additional U.S. economic sanctions aimed specifically at Haiti's wealthy elite. On June 8, Clinton cancelled all U.S. commercial flights to Haiti and froze all U.S. financial transactions and Haitian bank accounts including those of Haiti's National Bank. Clinton expected these sanctions to damage Haiti's wealthy classes that previously traveled to the U.S. for business and shopping tours. Their U.S. funds and investments would be unavailable as long as Cédras remained in power. To support Clinton's sanctions, Canada adopted similar measures against Haiti's commercial flights and financial transactions and, in July, the French halted all flights from Paris to Port-au-Prince, a favorite route of Haiti's French-speaking elite.

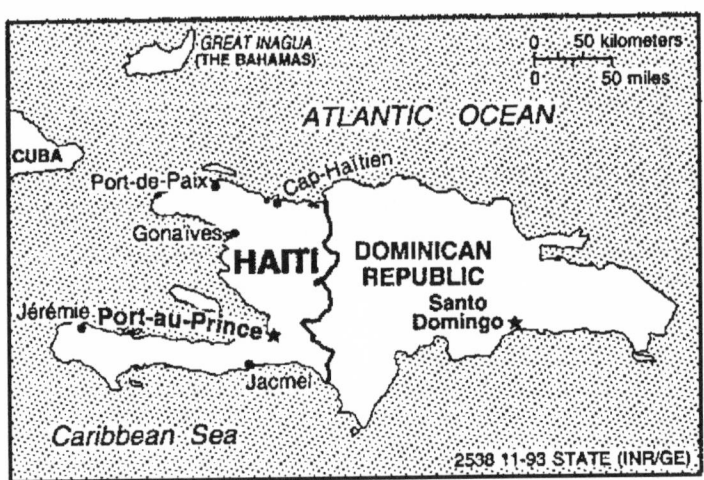

While ordering stiffer sanctions, Clinton also began preparing for military intervention and requested other nations to join the U.S. multinational force. The Pentagon publicized U.S. military exercises to confirm their serious intentions against Haiti while Clinton endeavored to overcome the opposition in Congress and the U.S. public. Clinton had as much difficulty in persuading other nations to join a UN force as he did with Congress. Excepting France, European leaders were reluctant to use force to intervene in another nation's civil conflict.

Latin American nations also hesitated to assist Clinton until Aristide publicly asked for a U.S.-led invasion if other methods failed to restore him to power. During a May meeting, OAS members, excepting

Argentina and Antigua, had opposed military intervention; but gradually some Latin American and most Caribbean nations agreed to join either a military intervention or a peacekeeping mission after Aristide was returned. By mid-July, Clinton announced fifteen OAS nations were contributing forces and, on July 31, the UNSC, voting 14-0 with Brazil and China abstaining, granted authority for the U.S. to lead an international force to restore Aristide.

The day the UNSC resolution passed, Clinton hinted that an intervention was only "weeks away" and publicized U.S. military preparations in order to impress Cédras and to solidify world opinion in favor of military action. Pentagon officials publicly described their preparations, telling reporters about secret exercises in the Gulf of Mexico involving over 2,000 commandos using air and naval personnel. In these rehearsals, U.S. troops practiced the seizure of Haitian-type seaports and airports that would precede a larger invasion. All of this was, of course, an effort to impress upon Cédras the seriousness of the situation and pressure him to negotiate.

Following the UNSC authorization of a U.S.-led force, the White House gave reporters details about Clinton's plans and reasons why the national interest required a military intervention. Clinton told a press conference on August 3 that the "fundamental interests of the U.S. justified an attack if it was the only method to restore democracy in Haiti. If the U.S. did not lead this effort, the nation faced both the continuation of gross human rights violations in a neighboring island and the continued refugee problems bringing more Haitians who fled whether for political or economic reasons."[20]

Not unexpectedly, Clinton faced opposition from members of congress who challenged his right to launch an invasion without prior congressional authority. This dispute between the president and congress had been waged since 1973 when the War Powers Act passed over President Richard Nixon's veto and, in August, the Senate approved a non-binding resolution requiring the approval of congress before Haiti was invaded. As had each president since Nixon, Clinton denied congress' right to restrict the commander-in-chief but he hoped congress would support any decisions he made.

Clinton delayed a final invasion decision because problems arose with Castro over Cuban refugees. Throughout the year, the arrival of Cuban refugees in Florida demonstrated the discriminatory policy that freely admitted Cubans while returning or detaining Haitian refugees. On

August 19, Clinton ended the twenty-eight year-old policy of allowing all Cuban refugees to become U.S. residents and said Cuban refugees would be processed in Guantanamo as political or economic refugees. But he also negotiated with Castro and, on September 9, announced an agreement with the Cuban government whereby Castro would deter the exodus of Cubans and the U.S. would legally admit up to 20,000 Cubans each year.[21]

As the Cuban question was being settled, the delay provided time for a final effort to persuade Cédras to negotiate. Several Latin American foreign ministers visited Haiti in August to plead with Cédras to compromise but, when he ignored the ministers, UN Secretary General Boutros-Ghali stated Cédras had rejected a "last attempt" to avoid an invasion. This estimate was wrong, however, because another U.S. military threat would persuade Cédras to accept last minute talks to avoid a U.S.-led invasion.

On September 14, Clinton told a national television audience that sanctions and negotiations had failed to budge Haiti's military rulers and a U.S.-led multinational force must act. He said the invasion would involve two stages. First, a force of 20,00 combat troops would attack in order to end the violence caused by Haiti's militant groups and to establish a new Haitian police organization. Second, a U.N. peacekeeping force would be deployed so Aristide could return and be assisted in setting up a government that would end the refugee problem.

The day Clinton spoke, Pentagon officers indicated a U.S. aircraft carrier with over 4,000 U.S. Army troops was leaving to join U.S. Navy vessels patrolling Haitian waters. Together with previous military preparations, the Pentagon's announcement finally got Cédras' attention because he knew his army was no match for the well-trained, well-equipped U.S. soldiers.

The day after Clinton's TV address, Cédras caved in and Clinton reported that he would negotiate with three U.S. envoys: ex-President Jimmy Carter, former Chairman of the JCS Colin Powell, and Georgia Senator Sam Nunn. These U.S. emissaries would arrange the departure of Cédras and other military leaders and Aristide would make a peaceful return. If Haiti's junta did not agree to terms in two days, the U.S. multinational force would invade.

The U.S. trio and Cédras had difficulty reaching a settlement, indeed, Cédras agreed to terms only in the last minutes of the 48-hour deadline. Under a pact signed by Haiti's President Jonassaint, Cédras and Army

Chief of Staff Brigadier General Philippe Biamby would resign and leave Haiti by October 15. Meanwhile, the 25,000 international forces would land immediately to prepare for Aristide's return on October 15. In addition, the UNSC would lift its economic sanctions against Haiti.[22]

The international forces began coming ashore on September 19 without resistance. U.S. Marines and paratroop units took control of Port-au-Prince's airport and docking facilities and, when the remaining forces landed the next day, crowds of Haitians cheered their arrival. Significant gaps in Carter's hastily drawn agreement soon became obvious as U.S. officers reported thugs and police were still beating and shooting Aristide supporters. Haiti's notorious police chief Michel Francois had not signed Carter's pact and although his police did not threaten U.S. troops, they attacked Haitians and frustrated U.S. soldiers who, under their rules of engagement, had to stand by and watch the armed gangs abuse innocent people.

The U.S. soldiers' frustration did not last long, for within 24 hours, Clinton changed the rules of engagement and declared that violence would not be tolerated. After General Hugh Shelton warned Cédras that his thugs must stop assaulting Haitian citizens or be punished, the multinational forces would use their weapons to prevent any "unreasonable force" by local militants. Under the new rules, U.S. Army and Marine personnel dismantled Haiti's best-armed units, and offered to buy guns and other weapons turned in by Haitians. The U.S. forces attacked the headquarters of army units that rejected Cédras authority and raided storage areas to confiscate weapons. U.S. military police were stationed in every Port-au-Prince police precinct to prevent violence. In Haiti's second largest city of Cap-Haitien, U.S. Marines clashed with militants, killing ten of them in a fight to restore order. These and other U.S. military actions brought security to Haiti, hastened the departure of Cédras and permitted the safe return of Aristide.[23]

ARISTIDE'S RETURN

The restoration of Aristide as president on October 15, 1994 did not restore the power he had held before his overthrow and exile. Now Aristide not only faced the problems of dealing with militants such as former Macoutes, FRAPH, and former army and police personnel, but he also was limited by provisions in the U.S. agreements he accepted before September 15. The agreements accomplished Aristide's return but also contained restrictions regarding U.S. and international financial activity which made Haiti's "democracy" dependent on foreign aid.

One unexpected benefit of the U.S. intervention resulted from the outbreak of violence in Port-au-Prince that led Clinton to approve measures to reform Haiti's corrupt police force and to buy guns held by Haitian gangs. The U.S. forces were able to control most of Haiti's militant irregulars, although the Pentagon rejected Aristide's request to disarm all militants and dismiss all former army officers. The U.S. sent some Haitian army officers abroad as attachés in Haiti's foreign embassies, but the Pentagon desired to retrain many Haitian army officers despite the fact that for years critics claimed Latin American officers schooled at U.S. Army bases never acted democratically upon returning home.

Aristide reduced the size of Haiti's army personnel but this presented a problem because approximately 5,000 former soldiers could not find new work and became a disgruntled faction. By 1996, the ex-soldiers were a disruptive threat because anyone with money could purchase their military talents. The veteran's formed the "Unjustly Discharged Soldiers" lobby that protested their failure to receive severance pay or pensions because those with savings in military-bank accounts discovered their funds were stolen by Cédras and other high-ranking officers when they left for exile. Cédras also destroyed the Ministry of Defense records, which made it difficult to determine what each soldier deserved, once Aristide collected sufficient funds to pay them. To minimize the veteran's threat, the U.S. and UN appropriated money to pay a Swiss agency to train former soldiers for new jobs, but Haiti's high unemployment made it difficult for the ex-soldiers to find jobs even with their new skills.

The reform of Haiti's police was also a formidable task. The U.S. recruited Haitians to attend the U.S. International Criminal Investigation Training and Assistance school at Fort Leonard Wood, Missouri. According to plans, after these police were trained and sent back to Haiti, U.S. forces could withdraw and UN peacekeepers commanded by a Canadian would supervise Haiti's reconstruction. To oversee the police work, the U.S. established an International Police Monitors group that a Pentagon official said would make "Haiti's police responsive to Washington's advice and control," not to Aristide.

Although the UN and Washington spent $65 million to train Haiti's police, Human Rights Watch reported in December 1996 that trustworthy police officers did not emerge from this training. After U.S. troops left

Haiti in March 1995, the U.S. deployed 5,000 police rookies with four months instruction rather than the year of training experts recommended. Moreover, Aristide's supporters said the new police force was infiltrated by members of SIN and FRAPH factions which the CIA-DIA had supported against the Lavalas reformers. Human rights observers reported a steady increase of incidents where Haiti's police used sadistic or stupid methods to mistreat civilians. In 1995-1996, at least 46 deaths resulted from police who beat or killed victims. On November 5, 1996, for example, police shot five men on a Port-au-Prince street, one of which was in handcuffs.

During 1996, the Clinton tried to rectify the mistake of too quickly replacing U.S. troops with Haitian police by setting up a program for Haitian-American police to instruct Haiti's rookies, a program which might help if supported for several years. Clinton also allocated $500,000 for a Human Rights Fund to assist Haiti's police victims. The fund paid for funerals of eleven police victims and medical care for sixty Haitians injured by police brutality. It also established a witness protection program to provide safe houses and living allowances for persons reporting police abuses but feared retaliation against their families.

When "police crimes" were reported in 1995 and 1996, Aristide blamed the CIA-DIA for placing SIN and FRAPH members on the force. Meanwhile prominent Republican senators, such as Robert Dole and Jesse Helms, accepted the CIA and DIA's claim that Aristide and the Lavalas police committed most of the police crimes. In fact, both Lavalas supporters and anti-Aristide Haitians suffered from violent attacks. In March, two prominent Lavalas activists were shot and killed, one an assembly member, the other a Lavalas peasant organizer. However when a prominent Aristide opponent, Mireille Durocher Bertin, was killed in April, Senator Helms insisted the U.S. Federal Bureau of Investigation find the killer. After six months investigation, the FBI was unable to arrest anyone and Helms blamed Aristide for obstructing justice.[24]

The U.S fared better in repairing Haiti's political structure. Shortly before Aristide arrived on October 15, the U.S. flew exiled legislators to Haiti to join those members in hiding since 1991. Under U.S. military protection, Haiti's Senate and Chamber of Deputies granted amnesty to persons involved in the 1991 coup d'état, as Aristide had agreed. This action permitted Cédras and other officers to leave the country as exiles.

There were, however, concerns raised about two elections during 1995. In June, Haiti's parliamentary and municipal elections caused trouble because the Lavalas-dominated Election Council (CEP) manipulated a Lavalas victory which opposing parties asked OAS observers to annul. Although the OAS monitors certified the election results, Robert Pastor of the Carter Center believed the vote was a step away from democracy. While the June election had shortcomings, the December 1995 presidential election seemed to be free and fair. Although Lavalas radicals urged Aristide to ignore the constitutional provision against a second term, he chose Rene Preval as the Lavalas candidate and Preval won easily. Experts were disturbed that only 28 percent of the electorate voted but attributed this to Preval's near-certain victory.[25]

Perhaps the most important agreements between Aristide and the U.S. related to Haiti's economy. After economic changes in the 1970s brought U.S. manufacturing to Haiti, the status of Haiti's commercial middle class declined while a group of technocrats prospered from U.S. investments. During Haiti's 1990 election, Marc Bazin was favored by the technocrats but Haiti's commercial bourgeoisie joined Aristide's coalition of students, workers, and peasants. The Clinton administration was divided between supporters of the Lavalas "bourgeoisie" in the State Department and AID and the proponents of Haiti's technocrats among CIA-DIA officers who had supported the orderly, if repressive, policies imposed by Haiti's army. The administration tried to reconcile the interests of the Lavalas "bourgeoisie" and Haiti's technocrats, but ignored the workers and peasants whose interests Aristide championed. Working together with a "reformed" army and Aristide's democracy, U.S. officials anticipated the Lavalas middle class and technocrats could restore order while increasing U.S. corporate benefits for Haiti's commercial-technocrat groups

To achieve these ends, the State Department told Aristide their plans would increase worker's wages in the long term with financial assistance from AID, the World Bank, and the IMF. Meanwhile to obtain these funds, Aristide would have to minimize social welfare programs, privatize Haiti's state enterprises, maintain low wages for workers, keep inflation low, and support budget measures which favored business profits and repayment of Haiti's loans. These restrictions and limitations corresponded to recent international banking practices for loans to developing countries that required a government to guarantee investment profits and banking needs at the expense of low-wage workers. Although financial experts, such as James G. Speth of the UN's Development

Program, cited studies which demonstrated that these World Bank-IMF policies failed to promote democracy and free trade in developing nations, bankers were slow to adopt the "capacity building" measures their critics recommended. They did not do so in Haiti.

After October 1994, Aristide, Preval, and Haiti's Assembly were slow to enact the policies demanded by the bankers who, in turn, became dissatisfied and withheld almost all the loans promised to rebuild Haiti's poor economic conditions. Because Preval and Aristide could not uproot Haiti's elite nor improve the economy more refugees sought to reach the United States. In November 1996, the Coast Guard intercepted 1,000 refugees whom were sent back to Haiti. A 1996 UN poverty report listed Haiti's living standard as lowest in the Western Hemisphere, a situation fraught with grave future dangers.

Haiti's economic plight worsened by early 1998 because of a split in the parliament between Preval and Aristide factions. This made it impossible to enact Preval's privatization legislation designed to satisfy international bankers who again stopped most loans to Haiti.

Because of these economic limitations, when the UNSC set November 30, 1997, for its withdrawal from Haiti, some Haitians had come to look upon the U.S./UN presence as "neo-colonization." The last of the 1,400 Canadian and Pakistani "peacekeepers" left on November 28 but at Preval's request 300 civilian police from the U.S. and seven other nations remained to complete their training of Haiti's National Police. The U.S. also agreed to keep over 300 specialists in Haiti to help with civilian projects such as road building.

Haiti had taken steps toward order and democracy but its economic problem posed a grave danger as unemployment affected two-thirds of the people and there was a lack of electricity and plumbing for the poor in cities and rural areas. In 1997 reports indicated that militants once more repressed those who worked to assist the poor and that the CIA had renewed aid to FRAPH in an effort to prevent Lavalas rejuvenating Aristide's programs. As Haitian historian Paul Farmer concludes, Aristide's return quieted Haiti's social order through political stability and lessening terrorism, but could not find a solution to the country's basic economic problems.

In the best scenario, Haiti's revived economic benefits would some day "trickle down" to peasants and workers. In the worst case scenario, Haiti's standard of living would not meet the rising expectations of low-income workers and peasants, and will generate another revolutionary movement in Haiti. Whether Clinton's political success in Haiti will prevail, despite the short sightedness of the international financial community, remains in doubt.[27]

NOTES

1. For the occupation era see: Hans Schmidt, *The United States Occupation of Haiti* (New Brunswick, NJ: Rutgers University Press, 1971); James H. McCroklin, *Garde d'Haiti* (Annapolis, MD: U.S. Naval Institute Press, 1956). Irwin P. Stotsky, *Silencing the Guns in Haiti* (Chicago: University of Chicago Press, 1997): 21-23 has an excellent explanation of problems between Haiti's creoles, mulattos, and blacks.

2. Anthony P. Maingot, "Haiti," in his, *The United States and the Caribbean* (Boulder, CO: Westview Press, 1994): 204-206. Also see: Michel-Rolph Trouillot, "Haiti's Nightmare and the Lessons of History," in Deidre McFayden, et.al. eds., *Haiti: Dangerous Crossroads* (Boston: South End Press, 1995): 121-132.

3. Maingot, "Haiti," 212-218; Greg Chamberlain, "Up From the Roots," in McFayden, *Dangerous Crossroads*, 13-40.

4. Bob Shacochis, "Our Hidden Haitian Problem," *WPNW* (Apr. 8-14, 1996): 24. Stotsky, *Silencing the Guns,* 222-224, 242-244, fn 38, 39.

5. Michael S. Hooper, "The Monkey's Tail Still Strong: the Post-Duvalier Wave of Terror," in McFayden, *Dangerous Crossroads*, 161-173 and Deidre McFayden, "FRAPH and CDS: Two Faces of Oppression in Haiti." Ibid., 153-160; Shacochis "Our Hidden Haitian Problem," 24. For examples of what later could be seen as misinformation based on the FBI's anti-Aristide reports see: Steven A. Holmes, "U.S. Seeks to Bar Retaliation," *NYT* (Jan. 28, 1993): A-1 and Lally Weymouth, "Haiti's Suspect Savior," *Washington Post* (Jan. 24, 19930): C-2. For a summary of congressional committee hearings see *Congressional Almanac for 1993* (Washington, DC: Congressional Quarterly, 1994): 449-450.

6. Greg Chamberlain, "The Aborted Election of 1987" and "An Interregnum," in McFayden, *Dangerous Crossroads*, 27-40; Anthony P. Maingot, "Haiti and Aristide: The Legacy of History," *Current History* 91 (Feb. 1992): 65-69.

7. J.P. Slavin, "Aristide: Man of the People," in McFayden, *Dangerous Crossroads*, 47-50; Mark Danner, "The Prophet (Aristide)," *New York Review of Books* 40 (Nov. 4, 1993): 25-30 and (Nov. 18, 1993): 27-36.

8. Marx V. Aristide and Laurie Richardson, "Haiti's Popular Resistance," in McFayden, *Dangerous Crossroads*, 181-194.

9. Série Livres Blues des Nations Unies, Vol.XI, *Les Nations Unies et Haiti, 1990-1996* (New York: Département de l'information Nations Unies, 1996): 10-20 and especially Document 15, pp. 153-183, for the UN observers report on the elections. Kim Ives, "The Lavalas Alliance Propels Aristide to Power," in McFayden, *Dangerous Crossroads*, 41-46.

10. Greg Chamberlain, "Haiti's 'Second Independence': Aristide's Nine Months in Office," and Anne-Christine d'Adesky, "Pere Lebrun (necklacing with burning tires) in Context," in McFayden, *Dangerous Crossroads*, 51-56 and 175-181. Also see: Maingot, "Haiti and Aristide," 65-69; Howard W. French, "Haiti's Democracy, Such as it Was, Is Swept Aside," *NYT* (Oct.6, 1991): E-2; J.P. Slavin, "The Elite's Revenge: The Military Coup of 1991," in McFayden, *Dangerous Crossroads*, 57-64.

11. Domingo E. Acevedo, "The Haitian Crisis and the OAS Response," in Lois F. Damrosch, *Enforcing Restraint* (New York: Council on Foreign Relations, 1993): 189-156; Nathanial C. Nash, "Latin Nations Get a Firmer Grip on Their Destiny," *NYT* (June 9, 1991): E-2; Kim Ives, "The Unmaking of a President," in McFayden, *Dangerous Crossroads*: 65-78; *Les Nationes Unies et Haiti,* 21-27.

12. Acevedo, "The Haitian Crisis" in *Enforcing Restraint*, 135-138; Al Kamen and John M. Goshko, "U.S. Eased Haitian Embargo Under Business Pressure," *Washington Post* (Feb. 7, 1992): A-1. Former Reagan advisor Elliot Abrams, a principal opponent of Haitian democracy movement, believed it more "realistic" for the U.S. to use neo-colonial methods in the Caribbean, see his, "Policing the Caribbean," *The National Interest* No. 43 (Spring 1996): 86-92 and "Policy Confronts Reality," *National Review* 44 (Mar. 30, 1992): 38-39. *Les Nations Unies et Haiti*, 21-27; Ives, "Unmaking of a President," in McFayden, *Dangerous Crosroads*, 74-79; Stotsky, *Silencing the Guns*, 24, fn 4.

13. Howard W. French, "The Refugees Match Wits with Uncle Sam," *NYT* (Dec. 8, 1991): E-2; Douglas Farah, "Boats in Search of a Safe Harbor," *WPNW* (Dec. 7-13, 1992): 15; Elizabeth Drew, *On the Edge: The Clinton Presidency* (New York: Simon & Schuster, 1994): 134, 332; Deborah Sontag, "Reneging on Refuge," *NYT* (June 27, 1993): E-1.

14. Kim Ives, "The Unmaking of a President," in McFayden, *Dangerous Crossroads*, 65-88; *Les Nations Unies et Haiti*, 28-48, et l'Accord Governer's Island, Document 74, pp. 314-16. Howard W. French, "Haiti's Future Can be Undone," *NYT* (July 11, 1993): E-4. General Powell did not know what to do in Haiti, because the military could win easily but would have trouble getting out as they had after 1915, *My American Journey*, 544.

15. Drew, *On the Edge*, 332-35; *Les Nations Unies et Haiti*, 45-48; Michael Wines, "Clinton Corners Himself," *NYT* (Sept. 18, 1993): E-1, 4-5; Howard W. French, "Haiti's Curse," *NYT* (Oct. 17, 1993): E-1, 3; Pamela Constable, "Haiti: A Nation in Despair, A Policy Adrift (including Aristide interview)," *Current History* 93 (Mar. 1994): 108-114.

16. Shacochis, "Our Hidden Haitian Problem", 23; Tim Weiner, et.al., "CIA Formed Haitian Unit Later Tied to Narcotics Trade," *NYT* (Nov.14, 1993): 1, 8; Jill Smolowe. "Haiti: With Friends Like These," *Time* 142 (Nov. 8, 1993): 44-45. The disinformation was effective especially in congress where they debated Aristide's incompetence, see the *1993 Congressional Quarterly Almanac*, 501. Also see: John Canham-Clyne, "How Anonymous Sourcing Hides Official Bias," *EXTRA* 6 (April/May, 1993):12

17. Howard W. French, "In Haitian Diaspora, Dreams of the Future are Dashed," *NYT* (Jan. 23, 1994): E-5; Tim Weiner, "A Policy Founders," *NYT* (May 1, 1994): E-2; Larry Rohter, "Remembering the Past, Repeating it Anyway," *NYT* (July 24, 1994): E-1, 4.

18. "Clinton's Gamble Pays Off," *Congressional Quarterly Almanac for 1994*, (Washington, DC: Congressional Quarterly, 1995): 449-451. Noting the high percent of opposition to an invasion, Lori Damrosch thinks the president should have had congressional approval, see "Constitutional Responsibility of Congress for Military Engagement," *American Journal of International Law* 89 (Jan. 1995): 58-87. Her article is followed by five others on the Haitian intervention.

19. *Les Nations Unies et Haiti*, 51-60; Kim Ives, "Haiti's Second U.S. Occupation," in McFayden, *Dangerous Crossroads,* 107-110.

20. The text of Clinton's comments is in *NYT* (Aug. 4, 1994): A-16. *Les Nations Unies et Haiti,* 61-65. Michael Gordon, "U.S. Hopes Talk of War Forces Out Haiti Army," *NYT* (Sept. 10, 1994): A-4. Some commentators noted that having UNSC approval changed the Monroe Doctrine's principles: see Elaine Sciolino, "Monroe's Doctrine Takes Another Knock," *NYT* (Aug. 7, 1994): E-6.

21. Paul Lewis, "Cuba Vows to End Exodus," *NYT* (Sept.10, 1994): A-1,4.

22. Mark Kramer, "The Case Against Invading Haiti," and The Case for Invading Haiti," *Time* 144 (Sept 19, 1994): 34 and (Sept. 26, 1994): 28; Murray Kempton, "The Carter Mission," *New York Review of Books*, 41 (Oct. 20, 1994): 71; Special Section, "The Carter Connection," *Time* 144 (Oct. 3, 1994): 30-38; Powell, *My American Journey*, 597-601. Larry Rohter, "Compromise is American, Not Haitian," *NYT* (Sep. 25, 1994): E-1, 23.

23. Gaddis Smith, "Haiti From Intervention to Intervasion," *Current History* 94 (Feb. 1995): 54-58 and Anthony Maginot, "Haiti: the Rot Within," ibid., 65-70; Ives, "Haiti's Second U.S. Occupation," 111-116; Robert Fatton, Jr., "The Rise, Fall, and Resurrection of President Aristide," in Robert Rotberg, ed., *Haiti Renewed: Political and Economic Prospects* (Washington, DC: Brookings Institution, 1997): 141-149.

24. John Kifner, "Aristide, in a Joyful Return," *NYT* (Oct.16, 1994): A-1, 6; Larry Rohter, "After the Homecoming, the Hard Part," *NYT* (Oct. 16, 1994): A-1, 6; Allan Narin, "Our Man in FRAPH," *Nation* 259 (Oct. 24, 1994): 458-461, and "Haiti Under the Gun," *Nation* 262 (Jan. 8/15) 1996: 11-15, and "Haiti Under the Cloak," *Nation* 262 (Feb. 26, 1996): 4-5; Elizabeth Rubin, "Haiti Takes Policing 101," *NYT Magazine (May 25, 1997): 42-45;* Tammerlin Drummond, "A Constabulary of Thugs," *Time* 149 (Feb. 17, 1997): 62-63 and follow-up letters in Mar. 10, 1997 isssue, pp. 12-13; Stotsky, *Silencing the Guns,* 159-181, 192-207.

25. Larry Rohter, "Haiti Takes the Next Big Step," *NYT* (Dec. 17, 1995): E-5 and Rohter, "President to Be Faces Tough Agenda," Ibid., pp. A-1, 9. Although critical of the June elections, an   excellent summary is Robert A. Pastor, "Elections for Parliament and Municipalities, June 23, 26, 1995," (Atlanta, GA: Carter Center of Emory University, Working Paper Series, July 17, 1995); Stotsky, *Silencing the Guns,* 143-147, 154-159.

26. Anthony T. Bryan, "Haiti: Kick Starting the Economy," *Current History* 94 (Feb. 1995): 65-70; Barbara Briggs and Charles Kernaghan, "The U.S. Economic Agenda: A Sweatshop," in McFadyen, *Dangerous Crossroads,* 145-152; Noam Chomsky, "Democracy Restored: Intervention in Haiti, its Meaning and Prospects," *Z Magazine* 7 (Nov. 1994): 55-61.

27. Stotsky, *Silencing the Guns,* 206-212; Larry Rohter, "Haiti's Little Kings' Again Terrorize the Populace," *NYT* (Aug. 15,1996): A-3 and Rohter, "Haiti Premier Quits," *NYT* (June 10, 1997): A-13; Douglas Farah, "When a 'Twin' Goes It Alone," *WPNW* (Aug. 19-25, 1996): 16; Sidney W. Mintz, "Can Haiti Change?" *Foreign Affairs* 74 (Jan./Feb. 1995): 73-86; "Scores of Haitians Jump Ship in Miami," Washington Post (May 13, 1998): A-12.

CHAPTER FOUR

THE DISINTEGRATION OF YUGOSLAVIA

During the 1990s, Yugoslavia dissolved into several states because since 1918 its politicians have been unable to devise an acceptable system to support political unity. Created by the Western powers in 1919, the South Slavic state's security and political structure was uncertain from the outset and handicapped further by Germany's invasion and partisan fighting during World War II.[1]

THE INTERWAR YEARS

The nation shortly to be known as Yugoslavia was formed in 1919 from territories taken from the defunct Austro-Hungarian and Ottoman Empires, two multinational empires that along with czarist Russia had long competed for hegemony in the Balkans. The assassination of Austria's Archduke Ferdinand, by Serbian nationalists seeking to create a "Greater Serbia", had ignited World War I. After the war, the 1920 Treaty of Rapallo created the Kingdom of Serbia, Croatia, and Slovenia. The South Slavs gained most of the Adriatic's Dalmatian coast, including Kosovo province where Albanians were a majority. In the 1920 Treaty of Trianon, the South Slavs received three districts including over 200,000 Hungarians in Vojvodina; and in the 1919 Treaty of Neuilly, they obtained strategic areas on the eastern border that had many Bulgarians. Both the Hungarians and Bulgarians claimed bitterly that they had lost too much territory.[2]

Slavic leaders could not agree about the structure of government for their nation. The Serbs wanting a strong centralized government, where they would have the most influence, while the Slovenes and Croats preferred a federation that gave local units most of the political authority. A Constituent Assembly approved the Constitution of 1921 that established the Kingdom of Serbia, Croatia and Slovenia, but the delegates disagreed about each entity's rights. The constitution gave some authority to King Alexander, a Serb, and legislative rights to a one-chamber parliament. The constitution also gave the king emergency powers, if the political situation required, an article King Alexander found useful in 1929.

For four years, some unity existed but opponents of the authority given King Alexander caused disruptions that turned violent in 1928 when an extremist assassinated the Croatian assembly leader. On January 6, 1929, Alexander declared an emergency and suspended the 1921 Constitution.[3]

Planning to be an enlightened autocrat, King Alexander assumed full political power and proclaimed a new constitution changing the nation's name to Yugoslavia. The 1931 Constitution abandoned the six ethnic-based states of Serbia, Croatia, Slovenia, Bosnia-Herzegovina, Montenegro and Macedonia and established nine banovines (provinces) based on geography with local councils that the monarch controlled. Parliament consisted of a senate, with one-half of the members appointed by the king and one-half elected, plus a lower chamber of elected members where two-thirds of the seats went to the party with a plurality of votes, enabling the Serbs to dominate. Alexander also strengthened his power by abolishing the freedom of dissent and creating a national police with power over all individuals.

The new regime remained orderly until the king's assassination in 1934 when a Regency assumed power because Crown Prince Peter II was only eleven years old. Opposition to the Regents grew after they signed unpopular treaties with Italy and grew closer to Nazi Germany. After Adolf Hitler invaded Poland in September 1939, the Yugoslav government announced neutrality, but subsequently signed a pact with Hitler on March 25, 1941 which ignited a revolution in Belgrade.

Led by Serb military factions and joined by peasants and workers in Croatia and Slovenia, a coup d'état overthrew the Regency and accepted King Peter II, who would come of age in November 1941. The population rallied around Peter II but leaders of the coup did not have a political program acceptable to all parties that could hold their loyalties. Mostly the rebels hated the Germans and they severed relations with Hitler who immediately ordered the invasion of Yugoslavia on April 6, 1941. The Nazis quickly occupied Yugoslav, but for four years the German forces faced strong resistance from guerrilla bands.[4]

WORLD WAR II AND THE RISE OF TITO

The Second World War brought bloody strife to Yugoslavia; both from the Nazi invasion and from conflict between two major South Slavic guerrilla forces—the Chetniks and the Partisans. These guerrilla units fought each other as well as the Nazis.

In April 1941, after King Peter and his officials fled to England, the Germans set up Yugoslav collaborators with "puppet" regimes in Serbia, Montenegro, Croatia, and Slovenia. What followed were brutal acts of "ethnic cleansing" inflicted on Slavs, Jews, and Gypsies by Hungarians in Vojvodina, by Bulgarians in eastern Serbia and Macedonia, and by Italians and Albanians along the Dalmatian coast including Kosovo. The most brutal outrages were committed by Croatia's pro-Nazi Ustashe, led by Ante Pavelic, who used racial, religious, personal, and irrational excuses to kill or deport non-Croatians especially Serbs and Jews. The number of Utashe victims is controversial with estimates ranging from 350,000 to 750,000 deaths, plus 300,000 deportees.

To combat the Nazis and their collaborators, two Yugoslav guerrilla forces fled to mountain strongholds. General Draza Mihailovic formed the Chetnik force of Serbs with elements of Yugoslavia's pre-war army and the support of Peter II's exiles. Although the Chetniks were organized to fight the Germans, Mihailovic later cooperated with the Nazis by attacking Croats, Slovenians, Muslims, and non-Serbs who were helping the Yugoslav Partisans led by Josip Broz (Tito).

Croatian by birth, Tito studied Marxian theory in Russia as a prisoner-of-war during World War I. Returning home, Tito formed a Communist Party in 1937 but during the German occupation, his Partisans advocated South Slavic unity and attacked all Nazi puppet regimes. In 1943, Tito also organized an anti-fascist parliament that created a Yugoslav federation where all South Slav groups were equal, including Muslims and Macedonians.

During World War II, Tito and Mihailovic also battled for control of Yugoslavia. While the Chetniks waited for Britain and its allies to defeat Germany, Mihailovic's campaign against Tito's Partisans led him to help the Nazis drive the Partisans out of Serbia in 1942. By collaborating with Nazis, however, Mihailovic lost support of many Slavs, including Serbians. In 1944, the British realized that Tito led the only effective resistance to the Germans and Prime Minister Winston Churchill withdrew all aid from Mihailovic's Chetniks as did the U.S. and the Soviet Union. On October 20, 1944, a joint Soviet-Partisan army liberated Belgrade from the Nazis and the monarchy was restored, although actual power was held by Tito's National Liberation Movement. In elections on November 11, 1945, Tito's party won a majority of assembly seats and proclaimed the Federal People's Republic of Yugoslavia.[5]

TITO'S RULE ESTABLISHED

Despite his post-war popularity and the creation a society of all South Slav nationalities, Tito's 34 years of rule became a facade for Yugoslav unity. It hid the interests of ethnic extremists who disliked the equality for all minorities. Perhaps, if Tito had permitted a debate about the South Slavs "national question" after World War II, the varied groups might have resolved their differences; but Marxian theory assumed nationality would disappear under a communist economic system. Minority interests and fears, however, did not disappear despite Tito's communist policies.

The Constitution of 1946 made Yugoslavia a socialist federated republic where a one-party government restricted political dissent, violated civil liberties, conducted "rigged" elections, and sacrificed individual rights to the "greater good" of the state. Tito did not solve the problem of South Slav separatism. He changed the constitution in 1953, 1963, and 1974 but the outward appearance that Yugoslavia's flexible adjustments had established a dynamic "self-managed" socialist alternative to the Soviet Union was belied by the growing dissatisfaction, fostered by traditional ethnic leaders, with the existing political system.

Tito's break with Stalin in 1948 prompted him to claim he had created a more humane socialist system. It also enabled Tito to gain economic aid from the U.S. and Western Europe although Yugoslavia remained a non-aligned neutral throughout the Cold War. In 1950, the Yugoslav Communist Party introduced the concept of "self-management" by workers, an idea that remained denominative of Tito's regime and gained favor among socialist thinkers outside the Soviet Union as an alternative to Stalin's rigid rule. However, Tito's implementation of the theory experienced problems because it advanced the economy but did not distribute prosperity equitably to each republic. The republics of Serbia, Croatia, and Slovenia became the most prosperous and wanted to reform federal policy to gain greater shares of the resources because the less advanced republics seemed to dissipate funds on wasteful projects.

Because of a declining economy in the 1960s, economic "reformers" in the three advanced republics claimed that central planning limited their funds for the research, technology, and modernization necessary to compete in world trade. The reformers were communist party members in Croatia, Slovenia, and Serbia but their resurgent local nationalism bothered conservative bureaucrats in the League of Yugoslav Communists (LYC). In 1971, these bureaucrats persuaded Tito to reject decentralization because neither he nor the LYC had ever yielded control over politics and the military.

Tito asserted his power in December 1971 by purging the economic reformers inside and outside the party. The purges began in Croatia where Miko Tripolo's rhetoric inflamed nascent nationalism, and soon included Marko Mikezic in Serbia and Stan Kavic in Slovenia all of whom were referred to as "anarcho-liberals", who damaged national unity. Tito also removed directors of successful enterprises, editors and journalists advocating reform, university professors, and senior reform-minded bureaucrats. The purges repressed the ideas of party reformers who had lost their jobs and this especially hurt Croatia in that it lost a generation of moderate leaders.[6]

Vojin Dimitrijevic believes the purges and the new Constitution of 1974 contained the germs leading to Yugoslavia's breakup after 1990. On the issue of central power or local rights to secede, the 1974 Constitution reads: "The nations of Yugoslavia, proceeding from the right of every nation to self-determination, including the right to secession, on the basis of their free will expressed in the common struggle of all nations and nationalities in the National Liberation War...." For some, this implied that any republic or nationality could secede from the union. For others, self-determination formed common interests in a brotherhood where unity was permanent and secession prohibited.

The 1974 Constitution further confused the situation by providing two presidencies—one with Tito, one without him. In the first case, Tito headed the government as the President of the League of Yugoslav Communists. In the second case, there was an eight-person presidency, with one representative elected by each republic and province's assembly, and a chairmanship that rotated annually. Following Tito's death in 1980, a constitutional amendment designated the president of LYC would be represented on the federal presidency but no one assumed Tito's powerful role.[7]

During the 1970s, outside observers praised Yugoslavia's self-management as a unique socialist pattern. In reality, however, there was no genuine electoral democracy and Yugoslavia's economy was floundering, as it had become dependent on United States and Western European loans or grants that were reduced in the 1970s because of declining world prosperity. In Yugoslavia the gap between the prosperous and poor republics widened.

Tito's legacy for Yugoslav unity was equivocal. For thirty-four years the nation worked together, except for the purges in 1971-1972. The divergent South Slav groups demonstrated they could work together but communist party rule did not develop the expected emotional support for a larger Yugoslav community.

PRECONDITIONS FOR DISUNION

Tito's death unleashed the growing economic discontent and ignited the long smoldering dissension among the six republics. Yugoslavia's economic failures reached a breaking point by 1987, leading to the federation's downfall. Although the federal government attempted changes in its socialist policies to receive international loans, the reforms came too late. Leaders of Yugoslavia's three major republics—Slovenia, Serbia, Croatia—already had devised their own "national" methods to thwart the central government's reforms. These three republics opposed federal assistance to the less developed republics and revived nationalist slogans to support their own republic's economy.

The political clash over Yugoslavia's economic resources disclosed a corruption infiltrating the central communist bureaucracy. Nevertheless, the World Bank and the International Monetary Fund would only deal with the central government and required the enactment of austerity programs that would move the country to a free market economy and a "sound budget". A "sound budget" was defined as the ability to repay loans which meant cutting social programs, ending inflation, and privatizing business—measures whose short term effects would be lower worker wages, unemployment, and a decrease in welfare benefits.

By 1989, Belgrade's federal government was caught between the demands by three major republics and the insistence of international financiers on austerity measures. Serbs who saw their social benefits cut blamed the government for allocating money to Albanians in Kosovo; Slovenes blamed Belgrade because factory managers lacked the foreign currency to purchase technology and support research to improve export products; and Croats feared austerity would raise prices and scare foreign tourists away. For all, higher interest rates and prices became a common complaint against the national bank.

Lacking a leader with power to command action, the federal presidency and assembly could not counter the demands of Slovenian, Serbian, and Croatian leaders for changes in the 1974 Constitution. As the most prosperous republic, the Slovenes wanted to strengthen their local economic control by reducing the federal authority's allocation of money to other republics. In contrast, Serbian leaders wanted a stronger federal authority to alleviate the unemployment problem, reaching 20 percent (50 percent in Kosovo), and municipal problems resulting from rural migration to Belgrade and other Serbian cities. Serbians also wanted a strong federal government to control the Albanians in Kosovo and to increase military expenditures because Serbians dominated the army's officer class. Thus, Serbian and Slovenian reformers put opposite pressures on the federal government.[8]

MILOSEVIC'S RISE

Although Serb "reformers" such as Strom Pavelic urged moderate changes in the Constitution to strengthen the presidency, radical Serbs such as Slobodan Milosevic advocated "reforms" designed to give the Serb Republic more authority within the federal constitution. Milosevic proposed a "democratic" federal government that would give the larger Serb population the dominant role they had had in the 1930s. Particularly, he wanted to give one federation vote to each republic and to the provinces of Kosovo and Vojvodina that Serbia controlled.

Although known as an economic reformer, Milosevic discovered greater glory in preaching Serbian nationalism. During a visit to Kosovo in 1987, his speech favoring Serb nationalism catapulted him to prominence. Serb nationalism had grown since 1981 as a result of Yugoslavia's economic problems and was promoted in 1986 by a Serbian Academy of Sciences publication emphasizing the Serbs historic victimization by Ottoman Turks and by Croats and Slovenians since World War II. The Academy denounced Tito's division of Serb peoples among other republics and proposed borders to unite all Serbs in a Greater Serbia. The Academy wrote that Serbs "have a historic and democratic right to establish full national and cultural integrity...." Although denounced for its falsehood by Croatian and Slovenian scholars, the report became a textbook for Serb schools in Milosevic's reform campaign.

As a minority in Kosovo, many Serbs never accepted Tito's attempt to have them live in harmony with the Albanian majority and lauded the

Academy's findings. Although Kosovo was Yugoslavia's poorest region, Serbs believed it was a sacred land from which the Ottoman Turks had chased them after the Battle of Kosovo-Polje in 1389. Serbs were a minority in Kosovo since the 17th Century but the Serbia's Eastern Othodox Church leaders created myths of Serbia's past making Kosovo the place for a Great Serbian Empire. Actually, Albanians and other South Slavs fought alongside Serbs in 1389, but Serb nationalists ignored this fact and described the battle as a lost opportunity for a Serbian empire. As Misha Glenny remarks, the Serbs devised myths to celebrate victimization and redeem a defeat, whereas most nations celebrated their historic victories.

Before Milosevic's 1987 speech, the Serbs in Kosovo had already gained influence. In April 1981, a year after Tito's death, a fight between Serbian and Albanian students at the university led Yugoslavia's government to declare martial law in Kosovo and send the Yugoslav National Army (YNA) to restore order. Serbian officers who dominated the YNA sided with Kosovo's Serbs in their disputes with local police who usually were Albanians. As a result, although Serbs were 13.2 percent of the population, the army let them have control of Kosovo.

Milosevic's 1987 speech aroused the Serb feeling of victimization under Yugoslavia's existing government and the Serb's need to gain their rightful positions of power because, he said, the Serbs' declining population in Kosovo resulted from Albanian terrorism which forced Serbs to emigrate to other Serbian lands. Although these charges were proven false by the studies of Branko Horvat, Serbians accepted the claims of Serbia's Orthodox officials and Serbs living in Kosovo who said the Albanians employed terrorist tactics against them.

As British author Charles Bennett indicates, most Serbs in Yugoslavia never believed the Kosovian Serbs charges of Albanian terrorism until Milosevic's 1987 speech launched a Serb media campaign calling upon Serbs to revenge their victimization. The media campaign adopted a nationalistic slogan from Milosevic's speech: "nobody would ever beat you again."

Although moderate leaders such as the Serb Republic's President Ivan Stambolic and Belgrade's Chief of the LYC Dragisa Pavlovic denounced such rhetoric, Milosevic used his position as Serbia's LYC leader to expel Pavlovic from the party and replace Stambolic as the Serb president in December 1987. Milosevic removed moderate leaders from Serbia's LYC and installed loyal followers from rural areas where his complaints about

Serb victimization were readily accepted. To spread his propaganda, Milosevic staged large rallies and used Serbia's radio, TV, and news media to condemn Pavlovic and Stambolic. His Kosovo message about Serb victimization was extended to include Serbs living in all of Yugoslovia as victims of Tito's system who continued to face genocide if they did not fight for the Greater Serbia.

Milosevic excluded dissenting views. With Pavlovic and Stambolic removed, moderate Serbs were purged from the government. The Serbian secret police transported vast crowds to rallies that confirmed their belief in Serbian victimization. Demonstrators received free food and paid holidays and the unemployed were hired as demonstrators to be bussed to meetings in Bosnia and Croatia as well as Belgrade and other Serbian towns.

By 1989, Milosevic moved toward the de facto demise of Tito's 1974 Constitution by bringing four of Yugoslavia's eight political units under Serbian control. His candidates took power in Vojvodina in October, in Kosovo in November 1988, and in Montenegro in January 1989. After Albanians in Kosovo staged a strike in February 1989, Milosevic had the YNA break the strike and destroy the fiction of Tito's equality. Milosevic's efforts to recreate a Greater Serbia had accomplished much by 1989.[9]

SLOVENIAN PROPOSALS

In contrast to Milosevic's stronger central regime, Slovenian leaders hoped to decentralize federal decision-making. As the most prosperous Yugoslav republic, Slovenians disliked the high federal taxes because the federal budget distributed a disproportionate share of the revenue to less developed areas such as Bosnia and Kosovo. Led by Milan Kuchan, Slovenians claimed that as eight percent of Yugoslavia's population, their taxes provided twenty-five percent of the federal budget of which nineteen percent went to less developed republics. Kuchan thought each republic should negotiate its share of federal contributions and federal benefits because each republic's income and needs varied. He also objected to the high army expenditures, contending international conditions did not require huge defense costs and local Territorial Defense Forces (TDF) should defend the republics.

By 1989, Kuchan's effort to change budget funding shifted to ways of separating Slovenia from the Yugoslav federation. Two basic developments caused this shift: the threat from Milosevic's Serbian nationalism; and Slovenia's economic recession due to the austerity measures required by international bankers before Yugoslavia could receive loans. Milosevic threatened Yugoslavia's political stability, while the World Bank and IMF policies ignored the political problems between republics and the central government and the worker demands for better wages and employment.[10]

FEDERAL GOVERNMENT FAILURES

From 1987 to 1990, Yugoslavia's central government failed to resolve the federation's economic and political problems. Although Prime Ministers Branko Mikulic and Ante Markovic struggled to revitalize Yugoslavia's economy and to counteract demands for constitutional changes, they found the austerity programs demanded by the World Bank and International Monetary Fund—lowering wages and cutting welfare programs at a time of growing unemployment—to be politically disastrous. The austerity measures benefited critics of the federal government and swelled the ranks of nationalistic reformers in Serbia, Slovenia, and Croatia.

In November 1988, Prime Minister Mikulic's proposals to meet the international requirements were passed by Yugoslavia's Federal Assembly, including deregulating socialist controls which hindered the "free market," privatizing business, and decreasing government funding for social welfare programs. From the Western bankers perspective, the reductions in social welfare and the rights of the working class was a "pro-growth" policy for Yugoslavia's long-term economy, as well as a guarantee for full repayment of Yugoslavia's foreign loans. Yugoslavian's who had experienced a decade of economic scarcity, strongly opposed the "free market" changes and joined in anti-government demonstrations and worker's strikes. In December, the public uproar against the "reforms" led to Prime Minister Mikulic's resignation and a three months delay before Ante Markovic agreed to replace him. The former director of a large Yugoslav business, Markovic favored free market reforms and proposed economic changes which, he said, would enable the country to become prosperous within five years.

Thus, while Croatia and Slovenia moved toward 1990 elections on secession and Milosevic advanced Greater Serbian nationalism, Markovic misguidedly, but enthusiastically, added to the unpopular changes desired by international bankers. Markovic restructured Yugoslavian banking practices which restricted business enterprise, abolished limitations on competition between socialized and private enterprises, and ended restrictions on foreign investments in Yugoslav businesses or joint foreign-Yugoslav economic ventures. Markovic further reduced social benefits to workers and the unemployed, and adopted austerity policies that inflated prices, added to the unemployment rosters, and prevented wage increases. These actions lowered the standard of living and increased the discontent among workers already working more hours for less pay.

Neither Milosevic nor Kuchan accepted Markovic's program. Milosevic announced opposition to the prime minister's policies and encouraged worker's to strike while Kuchan did not hesitate to reject Markovic's acts giving the government more authority. Under Kuchan, Slovenia abandoned attempts at constitutional changes and on September 17, 1989, the Slovenian Assembly amended the Slovenian Republic's constitution to declare its sovereignty and exercise its right to secede from Yugoslavia. The Assembly called for elections in April 1990 during which Kuchan's party won control of the government.

In 1989, Slovenia's relations with the Serbian Republic had also reached an impasse. Aware of Milosevic's nationalist activities, Kuchan decided to stop the spread of Serbian propaganda by banning a massive political Serb rally in Slovenia's capital of Ljubijana and ordering Slovenia's local defense force to prohibit the Serbian protests. Milosevic retaliated by terminating all Serbian business and political links with Slovenia.[11]

CROATIAN NATIONALISM REVIVES

Sometimes referred to as "the silent republic" after Tito purged so many of its leaders in 1971, Croatians also feared Serbian developments when it joined Slovenia in proposing secession from Yugoslavia. Milosevic turned pro-Serbian propaganda against Croatia in 1988 by claiming that Croatia's Serb minority were victims of Tito's policies since 1945. Using mass demonstrations and Serbian media control, Milosevic told Croatian Serbs to act against its government and revived stories of the Croat Utashe killing "one million" Serbs during World War II—a figure twice the accepted estimate of all Utashe victims.

Although Milosevic's Serb candidate failed to win control of Croatia's communist party, his nationalistic appeals attracted many Serb peasants living in Croatia's eastern border area known as the Krajina. Milsosevic helped Jovan Raskovic organize the Croat-Serb Democratic Party (SDS) in Knin in February 1990. During Croatia's elections in

April 1990, Raskovic's SDS was not successful but his anti-Croat nationalism was the major reason for the victory of Croatia's most radical anti-Serbian party, the Croat Democratic Union (HDZ). The HDZ was led by Franjo Tudjman who advocated Croatia's right to secede from Yugoslavia. Croatia's 1990 election resulted in Tudjman's HDZ gaining control of parliament although receiving only 41.5 percent of the vote—the Croat LYC received 34.5 percent and the Coalition of National Agreement 15 percent. By previous agreement, the HDZ's plurality of the votes gave it a majority of the seats in parliament.

In mid-1990 Yugoslavia was intact but the federal government's power had dissipated. Croatia and Slovenia proclaimed the right to secede and President Milosevic had expanded the Serb Republic's power over Montenegro, Kosovo, and Vojvidina thereby allowing him to retain control of the Yugoslavia rump state after Croatia and Slovenia seceded.

BOSNIA AND MACEDONIA

Following Tito's death in 1980, Bosnia and Macedonia had the greatest interest in maintaining Yugoslavia's unity because they were the least economically developed republics and benefited most from the federation's financial assistance. When discussions about reforming Yugoslavia appeared in the 1980s, Bosnia and Macedonia preferred the existing order with Bosnia especially wanting to avoid changes because its population in 1991 included 43.7 percent Muslim Slavs; 31.4 percent Serbs; 17.3 percent Croats; and 5.5 percent who identified themselves as Yugoslavs. No ethnic-religious group had a majority; however, Tito's practices had not resolved inter-group divisions except in cities such as Sarajevo that had daily interaction and intermarriages between ethnic groups. Moreover, because Bosnia lacked industrial development, it had the largest rural population of any republic and its rural villages were usually religious communities of Muslims, Orthodox Christians or Roman Catholic Christians who retained the community system Turkey had established after 1389.

Expecting Yugoslavia to survive whatever reforms were approved, Bosnia did not seriously challenge the political opposition to the federation or Serb President Milosevic's propaganda about alleged Serb victimization in Kosovo. As in Croatia, Milosevic targeted Bosnia's Serbian population with Greater Serbia propaganda and used the Serb Republic's secret police to stage protests against Bosnia's Muslim and Croatian politicians, including an alleged Muslim plot to dominate all

Serbians. Milosevic financed Bosnia-Serb propaganda for a Greater Serbia and the Bosnian Serbs Democratic Party (SDS), a political party led by a Sarajevo psychiatrist, Radovan Karadzic who accepted Milosevic's ideas. In contrast to one krajina of Serbs in Croatian territory, Karadzic's SDS set up six Bosnian krajinas among predominantly Bosnian Serb populations and Milosevic gave these krajinas miltary supplies to battle their enemies.

In 1989, Bosnia's government was led by President Alija Izetbegovic of the Party of Democratic Action (SDA) which was the more fundamentalist Islamic group of two Muslim factions in Bosnia. Izetbegovic tried to be neutral between Serbia, Slovenia, and Croatia by advocating Yugoslavian unity and maintaining a balance of interests among Bosnian Muslims, Serbs, and Croats. However, Bosnia's elections in November 1990 revealed the Bosnia's ethnic-religious divisions. Izetbegovic's Muslim SDA received 43 percent of the vote; Karadzic's Orthodox Christian SDS had 31 percent; the Bosnian Croats Catholic HDZ got 17 percent. Bosnia's ministry was a coalition of parties, but Karadzic's SDS rejected Izetbegovic's policy of unity and began to form a separate Bosnian Serb republic.

On June 3, 1991, President Izetbegovic joined Macedonian President Kiro Gligorov in proposing a compromise federal constitution that would retained Yugoslav unity, but this effort received no serious consideration. Slovenia's government refused to delay a declaration of independence and Croatia did the same. In 1991, Bosnia supported European efforts to rescue Yugoslav unity but the European commission asked the Bosnian and Macedonian leaders if they desired independence. Both republics opted for independence but the Bosnian government was limited by the Bosnian Serbs' demand for a separate state. Subsequently, in 1992 Karadzic's SDS Party declared independence for the Bosnian Serbs' Srpska Republic although a Bosnian referendum approved the independence of all Bosnia-Herzegovina.

In Bosnia's February 1992 election, 99 percent of those voting approved independence, but Karadzic's Bosnian Serbs boycotted the election. In March, Karadzic's irregular forces began murdering Muslims in rural areas and, on April 5, war began when Karadzic's army erected barricades and began an artillery bombardment of Sarajevo. Milosevic and Karadzic had been planning the destruction of Bosnia since September 1991 when the Yugoslav National Army (YNA) helped the Bosnian Serbs place the artillery that bombarded Sarajevo in April 1992.[13]

SUMMARY

By April 1992, Yugoslavia ceased to exist as a federation of six republics. The republics of Serbia and Montenegro, who joined together under Milosevic leadership, chose to retain the name of Yugoslavia for their state. Because most of the officers of the Yugoslavian National Army (YNA) were Serbs, Milosevic also was able to retain control of most of its units. The four republics of Slovenia, Croatia, Bosnia-Herzegovina, and Macedonia became independent states.

The Yugoslav Federation's disintegration was largely the result of Milosevic's aggressive tactics and of the foreign financial groups myopic desire to create a Yugoslav capitalist free market. Meanwhile, the United States left the European Union's leaders to deal with the fighting that broke out; first, between Croatia and Serbia, and later between the Serbs, Bosnian Muslims, and Croats.

NOTES

1. Literature on causes of the recent Balkan wars is controversial. Authors such as Robert Kaplan in *Balkan Ghosts* agree with Western politicians claim that the Balkans historic ethnic conflicts were inevitable and could only be settled through bloodshed. Historical accounts, such as Robert Donia and John Fine's *Bosnia and Herzegovina,* argue that Serb and Croat political leaders adopted myths of national ethnic conflict to promote their political goals during the decade following Tito's death. This was done because there was no glorious Serb or Croat past and the South Slavs principal problem in the 20th Century was finding a proper political order. Ambassador Warren Zimmermann believes that in East Europe, collectivist communist ideas were replaced by politicians using collectivist nationalism [see his conversation with David Binder, "Haunted by What the U.S. Didn't Do in Yugoslavia," *NYT* (June 14, 1992): E-9].

   For summations of the divergent views see the references cited in Robert Kaplan's April 1992 article in the *N.Y. Times Book Review* and Fouad Ajami's essay in *The Black Book.* Because Kaplan relied heavily on Rebecca West's study, students might also read Brian Hall's "Rebecca West's War," in the 1996 *New Yorker.* Details of the works cited above are in Chapter Nine's bibliography.

2. Robert J. Kerner, "The Yugoslav Movement" and "Yugoslavia and the Peace Conference," in Robert J. Kerner, ed., *Yugoslavia* (Berkeley, CA: University of California Press for the United Nations Series, 1949): 33-41 and 92-106; Ivo L. Lederer, *Yugoslavia at the Paris Conference, A Study in Frontier Making* (New Haven, CT: Yale University Press, 1963): 135-219; for the Italian issue see Dragan R. Zivojinovic, *America, Italy and the Birth of Yugoslavia, 1917-1919* (New York: Columbia University Press, 1972).

3. Vladimir Dedijer, *The Road to Sarajevo [1914]* (New York: Simon & Schuster, 1966); Ivo Banac, *The National Question in Yugoslavia: Origins, History, Politics* (Ithaca, NY: Cornell University Press, 1984).

4. Jacob B. Hoptner, *Yugoslavia in Crisis, 1934-1941* (New York: Columbia University Press, 1962); Christopher Bennett, *Yugoslavia's Bloody Collapse* (New York: New York University Press, 1995): 33-42.

5. Bennett, *Bloody Collapse,* 42-33: Fredrich B. Singleton, *A Short History of the Yugoslav Peoples* (New York: Cambridge University Press, 1985): 172-206; Aleksa

Dijlas, *The Contested Country: Yugoslav Unity and Communist Revolution, 1919-1953* (Cambridge: Harvard University Press, 1996).

6.   Bennett, *Bloody Conflict*, 51-66; Alvin Rubinstein, *Yugoslavia and the Nonaligned World* (Princeton, NJ: Princeton University Press, 1970); Alex N. Dragnich, *Serbs and Croats*, 117-173.

7.   Vojin Dimitrijevic, "The 1974 Consitution and Constitutional Process as a Factor in the Collapse of Yugoslavia," in Payam Akhavan and Robert Howse, eds., *Yugoslavia, the Former and the Future* (Washington, DC: Brookings Institution, 1995): 45-74; Sabrina Pedro Ramet, *Nationalism and Federalism in Yugoslavia, 1962-1991* (Bloomington, IN: Indiana University Press, 1992).

8.   Susan L. Woodward, *Balkan Tragedy* (Washington, DC: Brookings Institution, 1995): 47-113; John R. Lampe, et.al., *Yugoslav-American Economic Relations since World War II* (Durham, NC: Duke University Press, 1990): 148-207.

9.   Misha Glenny, *The Fall of Yugoslavia,* 3rd ed. (New York: Penguin Books, 1996): 31-37. For the 1986 Serb intellectual's favorable report on nationalism see Serbian Academy of Science, "Memorandum of the Serbian Academy of Sciences (SANU)," Trans. by. by Denison Rusinow in Peter H. Sugar, *East European Nationalism in the Twentieth Century* (Washington, DC: American University Press, 1995): 275-280. Leonard J. Cohen, *Broken Bonds*, 2d ed. (Boulder, CO: Westview Press, 1995): 45-58; Woodward, *Balkan Tragedy,* 114-145; Bennett, *Bloody Collapse*, 82-92.

10.   Cohen, *Broken Bonds*, 59-65, 89-94, 118-120; Jill Benderly and Evan Kraft, *Independent Slovenia* (New York: St. Martin's Press, 1994); Tomaz Mastnak, "Civil Society in Slovenia: From Opposition to Power," *Studies in Comparative Communism* 23 (Autumn 1991): 305-317.

11.   Woodward, *Balkan Tragedy*, 121-143; Cohen, *Broken Bonds*, 66-72; Mijat Sukovic, "Constitutional Changes in Yugoslovia," *Review of International Affairs* 39 (Jan. 20, 1988): 1-6.

12.   Cohen,*Broken Bonds,* 80-83, 94-102. On Serbs in Croatia see: Glenny, *Fall of Yugoslavia*, 1-30. For Croatia's earlier views see N.L. Karolvic "Croatia and its Future: Internal Colonialism or Independence?" *Journal of Croatian Studies* 22 (1981): 49-115.

13.   Cohen, *Broken Bonds,* 139-151; Glenny, *Fall of Yugoslavia*, 138-180; Loring F. Danforth, *The Macedonian Conflict* (Princeton, NJ: Princeton University Press, 1996).

Crisis in Bosnia-Hercegovina
April-July 1992

CHAPTER FIVE

THE U. S. & BOSNIA: DELAYED INTERVENTION

The Bush administration decided in 1989 that Yugoslavia had become less vital to U.S.'s national interest because the Cold War was waning. Thus when disputes began between Yugoslavia's federal government and its three largest republics, Washington policy makers focused on events in Moscow and expected the European Union (EU) to resolve Yugoslavia's difficulties.[1] Unfortunately, the EU did not have the political-military institutions to handle such a crisis.

Although Americans celebrated the end of Soviet communism, the Post-Cold War world still required U.S. leadership to maintain global security, and foster democracy and free trade. After 1989, Bush thought EU leaders should take charge of European affairs and some EU members welcomed this new stance as the "new age of Europe." They believed, falsely as it turned out, that mediation between Yugoslav parties would quickly end the fighting.

Both the EU and UN secured numerous cease-fires that were subsequently violated but, because they lacked the ability to enforce them, the fighting spread from Slovenia to Croatia and Bosnia. The results were not only mounting bloodshed, but increased "ethnic cleansings" that ravaged conquered populations in a manner reminiscent of the Nazi holocaust.

Although war crime reports in the Balkans provided a moral imperative for U.S. intervention, President Bush, and later Clinton, initially tolerated the atrocities because no vital U.S. national interest was deemed to be present. Reluctantly, but gradually in 1994-1995, Clinton employed the necessary force and persuasion to compel the warring factions to adopt peace accords and committed U.S., European, and Russian forces to implement their terms.

Key Figures

Bulatovic, Momir: President of Montenegro to 1997 who allies with Milosevic as part of the rump Yugoslavia.

Djukanovic, Milo: advocate of Montenegro's independence from Yugoslavia: becomes Montenegro president in 1997.

Draskovic, Vuk: leader of Serb Renewal Party, opposes Milosevic in 1996.

Izetbegovic, Alija: President of Bosnia, leader of Muslim Party of Democratic Action.

Karadzic, Radovan: Bosnian Serb president of Srpska Republic to 1996, indicted war criminal.

Kuchan, Milan: leads Slovene reforms, President of Slovenia after it gains independence in 1991.

Markovic, Ante: last Yugoslav prime minister; efforts to reform economy fails to gain support in 1990-91.

Mikulic, Branko: Yugoslav prime minister to 1989, replaced by Markovic.

Milosevic, Slobodan: raises banner of a Greater Serbia in 1987; de facto head of Serb Republic since 1987 and rump Yugoslavia (Serbia/Montenegro) since 1991.

Mladic, Ratko: Serb ultranationalist, commander of Yugoslav Army in 1990-91 and of Bosnian Serb Army 1992-96; indicted war criminal.

Pavelic, Ante: Croat leader of Utashe terriorist, collaborating with Nazis during World War II.

Plavsic, Biljana: Bosnian Serb who replaces Karadzic in 1996: she challenges his power in the Srpska Republic.

Rugovo, Ibrahim: advocate of non-violent Kosovo-Albanian party, seeking autonomy or independence in Serb Republic.

Seselj, Vojislav: Leads nationalistic Serb Radical party, opponent of Milosevic after 1995; favors Greater Serbia.

Silajdzic, Haris: Prime Minister of Croat-Muslim Federation after 1994, is a more secular Muslim than Izetbegovic.

Stambolic, Ivan: communist President of Serb Republic who Milosevic replaces in 1987.

Tudjman, Franjo: President of Croatia whose nationalist HDZ (Croat Democratic Community) coalition has controlled the Croatian Republic since 1990.

Zubak, Kresimir: represents Bosnian Croats in the Muslim-Croat Federation.

For four years, however, the errors and missed opportunities of the EU, UN, and U.S. provided examples of what interventions should and should not attempt.

THE BUSH AMINISTRATION POLICIES, 1989-1993

Yugoslavia's problems that began during Ronald Reagan's presidency, reached a serious stage when George Bush entered office. During the Reagan era, Tito's death, the growing tensions in Yugoslavia, and the rise of Serbian and Croatian nationalism were scarcely noticed. Nevertheless, as Susan Woodward indicates, Reagan's refusal to condemn human rights violations and willingness to accept "authoritarian" anticommunist regimes provided the breeding ground for authoritarian-nationalistic regimes such as Milosevic's Serbian Republic and Tudjman's Croatian Republic. In addition, Reagan's economic policies acerbated Yugoslavia's difficulties because he stopped aid to Yugoslavia in 1981 and encouraged World Bank-IMF and AID to allocate loans to Yugoslavia only if their government adopted austerity programs. These policies disrupted relationships between Yugoslavia's federation and its three major republics.[2]

In 1989, Bush appointed Warren Zimmermann as Ambassador to Yugoslavia and, judging by Zimmermann's memoirs, neither he nor Assistant Secretary of State Lawrence Eagleburger comprehended the severity of Yugoslavia's problems until early 1990. Both Zimmermann and Eagleburger had earlier served as foreign service officers in Yugoslavia, but they would misjudge the intentions of Serbia's Milosevic, whom they had known as a leading economist.

Before Zimmermann left for Yugoslavia in March 1989, he and Eagleburger agreed to the changes in previous U.S. policy that ended Yugoslavia's status as vital to the U.S.'s national interests because it no longer served as the geopolitical crossroads linking Western Europe with Greece and Turkey. Moreover, unlike Poland and Hungary where democracy had begun to flourish, Yugoslavia had been committing human rights violations against Albanians in Kosovo.

Upon arriving in Yugoslavia, Zimmermann was surprised at the intensity of Serb nationalism but initially did not consider this relevant. He found that Milosevic's "trampling on Albanian rights was almost universally popular among Serbs." He met an art historian, a "sensitive woman" who had lived in New York, who said solving Kosovo's problem was "simple, just line all the Albanians up against a wall and shoot them."[3]

The decision that Yugoslavia was not important to U.S. national interests limited Washington's backing for Yugoslavia's federal government at a critical time. In April 1989, Zimmermann realized that Prime Minister Markovic needed support to reform Yugoslavia's political and economic system but did not fully appreciate the dangers to Markovic's program from leaders of Serbia, Croatia and Slovenia. Markovic had Yugoslavia's Assembly carry out "structural adjustments" of the economy required by the World Bank-IMF but unemployment and cuts in welfare that followed persuaded many workers that the nationalist measures of Milosevic, Kuchan, and Tudjman would help them more.

To promote Markovic, Zimmermann arranged for him to visit the U.S. in October 1989, but unfortunately the journey simply underscored American's inability to understand Yugoslavia's discontent. Markovic's New York discussions with bankers and businessmen provided no economic investments to aid his government and, at the White House, Bush wasted Markovic's time by asking him about Mikhail Gorbachev's Soviet policies and showing no interest in Balkan problems. By December 1989, Zimmermann grasped Markovic's problems when Slovenia prohibited Serbs from staging anti-Albanian demonstrations in Ljubljana and Milosevic retaliated by embargoing Serbian trade and finance transactions with Slovenia. After Croatian leaders sided with Slovenia, Markovic could no longer restrain the leaders of these three dominant republics.[4]

Hoping to assist Markovic, Zimmermann persuaded Eagleburger to visit Belgrade in February 1990. In meetings with Markovic and leaders of the various republics, Eagleburger's efforts to convince Milosevic, Tudjman, and Kuchan that their best interests required Yugoslav unity met with no success. Because of Bush's passive policies, Eagleburger offered Yugoslav leaders nothing except statements in favor of Yugoslav unity—no economic, political or military incentives to change their behavior.

Eagleburger and Zimmermann agreed that Yugoslavia's menacing situation was a European problem and that the U.S. should urge the Europeans to help Markovic. Upon returning to Washington, Eagleburger requested all U.S. embassies to ask the European states to assist Markovic, but this too failed to produce satisfactory results.

Perhaps the underlying reason Bush desired to have the Europeans deal with the Yugoslav problem was his belief that U.S. intervention would pose a serious dilemma. In January 1992, Bush told an interviewer that " I don't want to send young men into a war where I can't see that we are going to prevail and prevail quickly"—a comment *Washington Post* columnist Jim Hoaglund dubbed the "Bush doctrine."[5]

Of course, European leaders share in the blame for failing to prevent Yugoslavia's break-up and the subsequent bloodshed. Europeans eager to displace American supervision had made some successful steps toward Europe's economic unity; but the EU had not achieved real political or military unification. Neither the European Parliament nor the three rotating heads of the European presidency had effective authority, while the European Council of Ministers represented the divergent national interests of Britain, France, Germany, and Italy, not "European" interests.

Although the Conference on Security and Cooperation in Europe (CSCE) represented Central and Eastern as well as Western European states, this group had to please a broad spectrum of members and was in the formative stage of devising war prevention and peacemaking operations. Permanent institutions to carry out CSCE programs began with the Charter of Paris for a New Europe signed on November 21, 1990 but were not set up until early 1991. The first Committee of Senior Officials (CSO) meeting was in January 1991; while the Secretariat's Offices opened on February 20 and the CSCE Conflict Prevention Center began operations in March 1991. Although the CSCE had potential, no CSCE military group existed to use coercion if necessary. NATO troops, led by the U.S., presented the only effective multilateral force available. Also, judging by their reception to the warning Eagleburger's sent in February 1990, European leaders were reluctant to become involved in Yugoslavia's complex problems. Zimmermann reports their reaction to the U.S. warning was "a yawn."[6]

While the European governments failed to help Markovic keep the Yugoslavia federation together, Zimmermann and Bush had to deal with well-intended but narrowly conceived interference from congressional members that weakened the already inadequate U.S. backing for Markovic. Influenced by Albanian-American and Croatian-American lobbyists, Congress held hearings on mistreatment of Albanians in Kosovo. Republicans led by Senators Robert Dole and Alfonse D'Amato and Representative Don Nickles and Democrats led by Representatives Joe Dioguardi and Tom Lantos apparently had little understanding of

Yugoslavian political affairs. They could not grasp that Markovic was unable to control the Serb Republic's use of terrorist methods against Albanians in Kosovo.

After visiting Yugoslavia, Dole, D'Amato and Nickles persuaded congress to pass the Nickles Amendment in November 1990 that would cut off U.S. aid of $5 million to Markovic's government on May 1, 1991 if Yugoslavia did not stop the repression in Kosovo. President Bush opposed it but failed to convince Dole to drop the idea because it satisfied Albanian and Croatian lobbyists. The Nickles amendment passed at the time when both Zimmermann and the Central Intelligence Agency warned the White House that Markovic's government was faltering. Zimmermann reported that if Slovenia and Croatia seceded, the other republics would be at the "mercies of Serbia" and Bosnia "would make democracy the first casualty." Only U.S. action, he said, might prevent violence and assist Yugoslavian unity. A CIA report was more pessimistic; it anticipated that Milosevic would try to block the secession of Slovenia and Croatia by unleashing civil war and ethnic violence throughout Yugoslavia. The CIA concluded that neither the U.S. nor Europeans could save Yugoslavian unity.[7]

As the June 1991 date for the secession of Slovenia and Croatia approached, the EU and the U.S. undertook last minute steps to preserve Yugoslavia's unity. In March, Markovic asked EU President Jacques Delors for assistance but EU members sent mixed messages to Belgrade. The EU Parliament responded with a resolution favoring the right of republics to secede if they did so peacefully. However, it also approved Delors' proposal for $4.5 billion economic aid to Yugoslavia if the government protected minority rights and reduced its military and social welfare budgets—policies that had already exacerbated Markovic's difficulties.[8]

The EU's inadequate assistance was followed by an equally ineffective U.S. effort when Secretary of State James Baker visited Belgrade on June 21, 1991. Baker had kept the Nickles Amendment from taking effect and, before arriving, he had attended a meeting of the CSCE which voted to support Yugoslav unity but offered no aid to Markovic. Baker met with Milosevic, Tudjman, Kucan, Izetbegovic, and Gligorov, but found that reason alone was insufficient to unite the interests of the Serbians, Slovenians, and Croatians. The lack of U.S. and European action was, however, seen as a virtual "green light" by Milosevic, Kucan, and Tudjman to break-up the Federation. Zimmermann called the U.S.

and European failure the "paradox of prevention" since they could not obtain the necessary domestic support to prevent Yugoslavia's demise because "circumstances that unambiguously justify such action have not yet arrived."

Shortly after Baker's visit, Slovenia and Croatia declared their independence, throwing Yugoslavia into turmoil. EU and CSCE officials had no plan for maintaining Yugoslav unity during the secession crisis. Both British Foreign Minister Douglas Hurd and U.S. Assistant Secretary of State Eagleburger restated support for Yugoslav unity, but neither government would commit their forces or NATO to assist a Yugoslav settlement. EU and CSCE representatives gained a cease-fire agreement on July 7 but shortly afterwards fighting broke-out between Croatia and Serbia.[9]

EARLY EUROPEAN UNION & UN PEACE EFFORTS

President Bush's decision to let Europeans deal with Yugoslavia's crisis dominated U.S. policy over the next eighteen months. Bush, Secretary Baker and Chairman of the Joint Chiefs General Colin Powell refused to involve American troops to stop the Serb-Croat conflict or to take strong action in April 1992 when fighting began in Bosnia. The State Department only supported the attempts of the EU and CSCE to gain a cease-fire. The reasons for U.S. passivity were several. They include the claim that Balkan conflicts were inevitable; the lingering "Vietnam Syndrome" that interventions will escalate; Powell's contention that any U.S. military intervention must result in a quick, decisive victory with few casualties; U.S. budget problems; and concern that military intervention would hurt Bush's presidential chances in the 1992 election.

Possibly the White House also wished to test the Europeans ability to act alone in the Post-Cold War world. Europeans such as Luxembourg's Jacques Poos had asserted: "This is the hour of Europe. It is not the hour of America." Together with Italy's Gianni DeMichelis and the Netherlands' Hans van den Broek, Poos thought negotiating a cease-fire between Serbia, Slovenia, and Croatia would be easy. As Susan Woodward explains, the EU-CSCE mediators talked about unity but in reality negotiated cease-fire terms that weakened Markovic's government, virtually approved Slovenia's independence, and resulted in the Serb-Croat war.

Following their declarations of independence, Slovenian officials were prepared to secede but Croatia and Markovic were not ready for war. Slovenia's Minister of Defense Janez Jansa had illegally purchased military equipment for the TDF and recruited Slovenians from the Yugoslavian National Army (YNA) to assist secession. After declaring independence, Jansa's TDF and YNA recruits took control of Slovenia's border control posts and customs houses and sought support from the Austrian and German governments.

In contrast to Slovenia's preparedness, Markovic and the federal parliament argued about responding to secession before parliamentary leaders instructed the Minister of Defense to send the YNA to attack Slovenia and regain control of the borders to Italy and Austria. In two days fighting, Slovenian forces had prevailed. The YNA suffered 37 deaths, while the Slovenians endured 14 deaths but captured 3,200 YNA prisoners.

In Croatia there were skirmishes between Tudjman's TDF and Croatian Serbs. Their fighting escalated in mid-July when Milosevic's Serb Republic and the YNA ignored the EU-CSCE's July 7 cease-fire and joined the Croatian Serbs to fight for a Greater Serbia. Knowingly or not, EU-CSCE mediators had treated Croatia and Slovenia as sovereign states equal to Markovic's government not as revolutionaries violating the Yugoslav Constitution. The EU-CSCE claimed to support Markovic but did not differentiate between the Federation and the separatists who used military force rather than peaceful negotiations to achieve independence.

Milosevic did not contest Slovenia's secession but rushed armies to help Croatian Serbs in the Krajina, in Eastern Slavonia and along the Dalmatian Coast. Tudjman vowed to fight Serbs to the bitter end and the Serb-Croat conflict became a fierce, bloody war where victorious Serbs began an "ethnic cleansing" program.

Poos and EU mediators could not resolve Yugoslavia's problems and, at the suggestion of France, they asked the UN to join peacemaking efforts. In September 1991, the UN levied an arms embargo on all Yugoslavia and Secretary General Boutros-Ghali appointed American Cyrus Vance to head mediations in Geneva while Lord Carrington of Britain led EU negotiations at The Hague.

The Europeans July cease-fire actually speeded up Yugoslavia's disintegration. The EU usually ignored Markovic and Yugoslav moderates such as the presidents of Bosnia and Macedonia who wanted unity. After being virtually ignored, Markovic resigned in December

1991, while Bosnian and Macedonian leaders prepared to declare their independence.[10]

Vance and Carrington believed in November 1991, that the Serbs and Croats had accepted a viable cease-fire and peace agreement. Vance concentrated on getting a Serb-Croat cease-fire while Carrington mediated terms for a settlement covering all Yugoslav republics. During these months, Milosevic's Serbs and Croatian Serbs conquered the Krajina of Croatia and most of East Slavonia before besieging the Dalmatian city of Dubrovnik. On November 23, Croatia's Tudjman and Serbia's Milosevic signed Vance's cease-fire proposal. Four days later, the UNSC assisted the agreement by approving the deployment of a United Nations Protection Force (UNPROFOR) to separate Serb and Croat armies and monitor the cease-fire. On January 2, 1992 fighting ended when the Serb and Croat military leaders finalized cease-fire zones and in March, 14,000 UNPROFOR soldiers—most of them from France and Britain but none, of course, from the United States—reached Croatia.

In November, Carrington prematurely believed a peace agreement had been reached which could merge with Vance's cease-fire. Carrington's plan held that Vance's cease-fire zones were temporary pending the final peace terms that would govern relations between the six republics and protect minority rights of all groups. However, Carrington's plans faltered on the issue of withdrawing YNA troops from Croatia. Because the YNA assisted Croatian Serbs, Tudjman wanted all YNA combat units to leave Croatia immediately. Milosevic objected to Tudjman's demands and sidetracked Carrington's peace pact although Vance's cease-fire went into effect in January 1992.

During December 1991, the Vance-Carrington proposals received an additional blow when an EU Commission concluded that Yugoslavia's unity could not be restored and recommended the recognition of Macedonian and Slovenian independence. After the Commission reported, German Chancellor Helmut Kohl proposed that Croatia should also be recognized because the Serbs were the aggressors. Kohl claimed the process of each republic in determining its future was "more democratic", although critics said he ignored a "democratic state's" responsibility to avoid war and pursue peaceful methods for settlements with neighboring republics.

Details of the 1991 diplomatic discussions between Bonn, Paris, London, and other European capitals have not been published. Apparently Kohl made deals with the British and French to gain their approval for his recognition policy. Britain voted for recognition in exchange for Kohl's vote for a British amendment to the Maastrict Treaty on economic unity. France accepted recognition after Kohl agreed to amendments by which the EU would recognize any Yugoslav republic which protected human and minority rights, accepted disarmament and nuclear non-proliferation, and approved regional security arrangements. The amendments also extended possible recognition to Macedonia and Bosnia. Thus on December 17, the EU voted to recognize independence for Slovenia and Croatia on January 15, 1992, and other former Yugoslav republics which met the stated standards on human rights, disarmament, and regional security.

The EU recognition of Croatia was badly timed, coming when the Vance Plan prepared the cease-fire between Serbs and Croats and the UNPROFOR mission prepared to monitor the Croat-Serb cease-fire. The EU ignored Carrington and Vance who protested that recognition left the negotiators without incentives to reach a broad peace agreement for all Yugoslav republics.[11]

The EU's resolution convinced Bosnian leaders to plan for immediate independence. Although President Izetbegovic was preparing a February 1992 referendum on independence, he was challenged on January 9, when Bosnian Serbs declared independence for their Republic of Srpska. This declaration prompted EU President Jose Cutileiro to propose negotiations in Lisbon on a plan for a confederation government along Serb, Muslim, and Croat ethnic-cultural lines in Bosnia. Neither the Bosnian Muslims nor the Bosnian Serbs liked the plan, but Ambassador Zimmermann indicates that the Bosnian Serbs would accept it if they could have two-thirds of Bosnian territory, an idea which neither Izetbegovic nor Cutileiro accepted.

The Bosnian government held its plebiscite on independence on February 29 and March 1 but the Bosnian Serbs boycotted it. Without Serb participation, two-thirds of Bosnia's total population voted and a majority of 99 percent approved independence. On April 5-6, the EU and the U.S. recognized the Republic of Bosnia-Herzegovina but ignored Karadzic's claim to have an independent Republic of Srpska.

When Bosnia was recognized on April 5, war had already begun because Bosnian Serb paramilitary groups, assisted by Milosevic's YNA, attacked Muslim and Croat villages. Using the YNA's heavy weapons, Serb artillery bombarded Sarajevo in early April and a conflict ensued which resulted in atrocities committed by both participants but most by the Serbian irregular military.

EU actions and Bush's recognition of Croatia, Slovenia, and Bosnia completed the dissolution of the Yugoslavian Federation. But during the remainder of 1992, neither the EU, the U.S., nor the UN used effective measures to stop the fighting despite reports about the Serbs extensive use of ethnic cleansing.[12]

RESPONSES TO BOSNIA'S WAR

The reports of atrocities in Bosnia escalated as Serbian attacks on villages and bombardment of Sarajevo resulted in the deaths of innocent women, children, and other non-combatants. By August 1992, these reported war crimes had established a moral imperative for international action but neither European nor U.S. leaders took effective action because they believed their vital national interests were insufficient to risk military action. Moreover, the atrocity reports provided a rationale for European and U.S. leaders to excuse inaction by claiming Balkan violence resulted from "traditional conflicts of its national groups"—a view of marginal merit which doomed these people to suffer in order to solve their differences.

As Bosnia's war began, the EU and UNSC limited intervention to the arms embargo and economic sanctions on Serbia and Montenegro, while the UN also shifted 1,100 UNPROFOR troops from Croatia to protect medicine and supplies arriving at Sarajevo's airport. The Europeans also sent naval vessels to the Adriatic to try to enforce economic sanctions—an impossible task since there were many overland routes. In July, the UNSC approved an airlift of humanitarian aid to Sarajevo and President Bush sent U.S. Air Force C-130 cargo planes to fly food and medical aid to Bosnia.

Although the UN aid saved lives and reduced suffering, the Carnegie report of 1996 indicated that UNPROFOR's mission, acting as a neutral group, had "the effect of dampening the public pressure for robust action in response to news of atrocities by Serb forces, and later Croat forces as well." As "neutrals", the UN and EU were reluctant to use force against Serb aggression even when the Serbs blocked aid convoys, refused to move heavy weapons away from Sarajevo's airport, and violated the no-fly zones and safe havens. EU-UN officials called the mission "peacekeeping" but, aside from Vance's cease-fire in Croatia, there was no peace or cease-fire in Bosnia.[13]

The UN humanitarian activities did not prevent fighting and atrocities. In early August 1992, both journalist Roy Gutman of *Newsday* and a British Broadcasting (BBC) documentary provided details about the war crimes committed principally, but not only, by Serbs against civilians and prisoners-of-war. These graphic reports outraged world opinion and inspired a U.S. congressional debate. In August 1992, Bush's officials claimed there was no intelligence data to confirm the atrocity reports. This seemed to be supported by a Red Cross group that visited ten POW camps in Bosnia and said all sides had committed some crimes. Experts on Bosnia sharply criticized the Red Cross for inspecting only camps opened to them, but not those in restricted Serbian areas seen by Gutman and BBC personnel.

In 1995, however, declassified CIA reports revealed the Bush administration withheld evidence of the atrocities. CIA satellite photographs taken in 1992 substantiated claims of Serb atrocities in Bosnia and they were available to the White House. One group of CIA photos showed three thousand Muslim prisoners being tortured and killed near the village of Brosk. By September 1992, the CIA had also compiled a list of Serb detention camps where war crimes were committed. After the photos were declassified, the International War Crimes Tribunal used the CIA data to indict war criminals. Perhaps the Bush team kept the data secret to avoid inflaming U.S. public opinion, but Clinton also withheld the reports until they were leaked to the *New York Times* in March 1995.

Without the CIA photos, the U.S. congressional debate resulted in two types of humanitarian aid for Bosnia. The House and Senate passed non-binding resolutions urging the president to work with the UN to send aid and use force, if necessary, to protect UNPROFOR supply routes. Congress also authorized $55 million to aid Bosnian refugees and displaced persons and $50 million to send military equipment to the embattled Bosnians if the UN lifted its 1991 arms embargo. During the next three years, congress kept returning to the idea of sending the Bosnian Muslims arms and ending the UN embargo, but neither Bush nor Clinton accepted the idea because nations with UNPROFOR soldiers in Bosnia claimed it would jeopardize their forces. Although EU-US humanitarian aid soothed moral feelings by doing something, politicians in these countries refused to reexamine their national interests about Europe's political stability.[14]

Secretary General Boutros-Ghali shares blame for handicapping effective EU-UN action. After his term as Secretary General began in

January 1992, Egypt's Boutros-Ghali claimed to speak for small Third World countries and spoke disparagingly about the U.S.-EU dominance of the UN. Boutros-Ghali contended Western powers wanted aid for European states such as Yugoslavia but ignored humanitarian needs of African nations such as Liberia, Somalia, and Rwanda where civil strife had caused refugees, starvation, and disease. The Western powers helped Christian nations, he said, but overlooked problems of other religious groups in allocating UN resources.

Correct or not, Boutros-Ghali obstructed UNSC action on Bosnia. In the U.S. critics argued that the Secretary General did not consider the proportion of UN resources transferred by Western powers to Third World countries since 1945. This "other side" included UN refugee funds, UNICEF aid to Third World children, World Health Organization funds to combat disease, and World Bank-IMF funding for Third World development. U.S. leaders such as Republican Senator Jesse Helms resented Boutros-Ghali's failure to reform UN agencies which they claimed misused UN funds, and Congress reduced or delayed U.S. contributions to the United Nations. In 1996, Clinton would successfully oppose Boutros-Ghali's reelection as Secretary General. Exactly how critical U.S.-UN friction was in decisions on Bosnia requires further study, but Boutros-Ghali's position made UN-U.S. decisions difficult. The U.S. State Department worked through British and French channels to obtain UNSC action and in 1995 Clinton by-passed the UN in pushing for a peace settlement in Bosnia.[15]

In 1992, Boutros-Ghali's views did not hinder UN assistance to Bosnian refugees and displaced persons. Aid to refugees was readily achieved and an estimated 1.5 million persons received food, housing, and admission to other European countries. The Europeans bore the costs of helping Balkan refugees with Germany accepting over 300,000. In October 1992, the U.S. accepted 1,000 Balkan refugees needing medical attention and released $6 million of the $55 million congress authorized for refugee relief. Yet, Bush insisted that the Bosnian refugees were Europe's problem.

Bush steadfastly rejected proposals for a U.S.-led military intervention in Bosnia. Ambassador Zimmermann describes August 1992 discussions with the Bush team regarding U.S. or NATO air strikes to deter Serbian bombing and promote a cease-fire. Zimmermann believes that early U.S. and NATO military threats against the Serbs could have prevented three years of bloodshed. While Bush opposed NATO air strikes, he did accept collective action to establish no-fly zones and a tighter naval blockade to enforce the UN arms embargo and economic sanctions. The French and British, however, opposed no-fly zones, arguing that if NATO planes shot down a Serb airplane violating the zone, the Serbs would retaliate against UNPROFOR personnel on the ground.

On no-fly zones, the United States compromised with the British and French. The ensuing UNSC resolution, which established no-fly zones in Bosnia, limited. NATO retaliation for violations and prevented NATO planes from attacking Serb ground forces or military installations without approval of the chief UN civil authority in the Balkans.

Bush's no-fly zone proposal preceded the November presidential election but he committed U.S naval forces to the Balkans on November 16, after losing the election. This first U.S. military commitment to the Balkans sent U.S. ships to join NATO's naval blockade that enforced the 1991 UN arms embargo and the UN's 1992 economic sanctions against Serbia and Montenegro. Although observers believed the naval blockade did not stop Serb arms supplies, Bush committed the U.S. to a restricted military role, a decision made at the time he also sent U.S. forces to Somalia on a "humanitarian aid" mission. Thus, Bush bequeathed to Clinton the U.S. interventions in Bosnia, Somalia, and Haiti.[16]

NOTES

1. The term European Union (EU) is used in Chapters 5 thru 7 because it replaced the term European Community (EC) in 1992. Likewise, the term Conference on Security and Cooperation in Europe (CSCE) is used throughout although after January 1, 1995, it became known as the Organization for Security and Cooperation in Europe (OSCE).

2. Susan Woodward, *Balkan Tragedy* (Washington, DC: Brookings Institution, 1995): 47-113. For Reagan's cutting Yugoslav military aid to zero in 1982, see Roy A. Werner, "The Burden of Global Defense," in William Snyder and James Brown, *Defense Policy in the Reagan Administration* (Washington, DC: National Defense University, 1988): 152-153.

3. Warren Zimmermann, *Origins of a Catastrophe* (New York: Random House/Times, 1996): 1-27, the quote on shooting Albanians is on p.17.

4. Ibid., 43-59, George Kennan added to Zimmermann's understanding, p. 52.

5. Ibid., 46-48; Jim Hoaglund, "It's All or Nothing in the New World Order," *WPNW* (June 22-29, 1992): 29. Also see: Thomas Friedman, "As the World Turns, U.S. Policy Stands Still," *NYT* (Mar.15, 1992): E-2; Anthony Lewis, "The New World Order," *NYT* (May 17, 1992): E-17.

6. Ibid., 58-65. On the policy of letting Europe be responsible see James A. Baker, III, *The Politics of Diplomacy* (New York: Putnam's, 1996): 636-638. On European differences of views see, Gerd Koslowski, "Bosnia: Failure of the Institutions and of the Balance of Power in Europe," *Aussen Politik* 47:4 (1996): 359-367 and John Tagliabue, "Old Tribal Rivalries in Eastern Europe Pose Threat of Infection," *NYT* (Oct. 13, 1991): E-2. Tindemans, Leo, et.al. *Unfinished Peace: Report of the International Commission on the Balkans* (Washington, DC and Berlin: Carniegie Endowment for International Peace, 1996): 55-68 which indicates the trans-Atlantic strains were the worst since the 1956 Suez Crisis.

7. Zimmermann, *Origins of Catastrophe,* 126-131 and 138-139.

8. Woodward, *Balkan Tragedy,* 153-162. For an excellent account of the first year of war, see Mark Weller, "The International Response to the Dissolution of Yugoslavia," *American Journal of International Law* 86 (July 1992): 569-606.

9. Zimmermann, *Origins of Catastrophe,* 133-138; Baker, *Politics of Diplomacy,* 479-483; Thomas Friedman "For the Nations of East Europe, the U.S. is More Symbol and Model," *NYT* (June 30,1992): E-1. David Gompert, who served on Bush's National Security Staff, indicates U.S. policy was not attached to Yugoslav unity but hoped Yugoslavia's break-up could be peaceful. Gompert also indicates that the easy experiences of the 1991 Iraq war influenced Bush's policies. Gompert, "How to Defeat Serbia," *Foreign Affairs* 73 (July/Aug. 1994): 33-34, 41-42.

10. Woodward, *Balkan Tragedy,* 162-173. According to James Gow, *Triumph of the Lack of Will* (New York: Columbia University Press, 1997): fn 11, p. 50; the correct, less dramatic, Poos quote is "If one problem can be solved by the Europeans, it's the Yugoslav problem. This is a European country and it's not up to the Americans and not up to anybody else."

11. Woodward, *Balkan Tragedy,* 173, 198; Baker, *Politics of Diplomacy,* 639-645; Mark Danner, "The US and the Yugoslav Catastrophe," *New York Review of Books* (Nov. 20, 1997): 60-62. Laura Silber and Allen Little, *Yugoslavia: Death of a Nation,* rev. ed. (London: Penguin, 1997): 198-201, offer a version of the 1991 recognition process, indicating the French and British yielded to maintain European unity. The authors conclude the U.S. played no role because President Bush did not understand the Yugoslav problem. Gensher's argument for recognition was that the Serbs negotiated to buy time to strengthen their army. For evidence about Germany's concern for Serbia's armament effort see Josef Bata, "Serbia's Secret Contacts Abroad," *Aussen Politik* 44 (Apr. 1993): 373-382 on Serb contacts with Iraq's Saddam Hussein and Russians who opposed Boris Yeltsin.

12. Noel Malcolm, "Bosnia and the West," *The National Interest* No. 39 (Spring 1995): 3-14; Zimmermann, *Origins of a Catastrophe,* 188-197; Tindemans, *Unfinished Tasks,* 42-48.

13. Woodward, *Balkan Tragedy,* 273-302; Tindemans, *Unfinished Peace,* 48-52.

14. Roy Gutman, *A Witness to Genocide* (New York: Macmillan, 1993) reprints his *Newsday* dispatches. Charles Lane and Thomas Shanker, "Bosnia: What the CIA Didn't Tell Us," *New York Review of Books* (May 9, 1996): 10-15; John F. Burns, "Tribal War? Bosnians Don't See It That Way," *NYT* (July 26, 1992): E-3; Jill Smolowe, James Graff and George Church have three articles in "Land of Slaughter," *Time* 139 (June 8, 1992): 32-39. On Congress and White House decisions see Woodward, *Balkan Tragedy,* 294-297 including fn. 36; and John Newhouse, "Dodging the Problem," *New Yorker* (Aug. 24, 1992): 60-71.

15. Woodward, *Balkan Tragedy,* 285-297, including fn. 37.

16. For details on the military problem of "no-fly" zones and "safe-zones" between the UN, the U.S. and Europeans, see Gow, *Triumph of the Lack of Will,* 127-155. On U.S. policy see Mark Danner, "America and the Bosnia Genocide," *New York Review of Books* (Dec. 4, 1997): 55-65. Zimmermann, *Origins of a Catastrophe,* 213-219 thought U.S. military threats or actions would have helped in August but Baker disagrees in *The Politics of Diplomacy,* 651, saying the national interest was not involved. On pages 648-50, Baker indicates he considered U.S. air strikes in June 1992, but Powell and Cheney opposed. Baker also closed the last Serb consulate in the U.S. and expelled the Serb ambassador before resigning as Secretary of State, being replaced by Lawrence Eagleburger in July. On Bush activity late in 1992 see Trevor Rose, "U.N. Bans Military Flights over Bosnia, Delays Enforcement," *Washington Post* (Oct. 10, 1992): A-17; John Goshko, "U.S. Shifts to Accept Balkan War Refugees," *Washington Post* (Oct. 27, 1992): A-25; Leslie Gelb, "Never Again," *NYT* (Dec. 13, 1992): E-17.

Bosnia and Herzegovina: The Dayton Agreement

CHAPTER SIX

CLINTON'S BOSNIAN POLICIES: THE 1995 ACCORDS

President Clinton had campaigned in 1992 on the slogan "It's the economy, Stupid!" but during his first term of office he could not ignore the policies inherited from Bush on Bosnia, Haiti, and Somalia. Of these, Bosnia was the most intractable and challenged the U.S. Post-Cold War role in European security and order—the traditional linchpin of U.S. foreign relations. Moreover, television pictures of atrocities in Haiti, Somalia, and Bosnia intermittently caught the eyes and hearts of the American public, recalling the nation's idealism toward human rights and democracy. When the scenes of Bosnian horror escalated during 1995 the president was compelled to accept his role as world leader in Bosnia's struggle.

CLINTON'S UNCERTAIN TRUMPET

As a presidential candidate, Clinton had criticized Bush's Bosnian policy and implied that he would play a stronger role in the Balkans. Following his inaugural, however, Clinton largely adopted Bush's legacy of relying on the United Nations-European Union to take the risks in the Balkans because of a lack of policy alternatives. Clinton's national security team was comprised of Secretary of State Warren Christopher, Secretary of Defense Les Aspin, and National Security Advisor Anthony Lake. Christopher was cautious about defending human rights and his demeanor suggested a person who preferred talk to action. Aspin accepted the Pentagon's continued reluctance to intervene unless it was to be a quick, decisive strike with overwhelming force. Lake's emotional reactions to the human tragedy made him more hawkish about Bosnia, however, his views received little attention until mid-1995 when Serbian atrocities came to dominate media reports.

By May 1993, Clinton had expanded Bush's proposal for a no-fly zone, scored a very minor victory with an air drop, and stumbled badly by proposing a "lift and strike" policy which was neither carefully planned nor forcefully carried out. The no-fly zones set in 1992 were extended when Clinton supported a UNSC decision for NATO aircraft to enforce the UN's no-fly limits on the Serbs through Operation Deny Flight.

On April 16, after Bosnian Serbs violated a UN order to stop bombarding Srebrenica, Clinton backed the UN Security Council in making Srebrenica and Sarajevo safe-havens for UNPROFOR in order to protect Muslim civilians. On May 6, the UNSC designated five other towns as safe-havens: Sarajevo, Tuzla, Zepa, Goradze and Bihac. The safe-haven policy worked until the Serbs escalated their attacks in May 1995 when UNPROFOR failed to protect the zones because the UN feared air attacks would endanger their troops. The EU-UN policy for protecting zones was finally changed in July 1995.

In early 1993, Clinton's "very minor" triumph was to use U.S. C-130 cargo planes to air-drop food and medicine to Bosnians Muslims living where Serbs barred UN relief convoys. The U.S. air drops began late in February and continued whenever the need arose to deliver supplies to stranded Bosnians.[1]

On May 1 Clinton asked the UN to lift its 1991 arms embargo on Bosnia and permit NATO air attacks against the Serbs, a policy stimulated because of Clinton's dislike for the January 2, 1993 Vance-Owen peace plan. This plan evolved when EU-UN delegates, in September 1992, combined Cyrus Vance's UN peace talks with Lord David Owen's EU negotiations. Accepting the EU-UN assumption that the Republic of Bosnia-Herzegovina should remain sovereign, the Vance-Owen plan divided Bosnia into ten provinces according to geography, history and ethnic ties with each province sharing political power with a weak central government. The plan also included a cease-fire that the leaders of Bosnian Serbs, Muslims, and Croats accepted in January 1993.

Although the EU backed the Vance-Owen Plan, the Clinton administration extended only limited support to it because the president believed the Serbian aggressors got too much land compared to the Muslims. Clinton's sympathy for the Muslims irritated European leaders who wanted to act as neutrals between the warring factions and hoped the civil war would end if the Bosnian groups accepted the plan. As David Owen said, neither the U.S. nor West Europeans wanted a military intervention, a fact that made achieving better terms impossible.

Although Clinton's half-hearted backing of the Vance-Owen plan was not helpful, it failed due to Serbian objections. The Bosnian Serbs demanded concessions that would give them the 70 percent of Bosnia their military controlled and the right to secede from Bosnia. In contrast, Christopher used population data to argue the Serbs should get 33 percent of the land while the Vance-Owen Plan gave them 43 percent. By the end of May 1993, the Bosnian Serbs had rejected the Vance-Owen Plan after its Assembly voted against it. During the Assembly meeting, the Serb army commander General Ratko Mladic strongly opposed the plan.[2]

Meanwhile, Clinton offered a "lift and strike" proposal on May 1. "Lift" meant ending the 1991 UN arms embargo that allegedly restricted the supply of military equipment to the Bosnian Muslims while it gave the Bosnian Serbs an advantage because they could draw from Serbian sources. According to Clinton's advisors this imbalance could be rectified by providing military aid to the Muslims and Croats. "Strike" meant Clinton wanted NATO to launch air attacks to rigorously enforce the UN no-fly zones and coerce the Bosnian Serbs into accepting peace terms. Inside the White House, General Powell and Admiral David Jeremiah, the Vice-Chairman of the Joint Chiefs, opposed such air strikes, believing they would not deter the Serbs but might embroil the U.S. in an escalation of the war that would ultimately require U.S. ground forces. More seriously, Christopher learned—before Clinton announced "lift and strike"—that the British and French opposed both ideas. The Europeans thought more military equipment in Bosnia would increase the fighting, endanger UNPROFOR personnel, and weaken UN peace talks. Although Clinton was willing to offer U.S. ground forces to implement a peace treaty all Bosnian factions approved, his offer did not risk American lives in the way the "lift and strike" proposal endangered European and Canadian forces in Bosnia.

Despite the British and French warnings, Clinton announced his "lift and strike" proposal thinking it was more politically astute to propose action and have it rejected rather than do nothing. According to journalist Elizabeth Drew, however, the ever flexible Clinton had decided against the "lift and strike" idea even before Christopher returned with word that European leaders rejected the plan. Clinton had just read Robert Kaplan's *Balkan Ghosts*, a popular but historically unsatisfactory account of Balkans tribal wars that offered excuses for not acting because the Balkan conflicts were inevitable. Thus, Clinton and Christopher played down the "lift and strike" fiasco; with Christopher suggesting that the intractable Bosnian plight could never be cured.

For the remainder of 1993, Clinton continued Bush's policies of letting the UN and EU seek solutions to Bosnia's problems and refused to deploy U.S. forces as part of UNPROFOR. In the fall of 1993, no peace seemed possible. The Vance-Owen plan was shelved and a latter plan devised by Owen and Norway's Thorvald Stoltenberg was also rejected. Clinton's problems in Somalia and Haiti during September and October 1993 also diminished his enthusiasm for assuming leadership in Bosnia.[3]

TOWARD U.S. LEADERSHIP

After UN-EU peace proposals failed in 1993, fighting intensified in Bosnia during 1994 and 1995. In response, President Clinton slowly committed the U.S. to a greater role that led to coercive policies and an effective cease-fire and peace plan in November 1995. The evolution of this involvement apparently was driven by the White House's gradual realization that Balkans problems could be resolved and European security reestablished only if the U.S. exerted a major role in directing the peace effort.

The first step in U.S. involvement came in February 1994 when the Washington Framework Agreement established the Bosnian Federation of Muslims and Croats that shifted the balance of power against the Bosnian Serbs. The 1994 agreement fell into Clinton's lap as the result of three developments between September 1993 and February 1994. The first was the expansion of Bosnian warfare following the rejection of the Owen-Stoltenberg peace plan. Not only did Bosnian Serbs renew their shelling of Sarajevo and launch new attacks against Muslim villages, but the Bosnian Croats began an offensive against Bosnian Serbs and Muslims, hoping to enlarge the Croat mini-Republic of Herzeg-Bosna created by Bosnian Croatians in 1992 with help from Tudjman. Bosnia's triangular conflict between Croats, Muslims, and Serbs precipitated more reports of ethnic cleansings and also endangered UNPROFOR personnel trying to remain neutral while extending relief and negotiating a cease-fire agreement.

The escalation of Bosnia's conflict affected U.S. policy in February 1994 after a Serb shell exploded in a Sarajevo marketplace, killing 68 people and wounding more than 100 others. Shocked NATO authorities gave the Bosnian Serbs ten days to remove heavy weapons within twenty kilometers of Sarajevo's center or two kilometers of Pale, the Serb's headquarters. The NATO ultimatum followed a U.S. request for air strikes to force Serbs to stop bombing Sarajevo. The Serbians averted NATO's air strike because Moscow persuaded them to withdraw enough artillery from Sarajevo to satisfy the UN observers. Nevertheless, on February 28, 1994 a NATO "first" took place when U.S. jet planes patrolling the Bihac safe zone shot down four Serbian planes violating the UN protective area. This NATO action set a precedent for other NATO attacks when Serbs violated no-fly or safe-haven zones on April 10, May 24, August 5, and November 21, primarily near the safe-havens of Goradze and Bihac.

More significant than the NATO attacks, the Washington Framework Agreement shifted the power-balance in Bosnia. Following the February 5th Sarajevo disaster, U.S. State Department negotiators persuaded the Bosnian Muslims and Bosnian Croats to stop fighting each other and concentrate on defeating the Serbs. The idea for the agreement originated during the fall of 1993 with a group of Muslim secularists and Croatians living in Sarajevo. This group's existence became known to Charles Redman, a U.S. diplomat who Clinton sent to Sarajevo in February to discuss peace with Bosnia's Izetbegovic. Both Izetbegovic and Croatia's Tudjman realized that Muslim-Croat warfare benefited the Serbs and they decided in favor of a cease-fire that would give the Croat Republic a breathing spell to re-supply its army for conflict against the Serbs.

Redman announced a Muslim-Croat cease-fire, then soon after he said delegates from Bosnia Croatians, Bosnia Muslims, and the Croat Republic would meet in Washington to finalize a Bosnia-Croat federation and discuss a confederation with the Republic of Croatia. On March 18, Tudjman and Izetbegovic formed a confederation while Bosnia's Prime Minister Haris Silajdzic and Bosnian Croatian leader Kresimir Zubak accepted a constitution for the Federation of Bosnia and Herzegovina. Clinton offered economic aid to the signatories and said the U.S. would help enforce the settlement though the good offices of NATO. Although the Washington Agreement's constitutional relationship between Bosnia's Muslims and Croats was denounced by some extremist Bosnian Croats, military cooperation between the two groups enhanced their forthcoming struggle against the Serbs.[4]

A final outcome of the Serb's February market attack was the formation of a "Contact Group" by five major powers: the United States, Russia, England, France, and Germany. Formed on April 25, 1994, the Contact Group's first contribution took place in July 1994 when it presented a Bosnian peace plan to divide Bosnian territory on a 51-49 ratio giving the Muslim-Croat Federation a majority of the land. The Federation's leaders accepted the plan but Bosnian Serbia's President Karadzic rejected it.

In response to Karadzic's rejection, the Russian members of the Contact Group asked the rump Yugoslavian (Serbia/Montenegro) leader, Milosevic, to persuade Karadzic to accept the plan. Milosevic sought to cooperate with the EU-UN in order to end the UN's economic sanctions and keep Russia's support; thus, when he failed to change Karadzic's mind, Milosevic severed the Serbian Republic's economic and political relations with the Bosnian Serbs. He cut off communications with Pale and forbade visits by the Bosnian Serb leaders. In September, Milosevic also allowed UN civilian teams to monitor the Serbian republic's borders with Bosnia to verify he had stopped assistance to the Bosnia Serbs. In response to Milosevic's cooperation, UNSC resolutions in September tightened its economic sanctions against the Bosnian Serbs, but lessened the sanctions on Milosevic's Yugoslavia.[5]

Throughout the remainder of 1994, the Contact Group pursued negotiations based on the 49/51 ratio even though the July cease-fire agreement lapsed and fighting resumed in Bosnia. During the fall of 1994, Bosnian Muslims and Croats cooperated in attacking Serbian forces in western and northwestern Bosnia while Tudjman's Republic imported military equipment for its self and for its Bosnian confederates. All sides in Bosnia defied the 1991 UN arms embargo. The lack of a seaport had hindered the Bosnia Muslim's acquisition of weapons, but after allying themselves with Tudjman, illegal arms moved readily from Croatia to Sarajevo. Bosnian Muslims also received financial aid and armaments from Middle Eastern nations such as Turkey, Egypt, Saudia Arabia, and Iran. Although U.S. intelligence knew about the illegal deliveries of armaments, as well as the arrival of Iranian fundamentalist "holy warriors" in Bosnia, Clinton did not publicize this assistance. The Bosnian Serbs had also received illegal arms from the neighboring Serb Republic and Russia as well as through Bulgaria and Macedonia.

By early 1995, the military balance swung in favor of the Bosnian Muslims and Croats as extensive fighting took place around the "safe-haven" of Bihac on the northwest border of Croatia and Serbia. The Bosnian Federation's offensive in 1994 conquered sixty square miles of land, chased out 7,000 Serbs, and, apparently, found Muslims and Croats using ethnic cleansing. The Bosnian Serbs counterattacked with aid from

Croatian Serbs crossing from Croatia's Krajina and regained most of the land taken by the Federation offensive. During this time, the UNSC permitted limited NATO air attacks against Krajina Serb aircraft over Bihac's no-fly zone, but NATO stopped their action because Serbs captured 350 UN soldiers and used them as human shields to protect their military installations.

On December 1, 1994, Tudjman reacted to the Serbian counterattack by ending the 1992 Vance cease-fire and ordering a Croatian artillery bombardment of the Krajina Serbs who fought Muslims and Croats near Bihac. Although the Croatian attacks presaged their future offensives in 1995, there was a temporary halt on December 28 when Jimmy Carter negotiated a cease-fire between the Federation and the Bosnian Serbs.[6]

U.S. ASSUMES LEADERSHIP

Jimmy Carter's cease-fire was largely a winter lull as snow and rain created muddy conditions before fighting could resume in March. When the Bosnian Muslims ended the cease-fire by attacking Serbs around Mount Vlasic, near Tuzla, in northeastern Bosnia, Bosnian Serbs responded with artillery barrages against UN safe-havens at Tuzla and other safe zones in eastern Bosnia. The Federation's armies put the Serbs at a disadvantage because they had to fight on three fronts—near Tuzla, Bihac, and Sarajevo.

With U.S. urging, NATO warned the Serbs to stop shelling safe-havens or risk air attacks but the air attacks failed to take place in April despite pleas from Dutch UNPROFOR officers in the safe-havens. After the Dutch at Srebrenica requested strikes against the Serbs, Yasushi Akashi, the UN civil officer in Zagreb, rejected an air attack claiming it would be "unneutral." In New York, U.S. Ambassador Albright protested Akashi's decision to Secretary General Boutros-Ghali but the Secretary upheld his envoy's decision.

Albright's complaint was one of many against Boutros-Ghali's passiveness in Bosnia and persuaded Clinton in May to lobby for NATO air attacks on Serbs. Clinton also sent diplomat Robert Frasure to Belgrade to gain President Milosevic's recognition of the Bosnian Federation and help in persuading Bosnian Serbs to accept the Contact Group's peace terms. Milosevic would not recognize the Federation, but did ask the Bosnian Serbs to respect the safe-zones.

Rather than comply with Milosevic's request, the Bosnian Serbs intensified their shelling of UN safe-havens. At Clinton's urging NATO finally approved air raids for May 25 and 26, largely flown by Americans, which attacked Serb ammunition dumps and military installations near the Serb headquarters at Pale.

The air strikes' military success became a near political disaster before French President Jacques Chirac stepped in. First, the Serbs took UNPROFOR soldiers hostage to use as human shields against air raids and, at British and French insistence, the NATO strikes ceased. However, President Chirac, who replaced Francois Mitterand on May 17, noted the defects of the EU-UN policies in Bosnia and persuaded UNPROFOR to revise its tactics. Previously, the EU-UN acted as neutrals in a civil war, not differentiating between Serb aggressors and Muslim-Croat victims. Thus, when Serbs blocked Sarajevo's airport and refused to let planes land, the UN waited for Serbs to voluntarily end the blockade.

Chirac challenged these methods, convincing the Contact Group nations to redeploy UNPROFOR soldiers from scattered positions to militarily defensible posts and to adopt rules of engagement allowing UN soldiers to shoot when necessary and to open obstructed supply lines. Chirac also asked but failed to get the U.S. to send helicopter gunships to help redeploy troops and protect UN safe-havens. However, British Prime Minister John Major backed Chirac's decisions and dispatched British forces with heavy artillery to assist UNPROFOR activity.[7]

Clinton approved Chirac's proposals for UNPROFOR's redeployment but would not send helicopter forces because he feared congressional opposition. In a May speech at the Air Force Academy, Clinton indicated the U.S. would assist the redeployment of UN soldiers, but would send ground troops only as peacekeepers to implement an agreement. While the U.S. aided the Bosnian redeployment by sending eight warships and an aircraft carrier to the Adriatic Sea with 2,000 U.S. Marines, Clinton did not meet Chirac's request for a helicopter Rapid Reaction Force.

After appearing to be ready for an assertive U.S. role, Clinton flip-flopped because Serb anti-aircraft units shot down a U.S. F-16 plane on reconnaissance near Bihac. A six-day search was needed to rescue pilot Scott O'Grady. This incident led Senator Dole to criticize Clinton, who in turn, stated that U.S. navy forces in the Adriatic would only help UNPROFOR personnel needing "emergency extraction."

Although lacking Clinton's aid, the French and British altered their Bosnia tactics between June and August. The British sent 1,500 troops armed with tanks and heavy artillery and France deployed 4,000 troops plus helicopter gunships. Although not completed until late August, the

UNPROFOR forces secured defensive posts, adopted rules to protect themselves, and cleared the supply routes. The new methods were demonstrated on June 5 when French soldiers took control of the Vrbanja Bridge in Sarajevo by evicting Serb troops blocking the route to the city. Additionally, Milosevic responded to Ambassador Robert Frasure's entreaty by persuading the Bosnian Serbs to release the UN soldiers who had been held hostages against NATO air attacks since May.

The change in UNPROFOR activity was a step in the right direction but did not solve Bosnia's broader problems because fighting continued between Serbs, Croats, and Muslims. The Europeans were divided about what further steps to take because they did not wish to use force to coerce the warring groups into a meaningless settlement. Reports circulated that Britain and France would withdraw their troops before winter set in.[8]

Knowing the dissension among Contact Group members, Bosnia's factions ignored cease-fire proposals while warfare near Sarajevo and in northern and eastern Bosnia became more intense. When the Muslim-Croat's attacked near Bihac, the Serbs launched assaults on the less defended Muslim safe-havens around Srebrenica, Zepa and Goradze where Dutch UNPROFOR forces waited for British and French reinforcements.

On July 11, the Serb conquest of the Srebrenica safe-haven gained world attention and persuaded Clinton to adopt a forceful U.S. leadership role. When the Serb assault was imminent, the Dutch commander in Srebrenica requested NATO air attacks but the UNPROFOR commander, Lieutenant General Bernard Janvier, refused to believe Serbs would attack. Later that day, Janvier changed his mind, but help for the Dutch and Srebrenica's Muslims was too little and too late. The Serbs had overwhelmed the Dutch and entered the city before Janvier approved an air attack limited to Serb tanks and artillery posts "if they fired" at UNPROFOR troops. Janvier's stubborn "neutrality" failed the Dutch and Muslim victims.

After Srebrenica fell, Bosnian Serb's under General Mladic rounded up over 25,000 Muslim men, women and children in the city and surrounding villages. Thousands of Muslim men and boys were tortured and killed, and women and girls were beaten and raped. The villagers at Nova Kasaba, Bradunac, and Kravica suffered a similar fate except for those able to flee to Tuzla for refuge.

On August 8, Ambassador Albright showed a UNSC session the U.S. satellite and U-2 aircraft photographs which substantiated the Serb slaughter of Muslims. Clinton advisor Strobe Talbott saw this as "another European holocaust." The photos and accounts of refugees who escaped the slaughter proved that Mladic and other Serb officials were directly involved in massacres. Moreover, the Serb attacks did not stop at Srebrenica as Serb terrorists also attacked the "safe-havens" of Zepa and Goradze.[9]

COERCION AND NEGOTIATION

After the Srebrenica massacres, Clinton decided in August 1995 to provide U.S. leadership for a multinational effort at peace in the Balkans. Six years of fierce conflict and separatist propaganda had deeply embittered relations between Croats, Muslims, and Serbs, making a multinational Bosnian state unrealistic. In 1995, the U.S. decided to seek a Bosnian government made up of three cultural entities. Assistant Secretary of State Richard Holbrooke was entrusted with the negotiations.

Clinton's decisions began on August 2, when National Security Advisor Lake presented "new policy ideas" to the president. Prepared by Lake and Peter Tarnoff of the State Department, in consultation with Joint Chiefs Chairman General John Shalikasvili, who replaced Colin Powell in 1993, the report urged Clinton to get the UN and Europeans to use coercion and to take the lead in negotiations for a Bosnian peace. The "new ideas" recommended direct U.S. activity in peace and cease-fire negotiations and in undertaking aggressive NATO air attacks against Bosnian Serbs to force them to accept peace.

Clinton was also advised of Croatian plans to attack Serbs in the Krajina after U.S. intelligence discovered Tudjman planned an attack for August 4. Although the attack widened the war, Holbrooke advised Clinton not to criticize the attack because it would succeed and it would eliminate problems between Croatia and its Serb minority in the Krajina as well as between the Serbian Republic and Croatia. Holbrooke believed that Milosevic would accept a peace agreement, would not intervene to help Croatian Serbs, and would abandon the "greater" Serbia he had once advocated. Milosevic had not helped Serbs against Croatia's offensive into Western Slavonia in February 1995 and would not do so when Croatia attacked the Krajina region.

Holbrooke's assessment of Milosevic was correct and Croatia's offensive succeeded. Because Milosevic had abandoned the Greater Serbia idea, Holbrooke's peace terms would call for two separate political-based entities in Bosnia. Although careful to avoid publicizing this policy, the U.S. decision to support the division of Bosnia's government became evident in September. After Croatia's success in the Krajina, Clinton sent Lake to Europe to explain the "new" U.S. policy and enlist EU support. He also sent Holbrooke to Belgrade, Zagreb, and Sarajevo to negotiate a cease-fire and obtain tentative peace terms between the Bosnian factions.[10]

Between August and October 31, Clinton persuaded NATO members to accept U.S. negotiations between Serb, Croat, and Bosnian leaders that resulted in a cease-fire and the basis for peace terms. In leading the negotiations, Holbrooke limited his demands on Milosevic and Tudjman to get their aid in persuading the Bosnian Serbs, Croats, and Muslims to accept the cease-fire and peace terms. Fortunately, these two presidents desired peace because Milosevic's Yugoslavia was feeling the impact of the UN's economic sanctions and Tudjman now controlled the Croatian Serbs in the Krajina and all but a slice of Croatia's Slavonia near Vukovar.

Holbrooke succeeded although his talks were delayed for a week after three members of his State Department team, including Robert Frasure, were killed when their vehicle slipped off a mountain road near Sarajevo, fell in a ravine, caught fire, and exploded. Following funeral services in the U.S., Holbooke continued to shuttle between Belgrade, Sarajevo, and Zagreb until Bosnian, Croatian, and Serbian delegates met in Geneva. Karadzic, the Bosnian Serb leader, never came to Geneva but agreed on August 29 that Milosevic would represent him.

On September 8, Serb and Croat delegates agreed to recognize Bosnia as a legal entity and all three delegates accepted the 51/49 land distribution formula for Bosnia without specifying exact boundaries. In addition, the Bosnia Federation recognized the Bosnian Serb's Republic of Srpska as an entity whose future relations with the Milosevic's Yugoslavia (Serbia/Montenegro) would be determined later. In a second Geneva agreement, delegates adopted a structure for a future Bosnian state having a three-member presidency, a parliament and a constitutional court. In these institutions, the Bosnia-Croat Federation would share power with the Republic of Srpska on a basis of two to one.

While the Geneva talks were underway, the three parties continued to battle for control of territory before intensive NATO air strikes compelled the Serbs to accept a cease-fire. After an August 28 Serbian artillery attack on Sarajevo killed 37 people, NATO planes bombed Serb ammunition dumps and military facilities. These strikes stopped momentarily when the Geneva talks opened but resumed because the Serbs did not remove their heavy artillery from Sarajevo. The second round of NATO air raids were intensive daily strikes from September 5 until September 21 when Bosnian Serb General Mladic removed his heavy artillery from Sarajevo and the UN safe-haven of Goradze. Although the shelling ended, fighting continued between Bosnian Serbs and the Muslim-Croat army in western Bosnia.

Gaining the Bosnian Serbs cooperation was difficult because General Mladic designated NATO an enemy of the Serbs. Holbrooke needed the efforts of Russia's President Boris Yeltsin and Milosevic, who withheld all military aid to Mladic, before the Serbs accepted the cease-fire on October 12.

By October 12, the Bosnia-Croat Federation had gained more territory for the Federation. Serbia's land control decreased from a 70/30 ratio in 1994 to approximately the Contact Group's 49/51 favoring the Bosnian Federation in 1995. Having been approved by the U.S. and European countries, including Russia, the 49/51 ratio became the basis for allocating land during the peace talks that convened at Dayton, Ohio, on November 1, 1995.[11]

DAYTON PEACE ACCORDS

Three weeks of intensive negotiations at Dayton, Ohio produced an agreement on November 21 that the presidents of Yugoslavia (Serbia/Montengro), Croatia, and leaders of Bosnia's three factions signed in final form at Paris on December 14, 1995. Guided by Holbrooke, who was assisted by Secretary of State Christopher and Lt. General Wesley Clark, Presidents Milosevic and Tudjman dominated the sessions while President Izetbegovic let his prime minister speak for Bosnia. The Bosnian Serbs were represented by Milosevic but other Serb delegates at Dayton refused to initial the document which Karadzic signed two days later at a meeting in Belgrade with Milosevic.

On November 10, Croatia's President Tudjman and Bosnia's President Izetbegovic reaffirmed their commitment to support the Bosnia-Croat Federation of 1994 although psychological tensions existed between Muslims and Croats in western Bosnia especially at Mostar. A second preliminary agreement resolved problems between Tudjman and Milosevic over East Slavonia, a strip of Croatian territory that Serbs occupied in 1991. Milosevic acknowledged Croatia's right to the eastern strip and the two reached a compromise for a transitional period of twelve months for the Serbian withdrawal plus an additional period "not to exceed the first one" for the Serbs final withdrawal from Slavonia under UN supervision by December 1997.[12]

On Bosnia, the three critical questions at Dayton were the future control of metropolitan Sarajevo, a road linking Goradze with Sarajevo, and the Posavina corridor in northeast Bosnia near Brcko that linked western and eastern territory of the Bosnian Serbs' Srpska Republic.

The Sarajevo issue was acute because Serbs in several suburbs, including the headquarters of Karadzic in Pale, planned to fight to prevent Muslim control. Prime Minister Silajdzic insisted on unity for the multiethnic city and promised the Serbs would be treated as equals, as they were before 1990. Despite an awareness that Serbs felt strongly about control of the suburbs, Milosevic thought they could adjust to Muslim-Croat rule. In the accords, Serbs retained Pale but the rest of Sarajevo came under the Bosnia-Croat Federation.

On Goradze and Posavina, the Bosnian Federation obtained a five mile corridor linking Goradze with Sarajevo but a compromise intended to resolve the issue of the Posavina corridor continued to be disputed. The compromise called for binding arbitration by three arbitrators, one Muslim, one Serb, and a third agreed to by the other two. If the two delegates did not agree on a third, the International Court of Justice would appoint that person. The status of this corridor became exceptionally controversial after Muslims tried to return to their former homes in Brcko but Serbs resisted.

In addition to these three issues, the Dayton Accords contained many other details. Regarding the government, Bosnia-Herzegovina would have two "Entities": the Bosnian Federation of Muslims and Croats and the Srpska Republic. The Dayton pact provided a constitution for Bosnia-Herzegovina including clauses on relations between Bosnian Serbs and the Republic of Yugoslavia and between Bosnian Croats and the Croatian Republic which stated the Entities could have "parallel relations" with neighboring states consistent with the "sovereignty and territorial integrity of Bosnia and Herzegovina." Whether or not these terms permitted the Srpska Republic to join Milosevic's government was left for another day.

The Bosnian constitution provided for a presidency, a parliamentary assembly, a constitutional court and a central bank. There would be a three member presidency (one from each group) to conduct foreign policy, formulate the annual budget and appoint a Council of Ministers having at least one third Serbians. The bicameral parliament would have one house directly elected, the other house selected by each Entities legislature with fourteen Serb members and 28 Bosnia-Croat members.

The first government elections under the Dayton Accords would be conducted by CSCE, now known as the Organization of Security and Cooperation in Europe (OSCE). The OSCE would appoint a Provisional Election Commission to ensure that free and fair elections would be held no later than nine months after the Paris signing. Bosnian citizens were eligible to vote in their 1991 municipalities on the basis of the 1991 census unless they petitioned to vote elsewhere.

Other sections of the Dayton Accords were designed to avoid conflict between the Entities and their ethnic groups. These sections included the following: an agreement to settle disputes through binding arbitration; a Human Rights Commission headed by an ombudsman appointed by the OSCE to investigate human rights violations; a guarantee that refugees and displaced persons could return to their previous homes or be compensated for their property; a National Monuments Commission to preserve monuments; and a Commission on Public Corporations to rebuild roads, railways bridges, energy and postal services for Bosnia-Herzegovina.

The Dayton Accords also provided for a Joint Civilian Commission chaired by a High Representative chosen by the UNSC to facilitate peace at the civilian level and obtain funds for rebuilding the economy of the former Yugoslavia. Civilian agreements also created a United Nations International Police Task Force(IPTF) to train, staff and equip local police for Bosnia-Herzegovina. The IPTF would advise local police about threats to the peace and assist the local governments and OSCE in conducting free and fair elections. For the immediate maintenance of peace, the Dayton Accords granted the stationing of the U.S.-led multinational Implementation Force (IFOR) which received broad powers to control the soldiers and weapons of Bosnia's three formerly warring parties. Within thirty days, these three factions were to withdraw behind existing cease-fire lines and notify the Joint Military Commission of IFOR about the location of all heavy weapons, mine fields and military sites within six miles of the cease-fire lines. In addition all prisoners-of-war would be released within thirty days of the December signing in Paris.

A second annex on IFOR's military provided that within seven days of the Paris signing, Bosnian, Croatian and Yugoslavian (Serbia/Montenegro) representatives would begin negotiations on arms control and arms limitations arrangements. If no agreements were reached in six months, IFOR officials would impose a limitation on arms.[13]

After the Bosnian Serbs joined Milosevic, Tudjman and Izetbegovic in accepting the Dayton Accords, Clinton joined UN and European leaders in preparing for the final signing of the pact and for implementing the agreement. The UN Security Council removed the economic sanctions for a period of 100 days that could be extended if the peace process was intact. The UNSC also lifted the 1991 arms embargo on Yugoslavia to take place ten days after the treaty signing in Paris and the UN Secretary General's Office issued a report on atrocities in Bosnia which condemned the Bosnian Serbs as the principal perpetrator. Following the Paris signing, the UNSC transferred responsibility for Bosnia to the IFOR authority, ending the UNPROFOR mission in Bosnia. The UN also renewed its commitment to having troops in Macedonia and in the East Slavonia part of Croatia which the U.S. refused to make a part of the IFOR mission.

President Clinton visited Europe in early December to cement the cooperation of NATO allies and France, and to visit U.S. troops in Germany. The Europeans were forthcoming with their backing but when Clinton returned to Washington, he faced the larger problem—gaining approval from congress. While constitutionally he did not need their prior approval, he wanted the Republican-dominated congress to pass a resolution of support.[14]

CONGRESS AND THE BOSNIAN MISSION

Since the 1994 congressional elections, Clinton had difficulty with the Republican majority in both domestic and foreign affairs. On Bosnia, both congressional and public opinion zig-zagged as much as Clinton. Opinion polls usually showed that Americans opposed foreign military adventures; but when Bosnian atrocities were reported Americans said they wanted the president to do something. Unfortunately, neither the public, congress, nor Clinton seemed able to determine what the president should do.

In June 1995, public opinion and congress turned against U.S. activity after the Serbs held UNPROFOR hostages and U.S. pilot Scott O'Grady was lost for several days. By mid-July, however, reports of Serb atrocities at Srebrenica prompted the public and congress to take a "do something" position. In August, Senator Dole and Speaker of the House Newt Gingrich pushed a joint resolution to end the UN arms embargo and rearm the Muslims. Where would Bosnia get the military equipment or the money to buy it? Would the U.S. rearm and train Bosnians to insure their success? How should the U.S. deal with British and French objections to ending the embargo? Because they had no answers to these questions, Dole, Gingrich, and Senate Foreign Relations Chairman Jesse Helms appeared to be simply trying to embarrass the president.

In August 1995, Congress passed Dole's resolution to end the UN arms embargo but Clinton vetoed it. In 1996, informants disclosed that neither Clinton nor Anthony Lake told the Congressional Oversight Committee that U.S. intelligence agencies knew that Bosnia's Muslims had been receiving military aid from Middle East sources including Iran. Because of the divisive nature of American politics, no one knows whether better communication between Clinton and Congress would have avoided the discord in December 1995 when Clinton sought congressional approval for the mission in Bosnia. To obtain support after October, spokespersons such as Ambassador Albright, Lake, Christopher, and Defense Secretary William Perry appeared on radio and TV, in public forums, and before congressional committees to state their case that a moral imperative *and* the national interest required the U.S. to implement the Dayton accords.

After October, however, congressional opposition to troops in Bosnia persisted. Although public attention in November focused on the Palestine-Israeli conflict following Yitzak Rabin's assassination, when the White House mentioned plans to send 20,000 American soldiers to Bosnia, both Democrats and Republicans in Congress clashed with White House leaders. Christopher, Perry, and General Shalikashvili explained that the U.S. national interest lay in maintaining European security, but both Democrats and Republicans said they did not make a clear case for involvement or explain how the U.S. would get out of Bosnia. Consequently, despite Christopher's and Holbrooke's appeals against the measure, on November 2, a House resolution denied funds for U.S. troops in Bosnia.

After the Dayton Accords were signed on November 21, Clinton emphasized the moral imperative to end Bosnia's strife and the nation's interest in keeping NATO as an effective force for European peace, security, and stability as America's most vital friend and trading partner. U.S. troops, he said, would not be fighting a war but "helping the people of Bosnia to secure their own peace agreement." He admitted the U.S. should not be the world's policeman, should not intervene in every conflict, but added: "My duty as President is to match the demands for

American leadership to our strategic interests and to our ability to make a difference." In Bosnia, "America and America alone can and should make the difference for peace." He added that Bosnia's conflict "has challenged our interests and troubled our souls. Thankfully we can do something about it....So let us lead. This is our responsibility as Americans."

Clinton's decision to intervene was approved by Pentagon officers, some of whom previously opposed involvement. These officers said the mission had clear goals for a powerful IFOR under NATO with "robust" rules of engagement allowing local military officers to order troops to shoot without asking approval from higher command. General Dennis Reimer, a Vietnam War veteran, stated the Bosnia mission did not resemble Vietnam, a comparison made by critics in congress. To prevent comparison to Somalia's hunt for Aideed, Christopher and Perry said IFOR would not hunt for war criminals, detaining them only if they obstructed military operations.

Despite Clinton's media efforts, U.S. polls indicated the public was uncertain about intervening in Bosnia. While an ABC poll after Clinton's TV address indicated 39 percent favored and 57 percent disapproved his decision, a Gallup poll showed 46 percent favoring and 40 percent against. A CBS survey found 33 percent favored intervening compared to a University of Maryland poll that found 50 percent favored and 47 percent opposed the idea. The Gallup Poll highlighted one reason for public uncertainty—most Americans knew little about Bosnia.

Ignorance and indecision also governed Congress's responses. Given the public's views on a Bosnian intervention, it is not surprising that Clinton only gained a favorable vote in the Senate because Republicans Dole and John McCain and Democrat Robert Kerrey produced a bipartisan resolution to support him. Although 29 Republicans and one Democrat opposed the resolution, enough Republican senators joined with Democrats to back Clinton by a vote of 69 to 30.

To obtain Senate support, Clinton issued a written statement that Bosnia's army would be armed to defend themselves after INFOR departed and that U.S. forces would enter Bosnia on December 20 and leave one year after. The arming of Bosnians presented problems because European leaders opposed this as discriminating between the three Bosnian groups and a violation of the Dayton arms control limitations. Clinton said the U.S. would act within the arms control agreements to arm the Muslims if the Serbs failed to comply with the Dayton Accords.

During debate on the Dole-McCain resolution, senators never questioned the moral needs of Bosnia's suffering, choosing to differ over the national interest at stake. Senator Phil Gramm said the U.S. had no national interest in Bosnia. Foreign policy was not "social work", Gramm stated; furthermore, NATO had been designed for defensive purposes. Gramm claimed Clinton sought to have the U.S. be neutral between Bosnia's factions. In contrast to Gramm, Democrat Senator Robert Kerrey of Nebraska argued that "It does fall to the President of the United States to define the nation's vital interests and ask to defend them. Such interests are at issue in the former Yugoslavia." Kerrey believed European stability was at stake because Europeans were unable to solve their problems alone. Kerrey said the U.S. formed NATO as a Cold War defensive measure but the alliance now must extend the "same cooperation to Eastern Europe and, I hope, eventually Russia and other former Soviet states."

In contrast to senators, House Republicans under Gingrich were uncompromising. On December 13, the House reversed its earlier action of November 2. Enough moderate Republicans joined Democrats to defeat a new bill to cut funds for troops by a vote of 210 to 218. The opposition to Clinton's decision stemmed from varied reasons. Freshman Republicans elected in 1994 followed Speaker Gingrich's tough stand against Democrats and Clinton. The Speaker's "faithful" allowed the government to shut down in November 1995 by refusing to compromise on a 1996-97 budget. On foreign affairs, the faithful freshman Representative Sue Myrick probably did not realize she was also criticizing French President Chirac and British Prime Minister Major when saying: "We have a peace agreement that is not worth the paper it is written on. If it was, there would be no need to send American troops over there. There is nothing President Clinton can say that will change my mind."

Other reasons for congressional opposition was that the current Congress had many fewer members with military experience. In 1975, 73 percent of senators and 70 percent representatives had experience in World War II, Korea, or Vietnam. In 1995, however, only 50 percent senators and 37 percent representatives had such experience. As Senator Kerrey said "this was the World War II-Vietnam link....We're the ones who were on the side of defending an unpopular war because it is right, and we'll defend an unpopular military effort now because it is right."

Finally, the Republicans differed about foreign policy after Patrick Buchanan revived the party's isolationist, non-interventionist policy of the

1930s and 1940s. Election politics definitely played a major role in the political debates. In December 1995, Buchanan had began his second bid for the presidential nomination and Senators Phil Gramm and Dole were announced candidates.[15]

Despite the lack of congressional enthusiasm, Clinton and the Europeans proceeded to deploy 60,000 troops and to undertake the other measures necessary for implementing the Dayton Accords after the December 14 Paris ceremonies. The hope of Clinton and European leaders was that the power brokers in the Balkans would seize their "last chance" for future peace and cooperate with IFOR.

NOTES

1. Elizabeth Drew, *On the Edge* (New York: Simon and Schuster, 1994): 138-153; Jackson Diehl, et.al., "Clinton is Inheriting a World of Troubles," *WPNW* (Jan. 25-31, 1993): 16-17. Mark Danner, "Clinton, the UN and the Bosnian Disaster," *New York Review of Books* (Dec. 18, 1997): 67-81 describes Clinton's 1993 policy and the Serbs near-conquest of Srebrenica before a UN safe-haven was declared in April. James Gow, *Triumph of the Lack of Will*, 132-145 says the first air drop was captured by Serbs but other drops were more successful.

2. David Owen, "The Future of the Balkans: An Interview with David Owen," *Foreign Affairs* 72 (Spring 1993):1-9 with greater details in Owen, *Balkan Odyssey* (New York: Harcourt Brace, 1996); Woodward, *Balkan Tragedy*, 304-309. For a critique of Owen's book by a Turkish scholar, see Hasan Unal, "Trop de Zele," *The National Interest* No.43 (Spring 1996): 93-96.

3. Drew, *On the Edge*, 153-163. Drew also describes (pp. 272-284) a few weeks of Washington excitement about using air strikes to end the siege of Sarajevo in August 1993, but Clinton only ordered more U.S. humanitarian aid to Bosnia. Powell, *American Journey,* 575-578. On the Kaplan book see Ch. 4, fn 1 of the present study. Thomas Friedman, "Any War in Bosnia Would Carry a Domestic Price," *NYT* (May 2, 1993): E-1, 4. Woodward, *Balkan Tragedy*, 309-310 and fn. 55, p. 501 indicates the May 1993 events caused more tension among U.S. political leaders, Boutros-Ghali, and the Europeans.

4. Cohen, *Broken Bonds*, 297-307; Woodward, *Balkan Tragedy*, 314-316 and fn. 63, p. 503; Silber and Little, *Death of a Nation*, 309-318.

5. Cohen, *Broken Bonds*, 307-321. On the Soviet role in the Contact Group see Andrei Kozyrev, "The Lagging Partnership," *Foreign Affairs* 73 (May/June 1994): 59-71.

6. John Promfret and David Ottaway, "Keeping the Pipeline Well Armed," WPNW (May 20-26, 1996): A-14 and Promfret, "An Arms Pipeline Uncovered," WPNW (Sept.30/Oct.6, 1996): 6-7. Richard Holbrooke, *To End a War* (New York: Random House, 1998): 50-51 indicates arms from Middle Eastern Islamic states began to reach Bosnia in 1992.

7. For data on Frasure's talks with Milosevic see Jan Honig and Norbert Both, *Srebrenica: Records of a War Crime* (London: Penguin, 1996): 160-174. Roger Cohen, "A Small Bite at the Bosnian Bullet," *NYT* (May 28, 1995): E-2: R.W. Apple, Jr. "How the World Makes Bosnia Safe for War," *NYT* (June 4, 1995): E-1, 6; Gow, *Triumph of a Lack of Will*, 260-276. British journalist Timothy Garton Ash, "Bosnia in Our Future," *New York Review of Books* (Dec. 12, 1995): 27-31 believes the Europeans failure indicates U.S. leadership must direct them.

8. Bob Woodward, *The Choice: How Clinton Won* (New York: Simon and Schuster): 253-260; Scott O'Grady and Jeff Coplon, *Return with Honor* (New York: Doubleday,

1995); Elaine Sciolino, "Congress Arms Bosnia With Gas," *NYT* (June 18, 1995): E-1, 4; George Church, "Pity the Peacemakers," *Time* 42 (June 5, 1995): 38-40.

9. On Janvier's problem with impartiality and safe-zones see Gow, *Triumph of the Lack of Will*, 127-155; Silber and Little, *Death of a Nation*, 347-350. Roger Cohen, "Honor, Too, Is Put to Flight in Bosnia," *NYT* (July 16, 1995): E-1,4. Elaine Sciolino, et.al. "Days of Slaughter: How the Serbs' Killing of Srebrenica Unfolded," *NYT* (Oct. 19, 1995): A-1, 6-7; Human Rights Watch Report/Helsinki Report "The Fall of Srebrenica and the Future of UN Peacemaking," No.7 (Oct. 13,1995). For a day-by-day version of Srebrenica's fall see David Rohde, *Endgame: The Betrayal and Fall of Srebrenica*, (New York: Farrar, Straus & Giroux, 1997).

10. Details of U.S. negotiations from July to November are in Holbrooke, *To End a War*, 79-314; Bob Woodward, *The Choice*, 260-270: Elizabeth Drew, *Showdown: The Struggle Between the Gingrich Congress and the Clinton White House* (New York: Simon & Schuster, 1996): 243-251; Thomas Lippman and Devroy, "Matching Policy...," 6-7; Craig Whitney, "Allied Extending Shield to Protect All Bosnian Havens." *NYT* (Aug. 2, 1995): A-14; Timothy Garton Ash, Bosnia in Our Future," *New York Review of Books* 42 (Dec. 12, 1995): 27-31.

11. Holbrooke, *To End a War*, 79-230; Roger Cohen, "From Greater Serbia to Lesser Serbia: A War Turns," *NYT* (Aug. 20, 1995): E-1, 3 and Cohen, "A Cycle of War and Illusion," *NYT* (Sept. 24, 1995): A-1; Mike O'Connor "Bosnian Serbs Say U.N. Force's Artillery Hit a Hospital," *NYT* (Sept. 10, 1995): A-8; Malcolm McConnell, "When NATO Went to War." *Reader's Digest* 124 (Sept. 1996): 91-96.

12. Holbrooke, *To End a War*, 238, 264-67; Roger Cohen, "Terms of Muslim, Croat Alliance are Set at Dayton," *NYT* (Nov. 11, 1995): A-3; Chris Hedges, "Serbs in Croatia Resolve Key Issue by Giving up Land," *NYT* (Nov. 13, 1995): A-1, 5; Barbara Crosette, "The Missions Not Accepted (Slavonia)," *NYT* (Dec. 31, 1995): E-10.

13. Holbrooke, *To End a War*, 231-314; "The Search for Peace in the Balkans: A Primer," *NYT* (Nov. 1, 1995): A-9; Richard Stevenson, "Yeltsin's Foes Use NATO Bombing to Press Him," *NYT* (Sept. 10, 1995): A-8; Craig Whitney, "Russia and U.S. Agree to Have Moscow's Troops in Bosnia Serve Under U.S. Unit," *NYT* (Nov. 9, 1995): A-4; Elaine Sciolino, "U.S. Tells Leaders of Balkan States to Wind Up Talks," *NYT* (Nov. 20, 1995): A-16; and Sciolino, Roger Cohen, Alison Mitchell, Eric Schmitt, "Accord Reached to End the War in Bosnia," four articles in *NYT* (Nov. 22, 1995): A-1, 6-7; Roger Cohen, "Taming the Bulls of Bosnia," *NYT Magazine* (Dec 17, 1995): 58-63 ff.; Marie-Janine Calic, "Bosnia-Herzegovina After Dayton," *Aussen Politik*, 47:2 (1996): 127-135.

14. Raymond Bonner, "In Reversal, Serbs of Bosnia Accept Peace Agreement," *NYT* (Nov. 24, 1995): A-1, 10; Eric Schmitt, "High-Tech Maps Guided Bosnia Talks," *NYT* (Nov. 24, 1995): A-10 and Schmitt, "Commanders Say U.S. Plan For Bosnia Will Work," *NYT* (Nov. 27, 1995): A-1, 6; Craig Whitney, "Success Has Many Fathers Among Allies," *NYT* (Nov. 23, 1995): A-9; Elaine Sciolino, Roger Cohen and Stephen Engelberg, "In U.S. Eyes, 'Good' Muslims and 'Bad' Serbs Did a Switch," *NYT* (Nov. 23, 1995): A-1, 11. The text of the Dayton Accords is in Matthew T. Higham et.al., *The ACCESS Issue Packet on Bosnia-Herzegovina* (Washington, DC: ACCESS, 1996): 41-46.

15. Drew, *Showdown*, 346-347; Woodward, *The Choice*, 332-333; Richard Morin, "Toning Down the Tough Talk on Bosnia," *WPNW* (June 12-18, 1995): 37; Michael Dobbs, "De Balkanizing the Balkans," and "Who's in Charge Here," *WPNW* (July 3-9, 1995): 24-25; John Promfret, "Some Heavy Lifting in the Arms Embargo," *WPNW* (Aug. 7-13, 1995): 17; William Clinton, "Clinton's Words on Mission to Bosnia, " *NYT* (Nov. 28, 1995): A-6; Eric Schmitt, "Key Bosnian Question: Where are the Exits?" *NYT* (Dec. 2, 1995): A-5; Katherine Seelye, "Clinton Gives Republicans Pledge on Army in Bosnia," *NYT* (Dec.13, 1995): A-8; Seelye, "Senate and House Won't Stop Funds for Bosnian Force," *NYT* (Dec. 14, 1995): A-1, 10; and Seeley, "How 2 Veterans Rallied Support for Military Role," *NYT* (Dec. 15, 1995): A-9; R.W. Apple, Jr., "Flimsy Bosnia Mandate," *NYT* (Dec. 14, 1995): A-1, 10.

CHAPTER SEVEN

IMPLEMENTING THE DAYTON ACCORDS

The Dayton Accords were formally signed in Paris on December 14, 1995, the day after the U.S. Senate approved Clinton's decision to send American soldiers as peacekeepers. The U.S. assumption that the Dayton agreement could be fulfilled and the Balkans peace restored in one year overlooked the fact that November's accords grossly underestimated the tasks that needed to be accomplished before the warring parties would accept their new political environment. Therefore, it was not surprising that the deadline for NATO troops to leave was initially extended from December 1996 to June 30, 1998; however, in December 1997 it was decided they would remain indefinitely as a Stabilization Force (S-For).

Although the U.S.-led NATO effort succeeded remarkably well in separating the warring Bosnian groups and obtaining a disarmament agreement, the civilian side of Bosnia's political, social, and economic reconstruction did not fare as well. Controversial elections inaugurated the two "Entity" Bosnian state on a shaky basis in October 1996, but the political and economic plans for rebuilding Bosnian society lagged far behind schedule and became the principal reason for the indefinite extension.

IFOR'S MILITARY SUCCESS

The Dayton Accords' military formula succeeded in bringing peace to Bosnia by separating the warring factions without a single combat casualty. The U.S. and European Implementation Force (IFOR) arrived in Bosnia between December 20, 1995 and January 15, 1996, entering a region torn by five years of internecine conflict that had created economic, social, and political disorder and destruction. IFOR leaders carefully limited their objectives to separating the three fighting factions, overseeing the prisoner-of-war exchange, and obtaining an agreement to limit armaments in the Balkans.

Following the Dayton signing in November, there were dire predictions about the dangers to NATO personnel from land mines and the warring factions. This threat never materialized and the awesome military power of IFOR combined with the war-weariness of the people made the military task relatively simple. Because the NATO contingents had received special training in working with local groups and treating all factions equally, their operations went smoothly in forming a buffer zone between the three·factions and obtaining an inventory of their weapons and military equipment. While a few soldiers were injured in accidents, the IFOR experienced no serious combat injuries or deaths in 1996.

With U.S. Admiral Leighton Smith as its supreme commander, the IFOR consisted of 60,000 troops plus the supporting forces outside Bosnia. The soldiers were from NATO nations, Russia, and fourteen non-NATO countries such as Poland and the Czech Republic. The American headquarters were near Tuzla in northern Bosnia, the British command was at Gorni Vakuf in central Bosnia, and the French were in the south near Sarajevo. Many British, French, and European soldiers simply changed their UN blue helmets for the national regalia of their home countries. Under special arrangements between Moscow and Washington, the Russian commander received orders from U.S. General William L. Nash at Tuzla, not from NATO. Of course, General Nash's orders came from the NATO commander U.S. General George Joulwan.

The NATO forces greatest initial difficulty was in adjusting to Bosnia's wintry weather. This was especially true for U.S. soldiers who came through Hungary and Croatia before crossing the Sava River into Bosnia. They encountered persistent fog, rain, snow, and the flooding river. The first U.S. platoon crossed the Sava River on a raft that became part of the pontoon bridge for the trucks, armored vehicles, and soldiers that followed them during the next two weeks. General Nash arrived on December 27 to meet with local Serbian, Croatian, and Muslim military commanders in the Tuzla area. These Bosnian leaders were exceptionally cooperative in carrying out Nash's instructions and keeping the Dayton Accords on schedule. They withdrew their troops to specified areas, provided Nash with maps to locate land mines, and reported the location and quantity of their armaments and heavy weapons.

British and French commanders reported similar cooperation in the central and southern regions of Bosnia. The British expected serious problems in disarming a Serbian anti-aircraft unit stationed on the peak of Kula Mountain but the take-over went smoothly. At Sarajevo where tensions continued between Serbs and Muslim, French military officers reported the Muslim and Serbian military officers complied with their directions for withdrawing from their positions around that city.

Except for scattered problems in the northern and central regions, the U.S. and British personnel found most Bosnians war-weary and eager for peace. The French, however, had difficulty with Serbian civilians in Sarajevo who resisted the Dayton provisions that awarded the Serb-held suburbs to the Bosnia's Muslim-dominated government. Voting on December 12, Serbians rejected the decision to unite Sarajevo and two incidents near Sarajevo marred the otherwise peaceful cooperation with IFOR. In one incident, where small arms fire from the Serb sector struck a C-130 cargo plane carrying humanitarian supplies, no one was injured but Admiral Smith condemned the attack and warned the Serbs against further attacks. In a second event, a British helicopter was fired at when it landed and later took-off from the airport. Again, no one was hurt but Admiral Smith issued a stronger warning, telling all parties to "knock off that stuff" and told the leaders of Bosnia's three factions they would be held responsible for gunfire attributed to their group. No more shots were fired at NATO forces.

The three Bosnian groups failed to meet the midnight, January 19th deadline for releasing all prisoners-of-war. Because of Serb-Muslim disputes about the number of prisoners, only 225 of the 645 prisoners registered by the International Red Cross were released on schedule: the Serbs freeing 68 and the Bosnian Federation releasing 157. The Muslims refused to free other prisoners until the Serbs accounted for an alleged 4,000 missing Muslims. In turn, the Serbs argued that over 500 Serbs were missing in northern Bosnia. After prodding from NATO officials, on January 28, the Federation released another 476 Serbian prisoners and the Srpska Republic released 82 Muslims.

Additional POW's were not liberated until April 1996. To end the delay, the five-power Contact Group met in Moscow on March 23 with the leaders of Serbia, Croatia, and Bosnia in a session that underscored Russia's role in Bosnia. Regarding the POW's, Russia's Foreign Minister Yevgeny Primakov told the Balkan leaders that: "If this aspect of the Dayton Accords is not fulfilled, the conference of economic donors set for mid-April cannot be convened." As described later, the donor conference was held on April 6 after the Serbs released another 28 POW's and the Bosnian Federation released 127 Serbs. Nevertheless, disputes continued regarding many missing persons who might be dead, refugees aboard, or simply lost in combat action after 1991.[1]

The POW settlement was important, but NATO found developing better relations between Serbs and Muslims in Sarajevo to be difficult. Although on January 26, Federation President Kresimir Zabak and the Srpska Republic's Momcilo Krajisnik encouraged all ethnic groups to retain Sarajevo as a multi-ethnic city, hard-line Serbs who opposed Muslim control sought to coerce those Serbs who were willing cooperate.

As the March 15 deadline neared for the Bosnian Federation's take over of Sarajevo, Serb gangs intimidated fellow Serbs who preferred to stay while Serb sniper-fire increased against Muslim targets. These localized incidents were supposed to be dealt with by civilian European and UN officials as part of Carl Bildt's rebuilding program. But Bildt's plans for international police experts to train and arm a new police force had barely begun in February and NATO commanders had no instructions for dealing with non-military conflicts in Sarajevo or other cities.

One incident in February focused attention on the aid which Iran's Islamic regime gave to the Bosnian Muslims. On February 15, French troops raided a Muslim training center where they arrested ten Muslims, three of whom were Iranians. The French discovered and confiscated large quantities of illegal weapons stored in the building, including explosive materials of the type used by terrorists. The French reported the Iranians were bombing experts who trained Muslim soldiers to commit terrorist acts.

Izetbegovic's government denied the French interpretation claiming the Iranians were training anti-terrorists in case of future conflicts with Serbs, an interesting twist that required NATO officials to compromise. The seven Bosnian soldiers were released and two Iranians were deported. The third Iranian carried a diplomatic passport and could not be deported but the passport connected him to Iran's direct assistance to the Bosnian Muslims.[2]

In addition to this incident near Sarajevo, the IFOR experienced problems between Muslims and Croats in Mostar, and between Serbs and Muslims in the Posavina corridor. Trouble began in Mostar on January 6 when Croatian police shot and wounded two Muslims. Other Muslims in the city retaliated by killing two Croat policemen, a situation which endangered the Croat-Muslim Federation that the U.S. had brokered in 1994 and which the Dayton Accords confirmed. The two ethnic factions remained embittered from their 1993 combat during which Croatia's President Tudjman had created the Herzeg-Bosna Republic for Bosnia's Croats, a ministate imitating the Bosnian Serbs' Srpska Republic. Radical Croatian nationalists disliked the Federation because they believed the Muslim majority wanted to destroy Croatia's cultural values.

Although the EU planned to train a police force for Mostar, the EU did not yet have the capability to do so. NATO officials rejected a Muslim request to take charge of Mostar, but IFOR troops stood by to ensure that EU mediators receive the cooperation of Mostar's Croatians. After further violence took place in Mostar and Sarajevo, Richard Holbrooke convened a "Dayton II" meeting in Rome on February 17 where Presidents Milosevic, Tudjman, and Izetbegovic reconfirmed their commitment to the November 1995 accords regarding the two cities. They signed four formal documents that affirmed Sarajevo and Mostar should be unified, all POW's must be exchanged, all refugees had the right to return to their homes, and war criminals should be prosecuted.[3]

Following the Rome sessions, the POW question lingered into April but Dayton's vision of a multinational city for Sarajevo and Mostar vanished because most Serbs left Sarajevo and Croats continued to cause trouble in Mostar. The enmity generated by four years of seige, together with the claims of Serb and Croat extremists that the Muslims would destroy them continued to precipitate problems in the major cities and elsewhere. In Sarajevo, local Serbs intimidated those who were reluctant to leave, persuading all but an estimated 100 Serbs to load their wagons, cars and trucks, and to exhume bodies from their ancestor's graves in order to move to Serb territory designated by the Dayton Accords. Young Serbian thugs threatened the elderly by using gasoline to set homes, apartments, and buildings on fire. Sarajevo's firefighters were afraid to enter the Serb areas and few buildings or people could be protected. A UN medical doctor from New York, Joseph Byrnes said Serbian thugs "see anyone who wants to stay here after the transfer as a traitor to the Serb cause. And it's the old people, the ones who have nothing to do with this war, who are paying the price." After the Serb departure, Muslims crowded into the suburbs, searching for their former living quarters that could be rehabilitated and occupied. Fortunately, French NATO forces occupied one suburban warehouse stored with humanitarian food and supplies which helped to feed the few remaining Serbs and the arriving Muslims; but the multi-ethnic, multicultural character of prewar Sarajevo had been lost.[4]

The Mostar situation was crucial to the Dayton Accords because the projected Bosnian Federation of Muslims and Croats would comprise a two-thirds majority in the confederation with the Serbs. The February Rome meeting confirmed the ideal of Croat-Muslim unity but did not end the Muslim-Croat conflict in Mostar, because President Tudjman was "half-hearted" in requiring Bosnian Croat's to comply with the Federation's authority. Consequently there was a serious crisis in Mostar on June 28 after municipal elections gave the Muslims a bare majority of city council seats. Although the EU and OSCE election monitors certified the election results as free and fair, Bosnia Croat hard-liners refused to recognize the Muslim's victory.

Although EU mediators thought the election dispute was settled on August 6 when Croat political leaders agreed to honor the city elections, radical Bosnian Croatians led by indicted war criminal Dario Kordic, continued their struggle for a separate Herzeg-Bosna ministate or union with the Croatian Republic. On August 14, Presidents Tudjman and Izetbegovic again stated support for the Muslim's election victory in Mostar and for the Bosnian Federation of Croats and Muslims. However not until October 1997, after the U.S. blocked World Bank-IMF loans to Croatia, was President Tudjman persuaded to have Kordic and nine other indicted Croat war criminals sent to the Hague for trial.

Cooperation between Croats and Muslims continued to be shaky. Following the September 1996 elections, the Bosnian Croat-Muslim Federation joined with the Bosnian Serb "entity" to form the Republic of Bosnia and Herzegovina. Nevertheless, Croatians in the Mostar sector continued to agitate for a separate state while Izetbegovic sought to solidify a Bosnian Muslim state. When schools opened in the Fall of 1997, the Muslim Croat Federation ignored the advice of OSCE and NATO officers by establishing separate schools for Muslims and Croats, claiming such schools would "protect minority rights." Although by December 1997, the OSCE persuaded Federation officials to reconsider the school plan, Croats and Muslims in the "Federation" remain as divided as they each are from the Serbs.[5]

While Holbrooke and Christopher gave special attention to Mostar, the EU turned the problem of the Posavina corridor and the city of Brcko over to an Arbitration Commission. Brcko's location at the narrowest part of the Posavina corridor was valuable to both Bosnian Serbs and the Bosnian Croats and Muslims. The latter had made up the majority of Brcko's population before the war but became victims of the Serbs ethnic cleansing program after the Serbian invasion in the summer of 1992. Izetbegovic insisted Muslim and Croat refugees must be returned to Brcko because it linked Bosnia to the eastern part of the Croatian Republic while the Serbs moved over 10,000 Serbs from Sarajevo to Brcko to swell their population in the corridor which linked east and west Bosnian Serb territory.

During 1996, the Brcko Arbitration Commission found it impossible to reach a compromise between the two "entities" making up the Bosnian government. When Muslim and Croat refugees tried to return to the city, Bosian Serbs repelled them and the violence had to be quelled by U.S. and Russian IFOR troops. The refugees camped in villages south of Brcko to await permission to return to their homes. From November 11 to 14, 1996, the worst fighting of the year occurred in these villages where Serbs tried to expel the Croat-Muslim refugees. Carl Bildt asked the Brcko Arbitration Commission to try again to solve the dispute but it was not successful. In February 1997, the commission appointed a temporary administrator for Brcko to oversee the return of refugees desiring to return to Brcko and it was hoped that the September 1998 elections might resolve the problem.[6]

Outside of Sarajevo, Mostar and Brcko, the IFOR had relatively minor problems involving contests between Muslims, Croats, and Serbs except when refugees wanted to return to their former homes in areas allocated by the Dayton Accords to a competing faction. When Muslims sought to move back to or visit their former homes in villages such as Dobaj, Mahaha or Trnovo, they were attacked by Serb mobs. At Trnovo on April 29, angry Serbs with rocks and sticks attacked seven buses loaded with Muslim refugees being escorted to the town by French troops. The Serbs killed three Muslims and injured dozens more before the Muslims took French advice and withdrew.

The Dayton provisions that all refugees could return to their former homes became a difficult decision to fulfill. Although the accords hoped to recreate Bosnia's multi-ethnic society, the effort to repair four years of violence and hatred between the warring groups, and return nearly one million displaced persons would require many years. The refugees return was complicated further because they could not be protected by local police forces which each of Bosnia's competing factions established. Although the Dayton Accords provided for the EU-OSCE to train Bosnian police to act impartially in internal incidents, this effort was inadequate because UN member nations sent only 600 police experts to train Bosnians rather than the 1,500 experts that were planned. Consequently, each Bosnia faction recruited its own "nationalistic" police some of whom were reported to be stockpiling armaments separate from the weapons inventoried by IFOR. Although IFOR and S-FOR troops sometimes intervened in local disputes, NATO commanders did not want their mission to include police duties.[7]

ARMS CONTROL MEASURES

Unlike the inadequate protection for returning refugees, the Dayton Accords offered a real possibility for limiting armaments in the Balkans. The November agreement included a timetable for Croatia, Yugoslavia, and Bosnia to negotiate and sign an arms limitation agreement by June 14, 1996. Although the treaty was signed within a week of the schedule, its enactment presented problems for the U.S. because of the Bosnian Muslims connections with Iran's Islamic regime.

The Arms Treaty was finalized in Florence, Italy on June 14 when the Balkan leaders signed a treaty brokered by OSCE personnel.

Chart A—Florence Arms Control Treaty

Arms Limited	Yugoslavia	Croatia	Bosnian Fed. Muslim-Croat	Bosnian Serbs
Tanks	1025	470	273	137
Armored vehicles	850	340	226	114
Heavy artillery	3750	1500	1000	500
Combat aircraft	155	62	42	21
Helicopters	53	21	14	7

As Chart A indicates, the Florence Pact adopted the arms formula accepted at Dayton which gave the Bosnian Croats and Muslims two weapons for every one allocated to the Bosnian Serbs, and the Yugoslav Serbs two and one-half weapons for each one received by the Croatian Republic. The agreement also provided methods to implement and verify the controls accepted by representatives of the Republics of Croatia and Yugoslavia (Serbia/Montenegro) and the three Bosnian factions. The

Yugoslav Republic would have a two and one-half-to-one superiority over the Croatian Republic in five weapons types and Bosnia's Muslim-Croat Federation would have a two-to-one superiority over the Bosnian Serbs.

The OSCE estimated that Yugoslavia and the Bosnian Serbs would feel the greatest reductions. Belgrade would reduce its entire inventory by about one-quarter. The Bosnian Serbs had greater reductions because their 400 existing tanks were limited to 263 and their 1,000 pieces of artillery to 500 over 75mm. The OSCE negotiators believed Milosevic accepted these reductions because Belgrade's weakened economy could not afford to purchase state of the art weaponry while the Croats and Muslims had foreign donor nations ready to supply them with the best modern equipment allowed.

The verification sections of the Florence agreement required each signatory to open their country for international experts to monitor their arsenals. After giving the international inspectors an inventory of their weapons, each entity would reduce its arms to its limit within sixteen months after July 1, 1996. Interim target dates for the gradual reductions were fixed and the parties could eliminate excess weapons by destroying them, selling them to other countries or using them as permanent museum displays. Combat aircraft could be used for training after all of its armaments were removed. After the treaty was completed, the OSCE monitors faced a serious problem in enforcing the arms agreement. At the end of 1996, both EU and U.S. intelligence reports indicated the three Balkan countries had taken few steps to destroy their weapons and, indeed, were adding smuggled weapons in case of renewed conflict when IFOR withdrew.[8]

Since December 1995, President Clinton had been committed to equalizing the Bosnian Federation's armaments with the Bosnian Serb armaments and committed $100 million for weapons to the Bosnian Federation. Nevertheless, U.S. leaders became alarmed after reports that Izetbegovic might establish an Iranian-style Islamic state appeared to be confirmed in December 1995 when some Bosnian officials expressed a desire to use Iran's "holy warriors" to create an Islamic state.

American opposition to Iran originated in February 1979 when the Ayatollah Ruhollah Khomeini overthrew the shah of Iran and later held American hostages at the Tehran embassy for fifteen months. The Ayatollah's anti-American rhetoric and assistance to Muslim terrorists around the world prompted the U.S. government to severe relations with Iran. Additionally, Washington embargoed all trade with Iran and tried to isolate Tehran from the international community. Thus American politicians were surprised in December 1995, when Iran inaugurated an "enormous new embassy" in Sarajevo and its visiting Foreign Minister told Bosnia President Izetbegovic that Iran would help rebuild Bosnia. The presence of Iran's "volunteer" soldiers helping Bosnian Muslims had become a well-known "secret" by 1995, but the Dayton Accords required all foreign military volunteers to leave Bosnia immediately after the Paris signing of the Accords.

Concerned by the words of Iran's Foreign Minister, Richard Holbrooke visited Sarajevo a few days later to obtain Izetbegovic's assurances the foreign soldiers would leave as scheduled but alarm bells again rang in Washington in February and March 1996. First, French NATO forces discovered Iranian explosive experts were training the Bosnian army and, secondly, American journalist investigators reported the Clinton administration had known about Iran's secret arms shipments to Bosnia's Muslims in 1994, but did not tell the Congressional Oversight Committee on Intelligence.

Although congressional leaders had wanted Clinton to arm the Bosnian Muslims in 1994 and 1995, both Republicans and Democrats in Congress now blamed Clinton for Iran's presence because he had remained silent. Clinton's dilemma was that Europeans opposed rearming the Muslims as a danger to UNPROFOR soldiers and Clinton's staff did not tell the Oversight Committee because the news of Iran's shipments might be leaked, a decision National Security Advisor Anthony Lake later said was a mistake.

In 1996, Congress established a special committee to investigate the 1994 events. The hearings disclosed that Croatia asked U.S. Ambassador Peter Galbraith if the U.S. objected to their acting as an agent for Iran arms to Bosnia. Anthony Lake informed the ambassador there were "n o instructions" for Croatia on this issue—this being tantamount to saying the U.S. would not object but could not officially approve an arms shipment. Thus, Croatia opened its ports to arms and oil shipments from Iran and other Middle Eastern countries, taking about one-third of the arms for the Croatian army and sending the rest to Muslim-Croat armies.

In addition to the arms shipments, other more recent events prompted congressional and White House concern about Iran's Islamic role in Bosnia's future. U.S. intelligence reports indicated some Bosnian groups favoring Iran had influential positions in Izetbegovic's Party of Democratic Action. Hasan Cengic, Bosnia's Deputy Minister of Defense, wanted Iranians rather than Americans to arm and train the Federation's army. Two other Iranian radicals were Irfan Ljevakovic, a senior officer in Bosnia's secret service who allegedly plotted to keep Iran's "freedom fighters" in Bosnia in violation of the Dayton Accords and Bosnian police chief Semsuden Mehmedovic who had formed Islamic paramilitary groups that intimidated Bosnians who criticized Izetbegovic's party. An estimated one hundred Iranian soldiers had relocated to small Bosnian cities such as Travnik and Zenic where they married local Muslim women to obtain Bosnian citizenship. In imitation of the Hamas Islamic radicals in Palestine's West Bank, these "Bosnians" gained followers by posing as social workers who fed, clothed, and educated Bosnians to "true" Koranic teachings that formed an Islamic Republic.[9]

The U.S. anxiety about Iranians in Bosnia impelled Secretary of State Christopher to demand that Izetbegovic dismiss his pro-Iranian officials before he could receive any U.S. military equipment or U.S. officers to train the Bosnian's to use high-tech armaments. Soon after the June 14 arms control pact was signed, the UN lifted its 1991 arms embargo on the Balkans, enabling Clinton to announce the U.S. would ship armaments to Sarajevo and ask other nations to help pay the cost of arming and training the Bosnian Federation's army. Although the EU opposed sending more weapons to the Balkans, countries such as Turkey and Saudi Arabia helped the U.S. finance Bosnian arms purchases.

Before delivering the arms, however, Clinton also demanded the merger of the Bosnian Croat and Bosnian Muslim armies, the Bosnian Croat's affirmation of their commitment to the Federation, and Izetbegovic's dismissal of government officers who advocated an Islamic state. The first two demands seemed to be fulfilled on July 9, when the Bosnian Federation's legislature passed a bill merging the Muslim and Croat armed forces and on August 2 when President Tudjman and the Bosnian Croatians agreed to dismantle the mini-state of Herzeg-Bosna. The army merger was finalized on January 11, 1997. But Tudjman's failure to promote peace between Bosnian Croats and Muslims surfaced again on February 2 when 700 Croatian Catholics attacked Muslims visiting their family graves near Mostar, killing one Muslim, wounding 22 others and evicting 28 Muslim families from their homes. Nevertheless, on May 9, 1997, the U.S. completed its $137 million arms delivery to the Federation by sending 116 heavy artillery pieces and 21 heavy transports.

If Muslim-Croat relations were shaky, Izetbegovic's views about an Islamic state were mysterious because he was reluctant to send Iran's volunteers home and to dismiss his pro-Iranian officials. Izetbegovic stalled the U.S. until November 19, finally removing Deputy Defense Minister Cengic after Clinton refused to release the U.S. arms intended for Bosnia which were held in Croatia. After Cengic was removed, Clinton released the arms shipment although other Muslim high officials remained.[10]

Two other Muslim actions frustrated Americans who dealt with Izetbegovic. In November, European intelligence officers reported the Bosnian army violated the arms control arrangements by secretly receiving heavy artillery from Turkey and Malaya. A week later, on November 14, Bosnian Muslim militia in Brnik, near the city of Brcko, attacked U.S. soldiers. Acting under the Dayton Accords, U.S. army officers had learned there was a suspected weapons arsenal near Brnik and raided the Muslim camp where they confiscated several tons of weapons and ammunition. The Bosnian Muslims retaliated by attacking the Americans with rocks and bottles. Although no Americans were seriously injured, the U.S. soldiers said they no longer saw the Muslims as the victims pictured by the U.S. media. Also, on June 9, 1997, John Promfret of the *Washington Post* wrote that Muslims stored military equipment and trained for an offensive against the Serbs while awaiting the IFOR's departure. Moreover, former defense minister Cengic was in charge of training Muslims refugees for war along the borders of Bosnian Serb-held territory to regain traditional Muslim areas south of the Drina River.

Although there were indications that Muslims were not alone in violating the arms agreement, the OSCE arms monitors issued an optimistic report in October 1997. The report said that in sixteen months Croatia, Yugoslavia, and the two Bosnian entities had destroyed over 4,220 tanks, jet aircraft, helicopters, and artillery pieces with more armaments scheduled for destruction. The report indicated the U.S. replaced outmoded Bosnian Federation weapons with modern arms that gave the Muslim-Croat army an advantage over the older weapons the Serbs retained. The Federation army's problem was that its top command had been unified to satisfy Washington's demands but, in fact, remained divided into Muslim and Croat units during training and exercises. Thus, the arms control treaty was only a partial success as the Croat-Muslim army division damaged Bosnia's civil-relations.[11]

BOSNIA'S CIVILIAN RECONSTRUCTION

If the IFOR attained some military success in Bosnia, the EU-OSCE civilian programs made slow headway. At Dayton, the EU-OSCE accepted responsibility for Bosnia's domestic reconstruction although Richard Holbrooke later complained they devised a "messy" bureaucratic system of operation. More seriously, the Dayton Accords did not offer details for financing reconstruction activity nor for the relations between IFOR members and EU-OSCE civilian personnel in Bosnia. One particular example of the difficulty was the EU duty to train police in "neutral" police methods to settle local Bosnian disputes. In fact, of course, few EU police experts arrived to conduct training exercises, meaning that few well-trained local police were deployed and police work remained limited throughout 1997.[12]

Bosnia's rebuilding programs may be divided into two major categories: political activity to include elections of new governments and to oversee their functioning; and socio-economic reconstruction projects to provide food, medical needs, housing, roads, trains, communications, revived industrial production, and improving relations between competing groups of returning refugees.

Of these two categories, the U.S. considered the elections as a primary means of establishing unity between the Muslim-Croat and the Serb entities under the Bosnian Constitution. The OSCE had the principal role in preparing for, and certifying, that "free and fair" elections had been conducted. It established an election commission chaired by former Swiss Foreign Minister Flavio Cotti and an international group of election monitors who operated in Bosnia under retired U.S. diplomat Robert Frowick. The monitors would determine if conditions existed for orderly elections in Bosnia and would supervise the election campaign and balloting to meet Dayton's September 14 deadline.

In the months preceding the September deadline, OSCE monitors experienced difficulty in evaluating order in the three zones where IFOR separated the warring factions and in interpreting free and fair election conditions. When OSCE monitors reported on conditions in June 1996, Frowick's monitoring teams gave divergent interpretations about "free and fair" conditions for elections. One group led by an American on Frowick's staff, William Stuebner, believed continued disputes between Bosnia's ethnic communities precluded "free and fair" elections. Stuebner's group cited frequent disputes in Sarajevo and Mostar which were duplicated in varying degrees in cities such as Bihac, Teslic, and

Tuzla as well as in some rural areas. Stuebner was also disturbed about the lack of freedom of movement in Bosnia and the absence of opposition newspapers, believing these conditions precluded proper elections. Steubner also complained that Frowick asked monitors to balance accounts of violations of the Dayton Accords with reports about proactive democratic activities where opposition parties could contest the election of existing office holders. Stuebner believed Frowick's "balancing" influenced a monitor's conclusions about fairness.

In contrast to Stuebner, the group finding "free and fair" conditions existed included Chairman Frowick who argued that Sarajevo, Mostar, Bihac, and Tuzla were relatively quiet in comparing conditions in January 1996 to June 1996. Frowick's supporters cited reports about Bosnian ethnic groups cooperating in cities such as Banja Luka, Vis, Jezerz, and Ljubinje. Regarding Steubner's "balancing" complaint, Frowick contended balance was needed because observers tend to be more impressed by one evil act than by several good acts.

On June 25, after considering Frowick's recommendations and listening to Steubner's negative conclusions, Flavio Cotti's OSCE commission decided to proceed with the election process. This decision was supported by President Clinton who told the Europeans that September's elections were necessary to activate Bosnia's government. Clinton also announced the U.S. would withdraw 1,200 soldiers in army tank units, replacing them with military police who could provide security at polling places. Defense Secretary Perry stated armored tanks were no longer needed in Bosnia.[13]

From May to July, however, President Izetbegovic obstructed the electoral process, contending Muslims would not participate in elections unless Bosnian Serb's indicted for war crimes resigned their leadership. The Bosnian Serb's President Karadzic and Army General Mladic had been indicted by the Hague Tribunal, but contrary to the Dayton Accords had not been arrested. With these men in office, Izetbegovic claimed the Serbs prevented Muslim refugees from returning to villages were they had been registered to vote before 1992, a provision of the Dayton agreements. He wanted the IFOR to arrest these two war criminals and send them to the Hague.

For IFOR officials the capture of war criminals held a low priority and, consequently, few of the indicted had been arrested. In February 1996, Izetbegovic's arrest of four Serbs caused problems while Croatia's Tudjman and Yugoslavia's President Milosevic argued about who should be the first to make arrests, probably because they feared being incriminated by the testimony of indicted officers. In addition, neither Clinton nor NATO leaders wanted IFOR soldiers to search for war criminals some of whom were still popular at home. The 1993 search for Somalia's Aideed, of course, had proven disastrous.

To placate Izetbegovic, the five-member Contact Group met in London on July 10 where they declared that Karadzic and Mladic must leave office. They threatened to renew economic sanctions on Milosevic if the two did not resign, an important declaration because Russia, as a Contact Group member, could help gain Serbian support. On July 17, Richard Holbrooke met with Milosevic who agreed that Karadzic's SDS party could not be allowed to participate in the September elections unless it chose another leader. The threat of economic sanctions, Russia's opposition, and the de-certification of the SDS persuaded Karadzic to resign. With Izetbegovic's approval on July 19, Holbrooke announced Karadzic's resignation as Srpska president and party leader. Although Mladic did not resign, Holbrooke and Clinton hoped the Bosnian Serb's moderates would have a better chance in the elections with Karadzic no longer an active leader. In fact, Biljana Plavic, who replaced Karadzic, proved helpful to the U.S. in 1997.[14]

Karadzic's removal allowed Bosnia's election campaign to move ahead although one more limit was placed on the local election process. Following Chairman Cotti's certification of satisfactory election conditions on June 15, the OSCE examined the refugee's ability to vote in local elections and found that absentee refugee ballots could be used in national elections but their participation in town and village campaigns would be restricted. As a result, the OSCE announced on August 27 that local elections would be delayed, but the national elections could be held. Local elections were scheduled for late October 1996, but delayed again before finally being held in September 1997.

Bosnia's national elections were conducted on September 14, 1996 with the results confirming that the ethnic-cultural divisions developed during the war had not been alleviated. The OSCE reported an excellent voter turnout of 60 to 70 percent of the 2.9 million eligible voters. As expected, the nominees of Bosnian's three dominant factions were elected to the three-member presidency: the Serb's Momcilo Krajisnik, a colleague of Karadzic; the Croat's Kresimir Zubak; and the Muslim's Alija Izetbegovic who became chairman of the presidency after receiving the plurality of votes for the position.

In the national parliamentary elections, the Federation of Bosnia and Croatia won the expected two-to-one number of seats over the Serbians. Hard line nationalists of each of the ethnic groups gained the most assembly seats but moderate opposition parties earned seven of the 42 House of Representatives delegates. Izetbegovic's Democratic Action Party dominated the House with 19 seats; the Serbian Democrat Party had nine seats; and the Croatian Democratic Union, seven seats. On September 29, the OSCE certified the election results that Secretary of State Christopher praised as a "landmark in promoting Bosnian stability."[15]

During the remainder of 1996 and 1997, the new Bosnian officials took a few steps towards creating a functioning government. In October, Izetbegovic met in Paris with Yugoslav President Milosevic to discuss the establishment of formal diplomatic relations. This meeting was part of a U.S. plan to empower the Sarajevo's government and enable Bosnian Serbs to realize they were separated from Milosevic's Yugoslavia. At Paris, the two presidents formulated plans for full political and economic relations following further negotiations. Izetbegovic dropped Bosnia's charges that Milosevic was responsible for genocide during the war and Milosevic promised to respect Bosnia's territorial integrity, an announcement which angered radical Serbs who continued to dream of a Greater Serbian state.

Following the September elections, Bosnia's central government began to work out details of its operations. On September 30, the three-member presidency met with the EU's Carl Bildt to set a timetable for appointing the council of ministers and convening the national legislature, events that were carried out in early January 1997. A glitch in these relations occurred on October 5, when the elected Bosnian Serb president and Serb parliament members refused to attend swearing-in ceremonies in Sarajevo because of insufficient security. Serb president-elect Krajisnik took the oath of office in a private meeting and regularly attended meetings with Izetbegovic and Zubak. On January 3, 1997, the new Bosnia-Herzegovina Parliament met and approved a cabinet ministry consisting of Muslims, Croats, and Serbs.

While these activities of the Bosnian government proceeded there were difficulties within the two state "Entities." As noted previously, the Muslim-Croat Federation experienced troubles in Mostar but political divisions also appeared in the Serb's Srpska Republic that became deeper during the summer of 1997. In November 1996, Srpska President Biljana Plavsic took steps toward creating a more moderate regime by taking civilian control of the armed forces. Plavsic removed General Mladic from office because he continually disagreed with her and, although Mladic initially rejected Plavsic's order, he resigned on November 27 after President Plavsic appointed General Pero Colic as commander.[16]

The army command problem of Plavsic's civilian government in Banja Luka expanded in 1997 to a conflict of Plavsic versus the Srpska Parliament and ex-president Karadzic whose headquarters were in Pale. Although Mladic's power disappeared, Karadzic maintained his influence over many Serb police and gained a monopoly over the importation of oil, cigarettes, and other products without paying taxes to Plavsic's government—a situation Plavsic sought to end in June 1997. With support from the Clinton administration, Plavsic publicly denounced Karadzic's corruption and his failure to bring peace. She dismissed parliament and called for new elections, but the Karadzic-dominated parliament rejected her dismissal and had the Supreme Court cancel the elections. Karadzic's Socialist Party also expelled Plavsic.

The Clinton administration's interest in supporting Plavsic evolved from White House decisions to play a direct role in implementing the civilian parts of the Dayton Accords. Early in 1997, after replacing Secretary of State Christopher with Madeleine Albright and National Security Advisor Lake with Samuel "Sandy" Berger, Clinton learned that Bosnia's civilian rebuilding required a stronger U.S. role if peace was to be lasting. To promote stronger action, Clinton appointed Robert Gelbard as his special representative on Bosnia and\ named General Wesley Clark as the NATO commander. Clark had been a consultant to Holbrooke at Dayton in 1995 and was greatly interested in having the Bosnian intervention succeed. Clinton also sent additional State Department personnel, U.S. special observer forces and CIA officials to Bosnia to assist the S-FOR. Most crucial, Clinton decided to aid President Plavsic although as a Serb nationalist she did not want Croat and Muslim refugees to return to their homes in Serb areas. Plavsic's virtues were opposition to Karadzic and endorsement of the Dayton Accords to bring peace.

Following Clinton's decision, NATO forces assisted Plavsic in her disputes with Karadzic. Helped by British troops, Plavsic gained extensive support from senior Serb army officers and Serb police in the western part of Serb territory near Banja Luka and S-FOR troops protected Plavsic's officials while they evicted a telephone-taping squad which allowed Karadzic's loyalists to monitor calls in Banja Luka. Most importantly, S-FOR identified the Serb Special Police protecting Karadzic in Pale as a military unit over which S-FOR could impose its control.[17]

The U.S. also supported Plavsic in holding elections for a new parliament. During talks with Yugoslav President Milosevic in September, representatives of Plavsic and Karadzic agreed to hold parliamentary elections in November which would be followed by elections in December featuring contests by Plavsic for reelection as Srpska president and Momcilo Krajisnik for reelection as the Srpska representative on the Bosnian presidency. In late October, however, OSCE election monitors objected to supervising two crucial votes within such a short time. Despite complaints from Karadzic'c followers, the U.S. and Plavsic agreed to delay the presidential elections until 1998, giving Plavsic's new party time to solidify. The September election agreements also required Karadzic to open Serb television and radio airwaves to programs sponsored by Plavsic's moderates. After Karadzic's Serbs violated these terms, NATO troops raided four key Serb TV transmission stations and turned over control to Plavsic's officials.

The November 22-23, parliament elections in the Srpska Republic had mixed success. On the positive side, Karadzic lost his majority in parliament where the Social Democratic Party held 24 seats and his Radical Party allies 15 seats in the 83-seat parliament. Plavsic's People's National Alliance won 15 seats, the Muslim and Croat refugees absentee ballots won 16 seats, Milosevic's Socialist Party won nine seats; Independent Social Democrats, two seats; and the Social Democratic Party won two.

Following the parliamentary elections, S-FOR assisted Plavsic in obtaining a Srpska Parliamentary majority to approve a moderate premier to head the ministry. After Plavsic's candidate, Mladen Ivanic, failed to get a majority, Carlos Westendorf the S-FOR civil authority in Bosnia set a deadline of January 18, 1998 for parliament to agree, threatening that S-FOR would remove any obstructionists in parliament. Subsequently, during a tense twelve-hour parliament meeting on January 17, Plavsic's new candidate, Milorad Dodik, received the necessary 42 votes to form a ministry, but only after Karadzic's 39 delegates walked out in protest. Dodik, a Banja Lukja businessman, believed the Srpska government should cooperate with S-FOR as the best way to obtain peace and over $5 billion in Western funds to rebuild the country's war-torn economy, funds which Westendorf promised to release as soon as it was clear the Serbs would cooperate.

While the U.S. continued to support Plavsic's moderates, elections in September 1998 demonstrated the persising influence of radical Bosnian Serbs. To assist the moderates, Westendorf ordered S-FOR troops to take control over the Srpska Republic's Interior Ministry building in Pale and police headquarters in Bijeljina which Karadzic's forces previously held. S-FOR troops in Bijeljina also arrested an indicted Serb war criminal, Goran Jelisic who had boasted of killing many Muslims and was known as the "Serb Adolf [Hitler]". S-FOR began acting effectively in the eastern section to control Karadzic's police and end his monopoly of the news media. But Bosnian Serbs remained divided between moderates near Banja Luka and radicals in the eastern sector near Pale. Subsequently, in the September 1998 elections, the moderates retained control of the Srpska Parliament but Plavsic lost the presidency to the more radical Nikola Poplasen.[18]

The other significant 1997 elections in Bosnia were 136 municipal council elections conducted under questionable circumstances on September 13-14, 1997 by the OSCE. These elections had been delayed from 1996 and, despite the fact that few of the 400,000 refugees had returned home to vote in their 1991 precincts, the OSCE allowed them to cast absentee ballots. In about 35,000 cases, NATO troops protected refugees who returned to "home" precincts controlled by opposing factions but left after casting their ballots. Thus, Muslims who previously lived in Pale voted there but were not welcomed by the Serb majority and, after voting, left under NATO protection. Similarly in Mostar, some Croats voted in Muslim areas and left, some Muslims voted in Croat areas and left. Not surprisingly, when the official OSCE certification of election results came on December 31, 1997, the results confirmed previous ethnic-religious divisions in the city and village councils.[19]

SOCIO-ECONOMIC REBUILDING OF BOSNIA

On a rating scale of one-low, ten-high, NATO's military role would receive an eight; the political process, four; and the socio-economic process, one. Although the EU had primary responsibility for the rebuilding, the low score was not entirely its fault because the Dayton Accords offered only a skeleton outline for the EU operation, lacking the details of the nineteen page military annex. Moreover, unlike the NATO forces who planned intervention with full funding by their respective governments, the reconstruction program began in December with no definite plans, no commitment of funds, and few personnel.

Although Holbrooke and the Dayton delegates realized that long-term peace depended on Bosnia's political and socio-economic rebuilding, this formidable task was difficult to envision and required an investigation of Bosnia's precise needs to calculate the daunting work ahead. Bosnia's economy had been among Yugoslavia's weakest before 1991 and five years of war caused destruction that was comparable to Europe's devastation at the end of World War II. Bosnia's war not only wrecked its industrial operations, but destroyed the entire network of its centrally directed economy.

World Bank officials who surveyed the ruins in December 1995 and January 1996 painted a bleak picture of Bosnia's economic capacity. Industries such as the Unis Holding Company in Vosges had, in 1990, produced over 50,000 Volkswagens a year with 9,000 workers and the Polietlenka food packaging and labeling plant near Bihac had prospered as a state-owned business with links to food processing industries elsewhere in Yugoslavia. In 1995, the Unis plant employed only 200 employees and required investments to modernize its machinery and find new products to replace its Volkswagen contract. A few elderly workers kept the Bihac plant's machinery clean in damaged buildings but the plant managers needed funds to replace their previous state-subsidized operations. As World Bank officials noted, Yugoslavia's pre-war socialist industrial network crossed ethnic lines and functioned as a unit such as making spare parts for the Volkswagen plant and having Serbian food processors buying Muslim food packages. Under Bosnia's present ethnic divisions, economists predicted each group would produce rudimentary textile and wood products to compete with each other for the export market. Moreover, because factories would be less profitable without Yugoslavia's network of interacting businesses, foreign investors shied away from a divided Bosnia. Bihac's Mayor Adnan Alagic who managed the packaging factory said that with 1996 conditions "The plant will never open again."[20]

Despite the prospects, the EU and World Bank sponsored two meetings in December 1995 and appointed Carl Bildt as general director of the reconstruction program. A former Swedish Foreign Minister, Bildt represented the EU at the Dayton talks and was considered the best choice for the job. At a London Conference on December 9, delegates from forty nations heard pessimistic reports about Bosnia's dependence on foreign assistance for 90 percent of its food. Its gross domestic product had dwindled by 80 percent since 1990, its industrial production had declined by 95 percent, its electrical generating capacity declined 70 percent, 80 percent of its housing units were destroyed or damaged, repairs were needed for 1,500 miles of the roads, and in 50 percent of the schools teachers had not been paid for two years. An estimated three million refugees were in foreign countries and the estimated casualty figures from the war were 250,000 people killed, 20,000 injured, and 13,000 permanently disabled.

Because EU members disagreed about the costs for Bosnia's rebuilding, the World Bank decided to investigate Bosnia's specific problems and prepare recommendations, a process slowing Carl Bildt's work another month. Because of delays in funding Bosnia's rebuilding, Carl Bildt reported in March 1996 that the reconstruction mission could not succeed by the December 20 deadline. A Defense Department report to Congress lauded the military success of IFOR, but Bildt's dismal civilian predictions appeared in a *New York Times* interview. Bildt explained that tensions between Bosnia's ethnic groups discouraged investors, that extensive economic problems needed to be solved quickly, and that donor money had not yet been obtained for Bosnia's civilian projects.[21]

Unlike NATO's military action, Bosnia's economic and social problems received little publicity from America's mass media until an April tragedy killed U.S. Secretary of Commerce Ronald Brown and 35 other passengers in an airplane crash near Dubrovnik, Croatia. Brown, members of his Commerce Department team, two Croatians, the U.S. Air Force crew, and a group of chief executive officers from America businesses died when their Air Force T-43 aircraft, flying in bad weather, crashed into a rocky Croatian hillside. Brown was playing a leading role in raising money to rebuild Bosnia and escorted executives of U.S. engineering and construction firms to examine the conditions in Bosnia.

One week after Brown's death, an EU and World Bank conference in Brussels obtained pledges to fund the first year of Bosnia's reconstruction program. The World Bank estimated that $5 billion would be needed over a three-year period. Its January report stated Bosnia's Muslim-Croat Federation required $3.7 billion and the Serb entity needed about $1.4 billion. The Bank's estimates did not include any funds to assist the Croatian and the Yugoslav Republic, nor did it consider what foreign business investments might be received. The four priority projects listed for the first year were repairs to bridges, mines, and water, sewage, and heating plants in major cities; medical treatment for war injuries, and rebuilding destroyed or damaged housing units.

At Brussels, donor groups pledged $1.8 billion to undertake the first year of funding for the $5 billion three-year plan. The U.S. contributed a total of $281.7 million that included previous pledges and a recent congressional bill providing $198 million. Among other pledges, the World Bank allocated $350 million, Japan $285 million, and the EU members $373 million. During the Brussels meeting, the U.S. delegation questioned the financial assistance given to the Bosnian Serbs who refused to extradite their indicted war criminals to The Hague. Although the Bosnian Serb's refused to send delegates to Brussels, the European delegates believed all Bosnian groups must be helped if peace were to be achieved. Nevertheless, the Brussels delegates accepted a statement that financial aid was intended for all Bosnian groups that complied with the Dayton Accords.

The United States provided no additional reconstruction money during 1996 but encouraged U.S. investments in Bosnia. Mickey Kantor replaced Ronald Brown as Secretary of Commerce and visited the Balkans to follow through on U.S. plans with American business begun by Brown. As a result, on July 13, the Clinton administration announced an agreement with the Bosnian Federation for the U.S. Overseas Investment Corporation to guarantee loans and insurance for U.S. investments in Bosnia which could stimulate the increase of U.S. economic relations with Bosnia. The expectation was that U.S. government protection and incentives would induce American corporations to invest in Bosnia's economic renovation.[22]

Because the EU-World bank programs were late in starting, Bosnia's economic situation showed few signs of recovery at the end of 1996. Nevertheless, some of the minimal improvements should be noted. The immediate consumer requirements brought a thriving marketplace to Sarajevo by February 1996 and to smaller cities such as Brcko by summertime. In May, Sarajevo's transit system began operating, thanks in part to the advice of three New York subway experts who helped the Bosnians. In August, Sarajevo's international airport opened for civilian passengers, about the same time that the city's main hospital appeared to be back to normal because it permitted some doctors and nurses to have their first vacation periods in four years. And in Dubrovnik, Croatians were nearly ready for the fall and winter tourist trade with the arrival of their former European customers.

Yet, the inadequacy of the rebuilding program was obvious and became the principal reason why U.S.-NATO forces will remain as peacekeepers beyond 1998. Bosnian groups did not yet compete economically for exports because their separate industries were not operating. None of Sarajevo's larger prewar industries were functioning and, therefore, could not hire former employees. Of Sarajevo's 300,00 population an estimated 47,000 were employed mostly as government workers. While foreign business officials studied which Bosnian factories and resources would be most profitable in the future, many Bosnian families lived by salvaging waste at Bosnia's city dumps. Clinton's reconstruction representative in Sarajevo, Richard Sklar asserted the "country is an economic basket case...It's below Third World levels now. In a few years, they can hope to climb to beneath a Second World level."[23]

Two other problems troubling Bosnia from 1996 to 1998 were undetected land mines and the status of refugees. The millions of land mines laid during the war were cleared from areas were IFOR personnel operated in buffer zones between the three factions but in the remaining rural regions there were frequent reports of exploding mines killing or maiming civilians. Few World Bank funds were spent on liquidating the land minds and cynics contended the former warring leaders wanted the mines in place for conflict after NATO left. To educate children and adults about the land mine dangers, the U.S. government sponsored the printing of Superman comic books prepared by Warner Brothers to describe the danger from mines. The comic books were distributed throughout Bosnia by NATO forces but their salutary influence was uncertain.[24]

Throughout 1996-97, the most critical problem in fulfilling the Dayton vision of Bosnia's future was the return of refugees. In December 1995, Carl Bildt was confident the refugee project would succeed because the United Nations High Commissioner for Refugees had extensive experience. In the case of Bosnia, however, refugee agents faced exceptional handicaps because Bosnia was divided into three ethnic areas without consideration for many towns and villages with a prewar mixture of ethnic groups. IFOR soldiers sometimes intervened to keep Muslims, Serbs, and Croats apart but neither IFOR nor S-FOR accepted the mission of forcibly settling Muslim refugees who had lived in Serb territory or, similarly, settling Serbs or Croats among competing ethnic groups. Although the Dayton policy sought to recreate Bosnia's mixed populations, the 1995 agreements did not indicate how this task could be accomplished and attempts at reestablishing multiethnic groups in Sarajevo, Mostar, and Brcko had failed.

Thus, the Refugee Commission found it impossible to resettle large numbers of refugees. Although the Federal Republic of Germany, which had the largest number of Bosnia refugees, offered to pay travel costs of their 320,000 refugees, Bosnia's political conditions delayed their return. In 1997 the U.S. hoped its support for Bosnian Serb President Plavsic would gain her cooperation with refugee resettlement, but she blocked their return, arguing that too many Serb refugees from Croatia already filled Banja Luka and other towns in Serb designated territory.

In November 1997, the UN Refugee Commission reported that of about 1.2 million who fled to other countries from 1990-1995, an estimated 250,000 refugees returned home in 1996 and another 200,000 should return by the end of 1997. Almost all returned to homes where their own ethnic group dominated and most returnees were in Muslim-Croat areas where local officials admitted them because they had received funds to rebuild the infrastructure under a joint U.S.-UN Refugee Commission program. This program provided $1.3 billion and at a July 1997 conference on refugees, the World Bank allocated $1.2 billion in loans to continue the rebuilding program. Bosnian Serbs received few of these funds until early 1998 because they had refused to cooperate in their areas.[25]

Bosnia's socio-economic reconstruction was a long-term venture that had barely started by June 1997 when Spain's Foreign Minister Carlos Westendorf replaced Carl Bildt. In fact, the inability of refugees to remain in their former "homes" after the September 1997 elections showed that the military separation of the three groups and the creation of a two "Entity" government did not provide the political and socio-economic circumstances for a multi-ethnic Bosnia state. The success of the extended U.S.-NATO mission thru 1998 and beyond depended not only on the return of refugees but on the EU-OSCE-UN's reconstruction work and long-term funding efforts by the World Bank-IMF and other donors.

THE CROATIAN AND YUGOSLAV REPUBLICS

In negotiating the Dayton Accords, Richard Holbrooke assumed that a viable Bosnian peace required cooperation between the Western powers and the authoritarian governments of the Republic of Croatia and the Yugoslav Federation of Serbia and Montenegro. Although the U.S.

preferred working with democracies, such governments did not exist in the Balkans so that in November 1995 the choice was between continuing to have war and terrorism or negotiations with Milosevic, Tudjman, and Izetbegovic. Moreover, Bosnia's future depended on good relations between Croatians and Serbians. Because the U.S. leaders hoped the three republics would adopt free market economies and democratic institutions, U.S. policies required the U.S.-NATO allies to find the proper balance between encouraging domestic changes and relying on the three leaders to promote peace, a difficult, perhaps impossible, mission. Since 1995, dissidents in Croatia and Yugoslavia had challenged their rulers to adopt democratic elections, but U.S. and Western leaders have had to rely on assistance from those authoritarian rulers who signed the Dayton agreements.

As noted previously, Tudjman did little to help solve Bosnia's problem in Mostar but in the Croat Republic, he succeeded in stifling domestic critics and was reelected as president in June 1997 in what OSCE observers called a "fatally flawed" election. Recent events had benefited Tudjman, however, because Croatia had not suffered from UN economic sanctions and his popularity increased after 1994 because the Croat army expelled Serbs from the Krajina and western Slavonia, while the Dayton Accords returned east Slavonia to Croatia. Also, he prevented Serbs from returning to their Croatian homes by violating the Dayton Accords and satisfied rabid Croat nationalists by denouncing Bosnia's Izetbegovic as a dangerous Islamic fundamentalist.

Croatia's opposition parties generally did not object to Tudjman's rabid nationalism but to his human rights violations and the HDZ's control over Croatia's mass communications. In June 1996, the government convicted two journalists for defaming the president and over the next four months the HDZ-dominated legislature imposed restrictions on political activities. Only protests from the U.S. persuaded him to cancel plans to close the independent Radio Station 101. Finally, Tudjman took no positive steps to promote democracy and dismayed Europeans and Americans by restricting foreign investments and free trade and by limiting the privatization of Croatian business except for those he sold to HDZ friends.

In May 1997, U.S. Secretary of State Albright warned Tudjman he would lose U.S. support unless he complied with the Dayton agreements on the return of refugees, sent indicted Croat war criminals to the Hague for trial, and liberalized his economy. To enforce Albright's words,

Washington blocked World Bank-IMF loans to Croatia in both April and August 1997 before Tudjman's policies changed by sending indicted Croat war criminals voluntarily to the Hague for trial: one in April and ten more on October 5.[26]

Tudjman's willingness in November 1996 to allow Radio 101 to continue broadcasting may have been influenced by events in Belgrade where successful protest demonstrations were staged against Milosevic. In 1994, Milosevic realized that the UN economic sanctions would end only if he gained international respect by abandoning the hope of creating a Greater Serbia, reducing his military supplies to the Bosnian Serbs, and negotiating with Holbrooke. At home, Milosevic's popularity had subsided because of economic scarcity and also because he did not assist the Croatian Serbs when Tudjman's army chased them from the Krajina to East Slavonia.

During 1996, Milosevic made another political sacrifice by agreeing to turn over Eastern Slavonia to UN negotiators who determined the best process for returning the area to Croatia. Slavonia had had a mixture of Serbs and Croats before Serb forces invaded in 1991 and displaced Croatians from their homes. In 1996, Croatians began to return home but Croatian Serbs who had lived in Slavonia before 1991 had to apply for permanent residence. Because Croatian officials set difficult residency standards for them, the Serbs complained that few applicants qualified; moreover, there were frequent reports of violence between Croats and Serbs. While some Serbs left Slavonia and even smuggled an entire textile mill to Yugoslavia by dismantling it, others preferred to stay in their ancestral homes. Thus, the UN transfer of power to Croatia was delayed until July 1997 while minority rights of Serbs were negotiated. Following UN supervised elections from April 13-15 in which Croatians won 18 of the 29 seats in Vukovar's city assembly, the UN withdrew one-half of its troops from the province pending Croatia's full compliance with guarantees for the rights of Serbs who won 11 seats in the assembly. About 100,000 Serbs remained in Slovonia as a minority whose rights the UN protected before returning it to Croatian rule early in 1998.[27]

While Milosevic yielded on Slavonia, his government did nothing to fulfill a Dayton promise to protect the rights of the Albanian majority in Kosovo. Although NATO officials expected Kosovo to remain part of the rump Yugoslavia, there were a few signs in 1996 and 1997 that the Serbs might change their past repression of Albanians. One sign was a 1996 Serbian Academy of Sciences report that altered that group's 1986 anti-

Albanian conclusions by urging Serbs in Kosovo to compromise either by sharing political power with Albanians or dividing the province into two ethnic enclaves. Another positive sign was the opening of a U.S. Information Center in Pristina to provide human rights data to Albanians and monitor human rights abuses against Albanians. And, finally, there was a July 1996 report indicating that many Serbs left Kosovo or were building homes in other parts of Yugoslavia.

But these signs were overwhelmed by other Serb actions amid reports that Albanian protests were turning from moderation to violence. Milosevic's martial law was not relaxed in 1996 as Serb police violations of Albanian human rights increased. Albanians killed by police acting during dubious circumstances grew from 14 in 1996 to 20 during the first half of 1997. Moreover, Milosevic refused to hold serious talks about the future with Albania's moderate leader Ibraham Rugova. Rugova was allowed to organize an Albanian governing body but the Serbs did not permit elections and continued anti-Albanian practices such as prohibiting the use of the Albanian language at the University of Pristina.

Continued Serb abuses weakened Rugova's program of nonviolence and in 1997 many young Albanians .joined the new Kosovo Liberation Army, a guerrilla organization ready to fight for Kosovo's independence and the right to join neighboring Albania. In October, the *New York Times* reported that much of rural Kosovo belonged to the rebels after nightfall. Guerrillas overran eleven Serb police stations in September and planned more demonstrations in Pristina.

Clinton and NATO faced a new dilemma as Serb violence escalated. Hoping Milosevic would negotiate with Rugova, Clinton opposed the KLA goal of independence, fearing it would encourage war in neighboring Albania and among Albanian minorities in Macedonia and Greece. Although Kosovo's status was not covered by the Dayton Accords, Western leaders could not tolerate Milosevic's terror tactics. In October 1998, the U.S., NATO and UN officials used threats of air attacks against Serbia to compel Milosevic to halt the assaults and agree to a settlement brokered by Richard Holbrooke. In addition to a cease fire and withdrawal of most Serb forces, Milosevic agreed to hold talks with Albanian leaders about Kosovo's future and accept international observers to verify Serb compliance.[28]

Kosovo's unrest threatened to reduce further Milosevic's claims to a Greater Serbia and damaged his popularity. Since 1992, Milosevic's Socialist Party had controlled the Serb Republic and Montenegro as

"Yugoslavia", retaining power by dominating the armed forces, the police, state-managed industry and the communications media. In March 1996, Milosevic undertook stricter police methods, harassed opposition leaders, nationalized all of Belgrade's private television stations and placed bans on the Soros Foundation, a philanthropic group set-up by Serbian-American George Soros to subsidize enterprises such as Belgrade's independent newspaper. Yet, Milosevic's tactics failed to suppress the opposition because the economy did not quickly revive after UN economic sanctions ended. From 1990 to 1996, a worker's average wage dropped from $800 to $40 per month and Yugoslavia's state-run automobile industry produced only a few thousand cars a year. In addition, the flood of Serb refugees from Croatia created not only a new government expenditure, but also increased the number of radical nationalists joining demonstrations against Milosevic in November.

Milosevic's opposition represented diverse groups ranging from radical Serb nationalists to ardent liberal democrats. The Radical Party led by Vojislav Seselj enrolled Serb nationalists and former paramilitary leaders who disdained Milosevic for deserting Serbs in Bosnia and Croatia and abandoning the idea of a Greater Serbia. But the cooperation of three parties as the Together (Zajendo) coalition made it the largest group in 1996. Of the three, the largest was the Democratic Party led by Zoran Djindjic whose rhetoric was often more rabid than Milosevic's in proclaiming Serb unity against the Croatians, Muslims, and Albanians. But Djindjic, who appeared to favor democratic elections and individual rights, was considered an opportunist who adopted popular ideas. A second Together member was the Civic Alliance Party led by Vesna Pesic, a strong civil rights advocate who attracted many university students. The third was the Serbian Renewal Movement led by Vuk Draskovic, who was described as a romantic nationalist simply wanting to end the power of Milosevic's neo-Communist Socialist Party.

The November 1996 demonstrations erupted after Together members won municipal elections in Belgrade and other Serb cities. When Milosevic refused to accept the victorious candidates, Together vowed to take over the city halls by staging daily strikes of 20,000 to 400,000 protestors in Belgrade and other cities. These protests aroused international criticism of Milosevic by the European Union, most European governments, the Clinton administration, and U.S. congressional members. Milosevic finally relented and, on February 4, 1997, the Democratic Party's Zoran Djindjic became mayor of Belgrade.

Other Together members controlled Belgrade's city Council and the governments of thirteen cities.[29]

The municipal elections did not disturb Milosevic's power in the Serb Republic and, after the Together coalition split apart in 1997, he moved to solidify his power in the Serb Republic and Yugoslavia. Because Serbia's Constitution prohibited a third presidential term, Milosevic had Yugoslavia's Parliament elect him president of Yugoslavia, resigned as the Serb Republic's president, and named a loyal lieutenant to that office.

During October 1997, however, Milosevic's manipulations ran into trouble in both the Serb Republic and Montenegro. In the Serb Republic's election, Milosevic's candidate, Milan Milutinovic, lost to Radical Party leader Vojislav Seselj. Milosevic had the Serb Supreme Court invalidate the election and called for new elections because fewer than 50% of the electorate voted. In a second election on December 6 more than 50% voted, but no candidate received a majority and in a subsequent December 23 runoff election, Milutinovic won but Seselj's complaint that less than 50% of the electorate voted was shunned by the Supreme Court.

More seriously for Milosevic's power in Yugoslavia, his candidate for president of Montenegro, Momir Bulatovic, lost in the October election to Milo Djukanovic who strongly advocates Montenegro's independence from Yugoslavia. Djukanovic's Party also gained control of Montenegro's voting block in the Yugoslav Parliament, enabling him to block legislation he disapproves. Advocates of Montenegro's independence have demanded economic concessions from Milosevic that Djukanovic may use as a bargaining chip. Without Montenegro, Milosevic loses his claim to be president of Yugoslavia's successor state.[30]

When Clinton and NATO extended the Bosnian mission in July 1998, Milosevic clung to power in Belgrade although Montenegro's leader sought independence and threatened to end the rump Yugoslavia's status. Also, the Serb Republic's control of Kosovo was being threatened by the increasingly violent protests of Albanians.

Since the former Yugoslavia's demise, Slavonia had prospered as an independent nation; Croatia had regained control of its Krajina and Eastern Slavonia province; and Bosnia-Herzegonia, under NATO protection, strived to retain its two entity state of the Muslim-Croat Federation and the Srpska Republic. In the Srpska Republic's sector, Serbs in Banja Luka had a tenuous ascendancy over the radicals at Pale who remained loyal to Radovan Karadzic. A key issue in Bosnia was whether the principal Serb war criminals, Karadzic and General Mladic could be brought to justice at the Hague Tribunal.

WAR CRIMES TRIBUNAL BEGINS WORK

The plans for a war crimes court began on May 25, 1993, when the UN Security Council created the International Tribunal for War Crimes in the former Yugoslavia Federation. From 1994 to 1996, South African jurist Richard Goldstone was its Chief Prosecutor and assembled data for court indictments. When his term ended in 1996, the UNSC approved Canadian Judge Louise Arbour as prosecutor and named Italian law professor, Antonio Cassese, as tribunal president.[31]

The tribunal's creation left unanswered the question of who would arrest indicted war criminals and present them for trial. The Dayton Accords, which required that signatories cooperate with The Hague, was carried out by Izetbegovic in the case of three indicted Muslims. Under U.S. pressure, Tudjman had sent most (12 of 18) indicated Croats to The Hague by October 1997. The Serbs and, especially indicted Bosnian Serbs, became the chief obstacle to war crimes trials because Milosevic had not delivered any Serbs to The Hague and leaders such as Karadzic and Mladic remained at large. Because IFOR and S-FOR commanders refused to search for war criminals unless they interfered with the military mission, the problem of Serb war criminals became a major concern of the NATO mission.

Although S-FOR officials remained reluctant to arrest war criminals, the British made a successful arrest on July 10, 1997. Acting under sealed court indictments, British troops surprised two indicated Bosnian Serbs, arresting Milan Kovacevic and killing Mimo Drljaca who pulled out a gun and shot a British soldier in the leg. After Kovacevic was sent to The Hague for trial, officials in London and Washington warned that other Serb and Croat war criminals might be arrested. Major war criminals such as Radovan Karadzic were not searched for by S-FOR, but in January 1998, U.S. troops seized a nortorious Bosnian Serb criminal, Goran Jelisic, for trial at The Hague and in April 1998, British forces captured two more indicated Serb war criminals.[32]

During 1996, the Tribunal began its first trial, returned a precedent-setting indictment regarding rape, and sentenced one prisoner who pleaded guilty under special circumstances. The first war crime trial started on May 7, for a Serbian police officer, Dusan Tadic, who was being tried on 31 counts of torturing and killing Muslim prisoners at

Omarska prison camp in 1992. To set precedents for future trials, the prosecutors sought to prove Tadic did not act in a Bosnian civil war but in an international war where Milosevic's Serb Republic controlled the Bosnian Serbs. In April 1997, the court found Tadic guilty of killing and torturing Muslims but two of the three judges ruled the prosecution did not prove his crime was part of a Milosevic-directed international war. The prosecution succeeded in the conviction of murder but needed more evidence to prove the crime was not a civil conflict but an inter-nation crime.[33]

While Tadic's trial continued in 1996, the Court set a precedent by indicting eight Serbian men for the war crime of raping Muslim women. Previously, sexual assault had not been prosecuted as a war crime although it was listed as a crime in the 1907 Hague Treaty. In 1996, the Hague prosecutors demonstrated to the court that, although all three Bosnian parties committed rape, the Serbs were the main perpetrators as part of a systematic strategy to take control of territory by terrorizing people, eliminating ethnic groups, and violating an estimated 20,000 Muslim women and girls. Eight Serb military and police officers not in custody were indicted for such activity near Srebrenica, Zepa, and Goradze. In March, however, the Court began a trial of three Muslims and one Croat for raping, torturing, or killing Serbs in a Bosnian prison, and in March 1998 a Serb pleaded guilt of a rape charge.[34]

Thirdly, the tribunal settled the controversial case of Drazen Erdemovic who surrendered and pleaded guilty because he took orders from a Serb army officer as an "ordinary soldier." After first refusing orders to shoot helpless victims, the Serb officer told him if he did not shoot prisoners he would be shot himself. His attorney argued this threat required him to obey. Although Erdemovic identified Serbs who took orders from General Mladic, the judges ruled he had not proved his claim, found him guilty, and sentenced him to ten years in a Scandinavian prison.[35]

By mid-1998, few of the 78 indicted criminals were in custody. While two war criminals were dead, The Hague held three Muslims whose trial began in February 1997, 11 Croats, and a Serb captured by the British in July 1997. Principally, it was indicted Bosnian Serbs who were at large because S-FOR seldom searched for them, claiming their primary goal was building an orderly society which might be jeopardized if those remaining popular with Serbs such as Karadzic were forcibly arrested. One new twist developed in 1997 when the International Tribunal asked

Germany to prosecute an indicted Serb they had arrested. The German court agreed and in September 1997, Nikola Jorgie was convicted on eleven counts of genocide and thirty counts of murdering Muslims in Bosnia. The Germans also issued warrants for five indicted Serbs believed to have entered Germany as "guest workers" after the Dayton Accords.[36]

EXTENDING THE DEADLINES FOR U.S. WITHDRAWAL

After Clinton decided to deploy troops to Bosnia in 1995, his commitment was plagued by congressional insistence on fixing deadlines for U.S. withdrawal. Although critics said deadlines favored Bosnian radicals who would wait for the U.S. exit to renew warfare, the Republican-controlled congress persisted so that until early 1998 Clinton had to equivocate or alter NATO's mission to gain long-term help for Bosnia's peace program.

After the initial deadline was set for December 20, 1996, Clinton's staff sought to convince Americans that an extended Bosnian mission was necessary although Clinton did not announce his decision until he was reelected in November. Public discussion of a probable extension began with a March 1996 NATO report that stated IFOR's military success could not be duplicated in one year by Bosnia's political and economic reconstruction teams and a smaller "follow-on force" was necessary to protect Bosnia's rebuilding. During the summer, Clinton's staff also hinted that one-year was not sufficient to guarantee peace. Secretary of Defense Perry said some U.S. troops should stay if NATO requested a U.S. presence and on July 24, U.S. Lieutenant General Patrick Hughes told a Senate committee that Bosnia's slow economic recovery and September election problems would make a U.S. presence necessary. In September, at a NATO meeting U.S. General George Joulwan, NATO's Supreme Commander, said NATO's likely option would be a "stabilizing force" to deter renewed fighting in Bosnian.

Joulwan's "likely option" became reality following the presidential election when Clinton announced a reduced IFOR would stay in Bosnia as a stabilizing force (S-FOR) until July 1998 because Bosnia's rebuilding took longer to achieve than anticipated. In December, NATO reduced its IFOR forces from 60,000 to an S-FOR of 30,000 troops including 8,500 U.S. soldiers.

Perhaps because the Bosnian intervention had no U.S. combat casualties, Clinton's extension of the U.S. mission received a quiet reception until the summer of 1997 when congressional Republicans expressed concern that NATO did not define the circumstances that would end the S-FOR mission. Madeleine Albright, who became Secretary of State in 1997, and Chairman of the Joint Chiefs General John Shalikashvili indicated exit strategies were hangovers from the Cold War era and should be replaced by flexible standards. In September, however, Congress passed the 1997-98 defense appropriations bill whose provisions stopped funding troops in Bosnia on June 30, 1998 unless Clinton explained to Congress by May 15, 1998 why and how the Bosnian mission would be extended.[37]

The crucial question on Bosnia's future was not answered until December 18, 1997, when President Clinton announced U.S. troops would remain *indefinitely* after June 1998. NATO finalized plans in March 1998, giving Clinton time to explain the mission before Congress' May deadline. Clinton stated that past deadlines were a mistake and NATO would not set a date to withdraw but would base exit decisions on achieving goals such as a suitable Bosnian national police force, an independent mass media, solving the refugee problem, and securing trials of war criminals.

Much remained to be done in Bosnia to avert the outbreak of another war. In December 1997, S-FOR nations met in Bonn to plan for action after June 30, 1998. The Bonn Conference gave Carlos Westendorf wider authority to "impose binding" decisions on the three Bosnian factions if they refused to agree on solutions to problems ranging from trivial items such as a common auto license plate to difficult ones concerning the return of refugees and arrest of war criminals. The conference ended on a sour note, however, because Bosnian Serb and Serb Republic delegates walked out to protest discussions about Albanians in Kosovo.[38]

By mid-1998, the possible lessons of Somalia, Haiti, and Bosnia suggested that the Cold War's simple "communist versus free world" decisions on intervention had become much more complex. The basic questions remaining was whether the U. S. and its allies could sustain peace, human rights, and stable conditions around the world as their foremost security ideal.

NOTES

1. Raymond Bonner, "G.I.'s Take Up Their Positions in Serb Held Bosnia," *NYT* (Dec. 27, 1995): A-7; Bonner, "U.S. Admiral Gets an Unexpected Welcome," *NYT* (Dec. 23, 1995): A-4; Kit R. Roane, "Bosnian POW Releases Gain Slowly," *NYT* (Jan. 30, 1996): A-4; "Bosnian Serbs Refuse to Free Prisoners," *NYT* (Apr. 7, 1996): A-8.

2. Chris Hedges, "NATO Says it Arrests Some Foreign Muslim Troops," *NYT* (Mar. 16, 1996): A-3; Kit Roane "NATO Links Bosnian Government to Training Center for Terrorists," *NYT* (Mar. 17, 1996): A-1, 4; Roane, "Bosnia to Deport 2 Iranians Caught in Raid by NATO," *NYT* (Mar. 18, 1996): A-18.

3. Mike O'Connor, "Tension in Mostar Eases With Bosnian Croat Pledge," *NYT* (Jan. 8, 1996): A-4; John Tagliabue, "Balkan Leaders Pledge to Carry Out Dayton Accords," *NYT* (Feb. 19, 1996): A-3; Kit Roane, "Muslims and Croats Sign Contract," *NYT* (Apr. 1, 1996): A-6.

4. Holbrooke, *To End a War*, 335-37 thought these events in Sarajevo were the "worst" in 1996. Stephen Kinzer, "Bosnian Serbs Pressed to Flee Areas Near Sarajevo," *NYT* (Feb. 21, 1996): A-3; Kit Roane, "As Bosnia Declares Siege of Sarajevo Over, Serbs Continue to Pack," *NYT* (Mar. 1, 1996): A-4; Chris Hedges, "NATO to Move Against Anarchy in Serb-Held Suburbs," *NYT* (Mar. 11, 1996): A-3; Reuters, "Bosnian Muslims Free 109 Prisoners," NYT (Mar 24, 1996): A-12; John Pomfret, "Coming Home in Sarajevo," WPNW (Mar. 26-31): 16; Pomfret, "Bosnian Serbs Refuse to Free Prisoners," *NYT* (Apr. 7, 1996): A-8.

5. Steven Erlanger, "Balkan Leaders Again Promise to Carry out Accords on Bosnia," *NYT* (Mar. 19, 1996): A-1, 6; Jane Perlez, "Divided Bosnia's City Croats Agree to Honor Vote Results," *NYT* (Aug. 7, 1996): A-6; Mike O'Connor, "In the Balkans Another Mini-State Digs In," *NYT* (Aug. 31, 1996): A-4; Ivica Profaca (Assoc. Press), "Croatian Officials Push for Solution to Mostar," *Peoria Journal Star* (Aug. 4, 1996): A-6; Lee Hockstadter, "In Bosnia Classes Open on School Segregation," *Washington Post* (Oct. 19, 1997): A-20

6. Raymond Bonner, "To G.I.'s Disputed Corridor will Test Path to Peace," *NYT* (Dec. 18, 1996): A-3; Michael Dobbs, "Bosnia's Intractable Passions," *WPNW* (July 1-7, 1996): 15-16; Mike O'Connor, "2d Day of Bosnian Fighting," *NYT* (Nov. 13, 1996): A-1, 3: O'Connor," Bosnian Town Held Hostage by Fear," *NYT* (Nov. 14, 1996): A-10; O'Connor, "Muslim Rioters in Bosnia Attack a U.S. Column," *NYT* (Nov. 15, 1996): A-3; Assoc. Press. "Arbitrators Loosen Grip on Brcko," *Peoria Journal Star* (Feb. 17, 1997): 3. For March 1998, see BBC on Internet Yahoo "Brcko Ruling Criticized," Mar. 16, 1998.

7. Mike O'Connor, "Threat to Bosnian Police: Rival Police," *NYT* (Jan. 12, 1997): A-8; Stephen Kinzer, "Bosnian Police Supplant Serbs in Capital Area," *NYT* (Feb. 14, 1996): A-1, 4; Kit Roane, "In Sarajevo Suburb, A Quest to Heal War's Hatreds," *NYT* (Feb. 28, 1996): A-7; Reuters, "Croats Jump Gun in Takeover of Sarajevo Suburb," *NYT* (Mar. 6, 1996): A-3: Mike O'Connor, "Bosnian Serbs Attack Muslim Croat Police," *NYT* (Mar. 30, 1996): A-4; "3 Muslims in Bosnia Die Going Home," *NYT* (April 30, 1996): A-10.

8. Chris Hedges, "Factions in the Balkans Sign an Accord to Limit Weapons," *NYT* (June 15, 1996): A-1, 7; Raymond Bonner, "Bosnia Serbs Said to Hide Big Supplies of Arms," *NYT* (Oct. 19, 1996): A-6; Hedges, "Bosnia Reported to be Smuggling Heavy Artillery," *NYT* (Nov. 8, 1996): A-1, 12; Bonner, "Who's Beating Swords into Ploughshares in Balkans?" *NYT* (Dec. 20, 1996): A-6.

9. Holbrooke, *To End a War*, 319-20, also see pp. 50-51. "What's Iran Doing in Bosnia, Anyway?" *NYT* (Dec. 10, 1995): E-4; Chris Hedges, "Bosnians Sending Soldiers to Iran to Get Training," *NYT* (Mar. 3, 1996): A-1, 4; Hedges, "A Secret Arms Deal Between Iran and Croatia," *NYT* (Apr. 24, 1996): A-4; Mike O'Connor, "Police Officials Methods Raise Ethnic Fears," *NYT* (June 16, 1996): A-6; John Pomfret, "The Ones [Islam Militants] That Got Away," *WPNW* (July 15-21, 1996): 17; Pomfret, "An Arms Pipeline Uncovered," *WPNW* (Sept. 30/Oct.6, 1996): 6-7; Pomfret and David Ottaway, "Keeping the Pipeline Well-Armed," *WPNW* (May 20-26): 14; George Mitchell, "Op-Ed on Iranian Arms," *NYT* (June 17, 1996): A-15; Steven Lee Myers, "House Republicans Say Administration Lied on Bosnian Arms," *NYT* (Oct. 11, 1996): A-3; Tim Weiner, "Senate Panel Finds Nothing Illegal on Clinton's Policy on Iranian Arms," *NYT* (Nov. 8, 1996): A-12.

10. Mark Thompson, "General for Hire," *Time* (Jan. 15, 1996): 34-36; Chris Hedges, "U.S.-Led Aid for Bosnian Army is in Jeopardy," *NYT* (Mar. 22, 1996): A-3; Mike O'Conner, "Bosnia Official's Methods Raise Ethnic Fears," *NYT* (June 16, 1996): A-6; O'Connor, "Under U.S. Pressure, Bosnia Dismisses Official Linked to Iran," *NYT* (Nov. 20, 1996): A-7: Mike O'Connor, "Spies for Iran Are Said to Gain a Hold in Bosnia," *NYT* (Nov. 28, 1997): A-1, 8.

11. Pomfret, John, "Waiting for the Next Balkan War," *WPNW* (June 9, 1997): 22, Raymond Bonner, "Success in Balkans: A Big Cut in Arms," *NYT* (Oct. 23, 1997): A-6.

12. Richard Holbrooke, "Backsliding in Bosnia," *Time* (May 20, 1996): 38; Reuters, "Croats Jump Gun on Takeover of Sarajevo Suburb," *NYT* (Mar. 16, 1996): A-3; Barbara Crossette, "U.N. Members Slow to Send Police," *NYT* (Mar. 21, 1996): A-1.

13. Chris Hedges, "Report on Bosnia Questions Ability to Hold Elections," *NYT* (June 2, 1996): A-1; Hedges, "U.S. Envoy Told Staff to Take Optimistic Line on Vote," *NYT* (June 5, 1996): A-1, 3; Steven Erlanger, "Bosnia Uproar: Why U.S. Pushes for Early Vote," *NYT* (June 12, 1996): A-3; Hedges, "Despite Doubts on Fairness, Official Gives Go-Ahead for Bosnian Vote," *NYT* (June 26, 1996): A-7.

14. Holbrooke, *To End a War*, 340-344. Craig Whitney, "Serbs Pressed on Ouster of Bosnian Leader," *NYT* (June 30, 1996): A-4; Jane Perlez, "Top Bosnian Serb Agrees to Resign," *NYT* (July 20, 1996): A-1, 4; Raymond Bonner, "With Karadzic out, 'Moderate' Serbs are Hopeful," *NYT* (July 24, 1996): A-3. Karadzic's resignation may have made him more popular among Serbs, see Christine Spolar, "The Canonization of Radovan Karadzic," *WPNW* (July 29/Aug 1, 1996): 17.

15. Chris Hedges, "Bosnia Holds Vote With Few Reports of Real Violence," *NYT* (Sept. 15, 1996): A-1, 10; Hedges, "Bosnia's Nationalist Parties Dominate Post-War Vote," *NYT* (Sept. 22, 1996): A-10. Michael Dobbs, "A Gap Between Rhetoric and Realism," *WPNW* (Sept. 23-29, 1996): 16. Three critical views of the elections are in Anthony Borden, et.al., "Bosnia's Democratic Charade," *Nation* 259 (Sept. 23, 1996): 14-20.

16. Mike O'Connor, "Bosnian Serb Leaders Boycott Unity Ceremony," *NYT* (Oct. 6, 1996): A-4; Chris Hedges, "New Bosnia Government Shows Few Signs of Life," *NYT* (Oct. 20, 1996): A-3; Craig Whitney, "Bosnia Foes Told to Make Peace in 2 Years," *NYT* (Nov. 15, 1996): A-3; "Bosnia's Ex-foes Pledge Peace, Start Governing Jointly," *NYT* (Jan. 4, 1997): A-3; John Promfret, "Serb Police Force Challenges Mladic," *Washington Post* (Nov. 14, 1996): A-23, 25.

17. Tracy Wilkinson and Tyler Marshall, two articles, "In Bosnia U.S. Creeps Deeper," and "U.S. Team on Bosnia Takes Peace Keeping to the Limit," *Los Angeles Times* (Nov. 11, 1997): A-1, 12 and (Nov. 12, 1997): A-12-13. Edward Cody, "Serb May Be Seized," *Washington Post* (Aug. 10, 1997): A-1, 20, 21; Guy Dinmore, "NATO acts Against hard-line Serbs," *Chicago Tribune* (Aug. 21, 1997): I-4; Steven Erlanger, "NATO Faces a Crossroads in Bosnia," *NYT* (Aug. 31, 1997): A-6; Edward Cody, "Finding an Unlikely Ally in Bosnia," *WPNW* (Sept. 8, 1997): 14.

18. Raymond Bonner, "Russia Fails to Block Bosnian Serb Vote," *NYT* (Oct. 10, 1997): A-3; Chris Hedges, "Bosnian Serb Leader [Plavsic] is Reported Balking," *NYT* (Oct. 17, 1997): A-13; Mike O'Connor, "NATO Says It Shut Serb Radio to Silence Serbian Propaganda," *NYT* (Oct. 21, 1997): A-3; Colin Soloway, "Bosnian Serb Hardliners Lose Ground [Nov. 23 election]," *Washington Post* (Dec. 8, 1997): A-22; "Bosnian Serb Parliament Meets and Begins Maneuvering," *NYT* (Dec. 28, 1997): A-4; Srecko Latal, "NATO Troops Bolster New Bosnian Serb Premier," *Washington Post* (Jan. 19, 1998): A-26; Ian Geoghegan, "NATO Arrests War Criminal," and "Bosnian Arrest 'Message' to War Criminals," Reuters News on Yahoo WWW (Jan. 22, 1998): 1-2; Mike O'Connor, "G.I.'s Seize their First Bosnian Atrocity Suspect," *NYT* (Jan. 23, 1998): A-5 and O'Connor, "West Seeing Payoff From its Support of Flexible Serb Leaders in Bosnia," *NYT* (Jan. 24, 1998): A-4. Steven Lee Myers, "Force in Bosnia Failed One Task: A Pullout," NYT (Oct. 4, 1998): A1, 8

19. Chris Hedges, "Serbs, Listless and Divided, Go to Polls," *NYT* (Sept. 21, 1997): A-4; OSCE Web Page, October 1, 1997: "The Results of the Municipal Elections," OSCE Press Office, Sarajevo, 2 pages.

20. Michael Dobbs and Dana Priest, "Now The Real Work Begins," *WPNW* (Dec. 18, 1995): 14; Dobbs, "Can We Make a Bosnian Miracle?" *WPNW* (Dec 25-31, 1995): 24-25; Christopher Wren, "The G.I.'s Don't Carry a Marshall Plan," *NYT* (Dec. 17, 1995): E-14; Chris Hedges, "Bosnian Serbs Trying to Jump-Start an Economy," *NYT* (Jan. 14, 1996): A-8; Raymond Bonner, "Bosnian Industries Face Obstacles to Recovery," *NYT* (Feb 4, 1996): A-4; Mike O'Connor, "Bosnia's Industrial Network Reels   from War Wounds," *NYT* (Oct. 27, 1996): A-6; Editors, "NATO's Missing Partner in Bosnia," *NYT* (Jan. 7, 1996): E-18.

21. Richard Stevenson, "Talks on Rebuilding Bosnia Squabble over Bill," *NYT* (Dec. 10, 1995): A-4. The Bildt interview which summarizes the slow economic process is in Chris Hedges, "In Bosnia, Securing a Peaceful Future Depends on Roads, Refugees, Elections," *NYT* (Mar. 26, 1996): A-10; Philip Shenon, "Pentagon Report Predicts Bosnia Will Fragment Without Vast Aid," *NYT* (Mar. 20, 1996): A-1, 12.

22. R.W. Apple, Jr., "Commerce Secretary Among 33 Lost in Croatia Plane Crash," *NYT* (Apr. 4, 1996): A-1, 8. On the U.S. companies involved see Leslie Eaton, "A Dozen Companies Await Word." *NYT* (Apr. 4, 1996): A-9 and "List of Passengers and Crew," *NYT* (Apr. 5, 1996): A-12. Chris Hedges, "Sober Farewell in Croatia for U.S. Victims," *NYT* (Apr. 7, 1996): A-8; Craig Whitney, "55-Nation Conference on Fund Raising is Split Over Serbs," *NYT* (Apr. 13, 1996): A-4; and Hedges, "$1.23 Billion Pledges In New Aid For Bosnia," *NYT* (Apr. 14, 1996): A-4; Reuters, "U.S. and Bosnia Sign Pact on Investment," *NYT* (July 13, 1996): A-6.

23. Philip Shenon, "3 New York Subway Veterans Help Restore Transit System," *NYT* (May 9, 1996): A-19; Ian Finnes, "Sarajevo Airport Reopens," *NYT* (Aug. 16, 1996): A-13; Jane Perlez, "Peace Brings New Kind of Work to Sarajevo Hospital," *NYT* (Aug. 16, 1996): A-1; Perlez, "Dubrovnik Is Seeking a New Path for Tourism," *NYT* (Aug. 18, 1996): A-4: Chris Hedges, "Gangs Descend to Pick Bosnia's Carcass Clean," *NYT* (Oct. 7, 1996): A-4: Richard W. Stevenson, "World Helps to Rebuild Bosnia But Work is Slow," *NYT* (Jan. 6, 1997): A-8; Fred Barbash, "Conference Hints Cutoff of Aid to Bosnian Rivals," *Washington Post* (Dec. 5, 1996): A-39.

24. Philip Shenon, "Main Peril for G.I.'s in Bosnia Lies Just Beneath the Surface," *NYT* (Dec. 10, 1995): A-1, 4; Mike O'Connor, "Bosnia is Strewn with Danger..." *NYT* (Oct. 28, 1996): A-8.

25. Alan Cowell, "For Bosnia's Refugees, Return May Be Illusion," *NYT* (Dec. 8, 1995): A-6; Cowell, "Bosnia's Muslim Refugees Find Election a Dilemma," *NYT* (June 25,1996): A-4; Cowell, "Germany Plans to Return Refugees," *NYT* (Sept. 20, 1996): A-4; Cowell, "Bavaria, Acting Alone, Begins to Expel War Refugees," *NYT* (Oct.10, 1996): A-14; Lee Hockstadter, "A Trickle Toward Progress in Bosnia," *WPNW* (Sept. 22, 1997): 16.

26. Ian Kearns, "Croatian Politics: The New Authoritarianism," *Political Quarterly* 67 (Jan./Mar. 1996): 26-35; Nikos Konstandaras, "Serbia, Croatia Agree on Diplomatic Relations," *Peoria Journal Star,* (Aug. 8, 1996): A-3; Jane Perlez, "Balkan Economic Stagnation in Grip of Political Leaders," *NYT* (Aug. 20, 1996): A-1; "Croatia reverses Closing of Radio Station," *NYT* (Nov. 20, 1996): A-4; Chris Hedges, "Ally in War, Burden in Peace," *NYT* (June 1, 1997): E-4 and Steven Lee Meyers, "Albright Chides Balkan Chiefs for Flaunting Peace Accords," *NYT* (June 1, 1997): A-8; Lee Hockstader, "10 Croats Surrender to War Crimes Tribunal," *Washington Post* (Oct. 10, 1997): A-11. On Dec. 19, The Hague Tribunal's Chief Prosecutor Louis Arbour announced that three of these Croats were being released due to lack of evidence regarding their guilt: "Tribunal frees former war crimes suspects," *Peoria Journal Star* (Dec. 20, 1997): A-6.

27. On Slovenia see Barbara Crossette, "The Mission Not Accepted," *NYT* (Dec. 31, 1995): E-10; Chris Hedges, "Serb Gangs Rule in Last-Chance Fief of U.N.," *NYT* (June 22, 1996): A-1, 3; Hedges, "Despite Treaty, Croatia is Denying Serbs a Right

to Live There," *NYT* (Nov. 17, 1996): A-8; *NYT* (Apr. 20, 1997): A-15; "Croatian Serb on Trial for Vukovar Killings," *Peoria Journal Star* (Jan. 17, 1998): A-3.

28. "Bomb Kills Boy and Injures Three (in Pristina)," *Peoria Journal Star* (Apr. 28, 1996): 3; Jane Perlez, "From Serbia, a Pragmatic Pullback," *NYT* (July 28, 1996): A-4; Aryeh Neier, "Impasse in Kosovo," *New York Review of Books* (Sept. 25, 1997): 51-53. Conflict broke out again in Kosovo during February 1998, see Chris Hedges, "Another Victory for Death in Serbia," *NYT* (Mar. 8, 1998): E-5; Warren Zimmermann, The Demons of Kosovo," *The National Interest* No. 52 (Summer 1998): 3-11; "U.S. Envoy in Switzerland for Kosovo Talks, *NYT* (June 28, 1998): A-4; Tim Judah, "Impasse in Kosovo," *New York Review of Books* (Oct. 8, 1998): 4-6; Jane Perlez, "In Kosovo Death Chronicles, Serb Tactics Revealed," and "U.S. Envoy Issues a Stern Warning on Kosovo," NYT (Sept. 27, 1998): A-10; Samuel R. Berger, "A Chance for Peace in Kosovo..." *WPNW* (Oct. 29, 1998): 26; Douglas Waller, "Holbrooke's Next Mission,"*Time* (Oct. 26, 1998): 59-60.

29. Michael Dobbs, "A Balkan Basket Case," *WPNW* (Aug. 12-18): 18; Chris Hedges, "Prospects for Change, Not Hope," *NYT* (Dec. 1, 1996): E-10; Hedges, "2 Powerful Serbs," *NYT* (Dec. 1, 1996): A-4; Hedges, "Serbs' Answer to Tyranny? Get on the Web," *NYT* (Dec.8, 1996): A-1,8; Hedges, "Belgrade's New Mayor," *NYT* (Feb. 23, 1997): A-10; Kevin Fedarko, "Taking to the Streets," *Time* (Dec. 16, 1996): 40-41. For a general summary of events from November to March see Timothy Garton Ash, "In the Serbian Soup," *New York Review of Books* 45 (April 24, 1997): 25-30.

30. Jonathan C. Randal, "Confounding Critics, Milosevic Thrives," *WPNW* (June 23, 1997): 17; Jane Perlez, "Serbian Media is a One-Man Show," *NYT* (Aug. 10, 1997): E-5; Reuters, "Big Powers Meet in Rome on Bosnian Serbs," *NYT* (Oct. 18, 1997): A-5; Laura Silber and Veran Matic, "Radio Free Yugoslavia," *New York Review of Books* (Nov. 6, 1997): 67; Chris Hedges, "Foe's Victory in Montenegro Threatens Milosevic's Hold," *NYT* (Oct. 21, 1997): A-6; Hedges, "Serb Election Again Seems Inconclusive," *NYT* (Dec. 8, 1997): A-8; "In Flawed Vote, New Serb Chief is Named," *NYT* (Dec. 24, 1997): A-6: "Serbia's New President Takes Up Office," *NYT* (Dec. 30, 1997): A-4; Tim Judah, "How Milosevic Hangs On," *New York Review of Books* (July 16, 1998): 44-47; Chris Hedges, "Montenegro Chiefs Widen Rift with Belgrade," *NYT* (June 2, 1998): A-10.

31. James C. O'Brien, "The International Tribunal for Violation of Humanitarian Law in the Former Yugoslavia," *American Journal of International Law* (AJIL) 87 (Oct. 1993): 639-658; Theodore Meron, "War Crimes in Yugoslavia and the Development of International Law," *AJIL* 88 (Jan. 1994): 78-87; Barbara Crossette, "U.N. Seeks Accord on Permanent War Crimes Court," *NYT* (Apr. 7, 1996): A-8; Marlise Simons, "Italian Who Heads War Crime Tribunal Angrily Warns of Future Genocide," *NYT* (July 26, 1996): A-4. Support for the arrests and war crime trials is described by Theodore Meron, "The Case for War Criminal Trials in Yugoslavia," *Foreign Affairs* 72 (Summer 1993): 122-135; and Kenneth Roth, "Why Justice Needs NATO," *Nation* 265 (Sept. 22, 1997): 21-24. For opposition to the trials and a critique see David Rieff, "The Case against the Serb War Criminals," *WPNW* (Sept. 16-22, 1996): 25 and Diana Johnston, "Selective Justice in The Hague," *Nation* 265 (Sept. 22, 1997): 16-21.

32. John Pomfret, "For the War's Victims, the Search for Justice Begins," *WPNW* (Dec. 25-31, 1995): 8-9; Christine Spolar, "Digging into Bosnia's Dirty Secrets," *WPNW* (Aug. 12-18, 1996): 16-17; Philip Shenon, "G.I.'s in Bosnia Shun Hunt for War-Crime Suspects," *NYT* (Mar 2, 1996): A-3; Shenon, "G.I.'s to Provide Security for War Crimes Investigators," *NYT* (Apr. 1, 1996): A-6; Shenon, "Some Mixed Signals by the U.S. On Pursuing War Crime Suspects," *NYT* (June 4, 1996): A-1, 4; Chris Hedges, "Diplomats Fault NATO Chief," *NYT* (Apr. 18, 1996): A-13; Stacy Sullivan, "Wanted, But Easy to Find," *WPNW* (Dec. 2-6, 1996): 17; Marcus Tanner and Fran Abrams, "Commando Swoop on Serbs," *Independent* [London] (July 11, 1997): 1; Edward Cody, "Has the Balance Tipped in Bosnia?" *WPNW* (July 18, 1997): 16; Mike O'Connor, "G.I.'s Seize their First Bosnian Atrocity Suspect," *NYT* (Jan. 23, 1998):

A-5; "Bosnian Serb Suspects Arrive in Custody," *Peoria Journal Star* (Apr. 10, 1998): A-2.

33. George Aldrich, "Jurisdiction of the International Crimes Tribunal for the Former Yugoslavia [Case of Tadic]" *AJIL* 90 (Jan. 1996): 64-68; Leigh Monroe "The Yugoslav Tribunal's Use of Unnamed Witnesses Against Accused," *AIJL* 90 (April 1996): 235-237; Marlise Simons, "At War Crimes Trial, A Disputed Definition," *NYT* (May 12, 1996): A-8 and "Defining a War to Determine a Crime," *NYT* (May 18,1997): E-4; Peter Maass, "Suddenly They are Killers," *WPNW* (May 20-26, 1996): 27. During Tadic's trial, "pro-Serbs" disputed the validity of BBC pictures of "refugee" camps in 1992: see Eric Alterman, "Bosnian Camps: A Barbed Tale," *Nation* 265 (July 28, 1997): 17-20.

34. Marlise Simons, "For First Time, Court Defines Rape as War Crime," *NYT* (June 28, 1996): A-1, 7; Marlise Simons, "An Ex-Bosnian Serb Commander Admits Rape of Muslims in War," *NYT* (Mar. 10, 1998): A-10. Theodore Meron, "Rape as a Crime Under International Law," *AJIL* 87 (July 1993): 424-28. "War Crime Trial for 3 Muslims, One Croat," *NYT* (Mar.11, 1997): A-10. For a documentary about women raped in Bosnia see Walter Goodman, "Review of *Calling the Ghosts: A Story about Rape, War, and Women*," *NYT* (Mar.3, 1997): C-16.

35. Jane Perlez, "Serb Chief Seen Aiding on Key War Crimes Suspects," *NYT* (Mar. 13, 1996): A-5; Marlise Simons, "War Crimes Panel in First Verdict," *NYT* (Nov. 30, 1996): A-1, 8ff.

36. On the arrest of Muslims and Croats, see Alan Crowell, "Serbs as Victims: Tribunal Files First Charges in War Crimes against Serbs," *NYT* (Mar. 23, 1996): A-1, 4; "Bosnia Extradites 2 Muslims to Hague Tribunal," *NYT* (June 14, 1996): A-6: Lee Hockstadter, "10 Croats Surender to War Crimes Tribunal," *Washington Post* (Oct. 10, 1997): A-11. On the German Trial see William Drozdiak, "German Court Convicts Bosnian Serb of War Crimes," *Washington Post* (Sept. 27, 1997): A-14.

37. Rick Atkinson, "The Year of Living Dangerously," *WPNW* (Mar. 11-17): 19; Craig Whitney, "NATO Urges to Keep Force in Bosnia," *NYT* (Mar. 21, 1996): A-1, 10; Susan Woodward, "Bosnia After Dayton: Year Two," *Current History* 96 (Mar. 1997): 97-103; Shenon, "Official Says U.S. Exit May Undo Bosnia Pact," *NYT* (July, 25, 1996): A-1: Elaine Sciolino, "Loosening the Timetable for Bringing G.I.'s Home." *NYT* (Nov. 17, 1996): E-3; Craig Whitney," NATO Clears Small U.S. Led Forces," *NYT* (Dec. 18, 1996): A-11; "Congress Gives Clinton Leeway to Extend Bosnian Mission," CQ *Weekly Report* (Sept. 27, 1997): 2321.

38. Bradley Graham, "Cohen Plays Skeptic Role on Bosnia," *Washington Post* (Nov. 30, 1997): A-1, 10-11; Craig Whitney, "NATO Is Weighing the Need for Troops in Bosnia After Mid-Year," *NYT* (Dec. 2, 1997): A-4; Steven Lee Myers, "U.S. Links Staying in Bosnia to Larger NATO Police Role," *NYT* (Dec. 3, 1997): A-11; William Drozdiak, "Bosnians Told to Adhere to Peace Process," *Washington Post* (Dec. 10, 1997): A-31. Internet RFL/RL (Radio Free Europe) News, Dec 12, 1997; Lee Hockstader, "In Bosnia, Peace is Only on Paper," *WPNW* (Dec. 15, 1997): 14; John Harris, "Clinton Says Troops to Stay in Bosnia Indefinitely," *Washington Post* (Dec 19, 1997): A-1, 45: Jeffrey Ulbrich, "NATO Extends Mission; 34,000 troops will remain in Bosnia beyond June," *Peoria Journal Star* (Feb. 19, 1998): A-3; "House Shies Away from Conflict with Clinton Over War Powers, *CQ Weekly* 56 (Mar. 21, 1998): 760-61.

CHAPTER EIGHT

EPILOGUE

Presidents George Bush and William Clinton's dealings with Somalia, Haiti and Bosnia highlight many of the factors that continue to influence America's Post-Cold War policies. Neither president initially gave these three regions a high priority despite scandalous violations of human rights and widespread suffering among civilians.

Schooled in the politics of the Cold War that permitted U.S. leaders to blame "communists" for foreign policy problems, Bush and Clinton focused their attention on fostering international market economies, Germany unity and reform possibilities in Moscow and Beijing, while protecting the availability of oil from the Middle East. Although they each accepted a Pentagon strategy for reduced defense budgets that would preserve a capability of simultaneously fighting two small-scale Third World wars, neither Bush nor Clinton initially saw the civil conflicts in Somalia, Haiti and Bosnia as a priority concern. They both expected the United Nations, the European states, the Organization of African Unity or the Organization of American States to deal with problems in these "fringe" areas.

Unwilling to deal adequately with the human tragedies in Somalia, Haiti and Bosnia, Bush ultimately bequeathed these problems to Clinton. Not until Bush lost the 1992 election did he hastily prepare an inept effort in Somalia, leaving Clinton and the UN to deal with the militant factions that had been disrupting their country since January 1991. Likewise, Bush left Clinton to deal with the large numbers of Haitian refugees fleeing the military government that overthrew Haiti's democratically elected president in September 1991, and the Serb-Croat ethnic cleansing that began in 1991 and spread into Bosnia in 1992. Although during the campaign he had criticized Bush's handling of Haiti and Bosnia, Clinton initially chose to concentrate on domestic affairs and adopted Bush's foreign policies in these two nations.

In announcing the Somalian intervention, Bush claimed to have a "purely humanitarian" purpose but he failed to explain why U.S. military force was needed and how it could alleviate the UN's problems with the militant groups who prevented resolution of the conflict. The Clinton administration also failed to come to grips with the fundamental issues in Somalia before it threw up its hands and bailed out. In Haiti, the long-standing U.S. interest in promoting democracy in the Western Hemisphere did not persuade Bush to forcefully oppose military regime that overthrew Aristide and precipitated a new flow of Haitian refugees. Bush hoped the UN and OAS would resolve this problem and Clinton continued this policy until deciding in mid-1994 that a multinational military threat was necessary to restore democratic institutions and, hopefully, stop the refugees. Finally, in Bosnia Bush and Clinton delayed taking action for four years while believing that European nations and the European Union should take the lead in finding a solution to the Balkan problems. Not until the summer of 1995, when large-scale killings took place at Srebrenica, did Clinton agree to use U.S. and NATO air strikes and to take the diplomatic lead in obtaining the peace accords.

Although humanitarian problems were publicized in Somalia, Haiti and Bosnia, Bush and Clinton never responded as quickly as Bush had when Iraq invaded Kuwait in 1990 and threatened the U.S.'s oil supply. The two presidents never clearly identified U.S. national interests in the domestic turmoil of small countries and were reluctant to become the world's policeman. Neither president favored an isolationist attitude, but both were uncertain about what type of a new world order to seek and what role the U.S. should play as the remaining superpower.

Several observers have concluded that the American public seems ready to support collective action when their political leaders explain the circumstances requiring U.S. leadership. Yet neither Bush nor Clinton have proposed a set of guidelines that would enable policymakers and the public to determine when action should be taken to prevent or end domestic strife and human suffering in small countries. In all probability, the so-called "Vietnam syndrome" has caused these two presidents to hesitate in calling for military intervention in such civil conflicts. They undoubtedly fear that the sight of American casualties on TV could easily reverse initial public enthusiasm.[1]

NOTE

1. On such observers see: James Chace, "New World Disorder," *New York Review of Books* (Dec. 71, 1998: 58-63; John Mueller, "The Common Sense," *National Interest* No. 47 (Spring 1997): 81-88.

CHAPTER NINE

SELECTED BIBLIOGRAPHY

Note: For citations from the *New York Times* (NYT) and the *Washington Post National Weekly* (WPNW), see the chapter notes.

GENERAL–U.S. POST-COLD WAR POLICIES

Principally, these are theoretical studies that form a framewok for historical considerations.

Blacker, Coit D. "A Typology of Post-Cold War Conflicts," in Arnold Kanter, et.al. *U.S. Intevention Policy for the Post-Cold War World* (New York: Norton, 1994): 42-62.

Blackwell, Robert D. "A Taxonomy for Defining U.S. National Interests in the 1990's and Beyond," in Werner Weidenfeld and Josef Janning, eds. *Europe in Global Change* (Gutersloh, Germany: Bertlsmann Foundation, 1993): 100-119.

Chomsky, Noam. *World Orders, Old and New.* New York: Columbia University Press, 1994.

Cox, Michael. *US Foreign Policy after the Cold War: Superpower Without a Mission?* London: Pinter, 1995.

Damrosch, Lois Fisler, ed. *Enforcing Restraint: Collective Intervention in Internal Conflicts.* New York: Council on Foreign Relations, 1993.

Fukuyama, Francis. "The End of History." *National Interest* No.16 (Summer 1989): 3-18.

———. *The End of History and the Last Man.* New York: Free Press, 1992.

Haass, Richard. *Intervention: The Use of American Military Force in the Post Cold War World.* Washington, DC: Carneigie Endowment for International Peace, 1994.

Heiberg, Marianne, ed. *Subduing Sovereignty: Sovereignty and the Right to Intervene.* London: Pinter, 1994.

Hogan, Michael J. *The End of the Cold War: Its Meaning and Implications.* New York: Cambridge University Press, 1992.

Hoge, James, Richard K. Betts, Tony Smith and Andrew Kohut, and Robert Toth. 4 articles in "Springtime for Intervention." *Foreign Affairs* 73 (Nov./Dec. 1994): 20-61.

Huntington, Samuel P. "The Clash of Civilizations." *Foreign Affairs* 72 (Summer 1993): 22-49.

Ikenberry, G. John. "The Myth of Post-Cold War Chaos." *Foreign Affairs* 75 (May/June, 1996): 79-91.

Johnson, Robert H. *Improbable Dangers: U.S. Conceptions of Threat in the Cold War and After.* New York: St. Martin's, 1994.

Kaplan, Robert D. "The Coming Anarchy." *Atlantic Monthly* 273 (Feb. 1994): 44-76.

Kennedy, Paul. *Preparing for the Twenty-first Century.* New York: Random House, 1993.

Lund, Michael. *Preventive Diplomacy and American Foreign Policy.* Washington, DC: U.S. Institute for Peace, 1994.

Mansfield, Edward D. and Jack Snyder. "Democratization and the Danger of War." *International Security* 20 (Summer 1995): 5-38; and Reinhard Wolf, et.al. "Correspondence." Ibid. 20 (Spring 1996): 176-207.

Reed, Laura W. and Carl Kaysen, eds. *Emerging Norms of Justified Intervention.* Cambridge, MA: American Academy of Arts and Science, 1993.

Roberts, Brad, ed. *U.S. Security in an Uncertain Era.* Cambridge, MA: MIT Press, 1992.

Sassen, Saskia, *Losing Control: Sovereignty in an Age of Globalization.* New York: Columbia University Press, 1996.

Zakaria, Fareed. "A Framework for Interventionism in the Post-Cold War Era," in Arnold Kanter, et.al. eds. *U.S. Intervention Policy for the Post-Cold War World.* New York: Norton, 1994, pp. 177-194.

U.S. POST-COLD WAR POLICIES ADVOCATED

These works favor such policies as isolationism, strong U.S. unilaterialism or cooperative internationalism as well as realism or idealism.

Albright, Madeleine K. "Realism and Idealism in American Foreign Policy Today." *U.S. Department of State Dispatch* 5 (June 27, 1994): 434-437.

Anderson, Kurt. "The Watchword is Wariness: Weinberger Outlines Six Criteria for Sending Troops into Combat." *Time* 129 (Dec. 10, 1984): 13.

Bandow, Doug, "Keeping the Troops and the Money at Home." *Current History* 93 (Jan. 1994): 8-13.

Buchanan, Patrick. "America First, and Second and Third." *National Interest* No. 19 (Spring 1990): 77-82.

Callahan, David. *Between Two Worlds: Realism, Idealism and American Foreign Policy after the Cold War.* New York: Harper Collins, 1996.

Cohen, Eliot A. "Playing Powell Politics." *Foreign Affairs* 74 (Nov./Dec. 1995): 102-111. Review of Powell's *My American Journey.*

Draper, Theodore. "Mission Impossible." *New York Review of Books* 41 (Oct. 6, 1994): 31-34. Reviews Tony Smith's *America's Mission*

Farber, Henry S. and Joanne Gowa. "Politics and Peace." *International Security* 20 (Fall 1995): 123-146; and relationship of democracy to peace in Charles S. Gochman, "Correspondence." Ibid. 20 (Winter 1996/97): 177-187.

Harries, Owen. "Pat's World [Buchanan]." *National Interest* No. 43 (Spring 1996): 108-111.

Huntington, Samuel P. "Why International Primacy Matters." *International Security* 17 (Spring 1993): 68-83.

Jervis, Robert. "International Primacy: Is it Worth the Candle?" *International Security* 17 (Spring 1993): 52-67.

Kegley, Charles W., Jr., ed. *Controversies in International Relations Theory: Realism and the Neoliberal Challenge.* New York: St. Martin's Press, 1995.

Kissinger, Henry. *Diplomacy.* New York: Simon & Schuster, 1994.

Krauthammer, Charles. "The Unipolar Moment." *Foreign Affairs* 70 (Winter 1990-91): 23-33.

Layne, Christopher. "The Unipolar Illusion: Why New Great Powers Will Rise." *International Security* 17 (Spring 1993): 5-51.

Miller, Stephen E., ed. "Promises, Promises: Can Institutions Deliver." *International Security* 20 (Summer 1995): 39-92. Articles on realism and collective action by Robert O. Keohane and Lisa L. Martin; Charles A. and Clifford A. Kupchan; John G. Ruggie; Alexander Watt; and John J. Mearsheimer.

Muravchick, Joshua. *The Imperative of American Leadership: A Challenge to Neo-Isolationism.* Washington, DC: AEI Press, 1996.

Nordlinger, Eric A. *Isolationism Reconfirmed: American Foreign Policy for a New Century.* Princeton, NJ: Princeton University Press, 1995.

Nye, Joseph S., Jr. "What New World Order?" *Foreign Affairs* 71 (Spring 1992): 83-96.

———. "The Case for Deep Engagement." *Foreign Affairs* 74 (July 1995): 90-102.

Powell, Colin with Joseph Persico. *My American Journey.* New York: Random House, 1995.

———."U.S. Forces: Challenges Ahead." *Foreign Affairs* 71 (Winter 1992/93): 32-45.

Posen, Barry R. and Andrew L Ross. "Competing Visions for U.S. Grand Strategy." *International Security* 21 (Winter 1996/97): 5-53.

Ravenal, Earl. "The Case for Adjustment [to Isolation]." *Foreign Policy* No. 81 (Winter 1990-91): 3-19.

Ruggie, John G. "Third Try at World Order? America and Multilateralism after the Cold War." *Political Science Quarterly* 109 (Fall 1994): 553-570.

Smith, Tony. *America's Mission: The United States and the Worldwide Struggle for Democracy in the Twentieth Century.* Princeton, NJ: Princeton University Press, 1994.

Summers, Harry G. *The New World Strategy: A Military Policy for America's Future.* New York: Simon & Schuster,1995.

Talbott, Strobe. "Democracy and the National Interest." *Foreign Affairs* 75 (Nov./Dec.1996): 47-64.

ETHNIC AND HUMANITARIAN INTERVENTIONS.

Interventions in humanitarian and ethnic conflicts are estimated to be most likely in the Post-Cold War era. How should the U.S. react to these issues?

Brown, Michael, ed. *The International Dimensions of Internal Conflict.* Cambridge, MA: MIT Press, 1996. Essays indicating problems beyond popular jounalist's "ancient hatreds."

Caufield, Catherine. *Masters of Illusion: The World Bank and the Poverty of Nations.* New York: Holt, 1997.

Feinberg, Richard E. and Valeriana Kallab, eds. *Uncertain Futures: Commercial Banks and the Third World.* New Brunswick, NJ: Transaction Books, 1984.

Gurr, Ted Robert. "Peoples against States: Ethnopolitical Conflict and the Changing World System." *International Studies Quarterly* 38 (Sept. 1994): 347-377.

Halperin, Morton H., David J. Scheffer, and Patricia Small. *Self-Determination in the New World Order.* Washington, DC: Carnegie Endowment for International Peace, 1992.

Hoffman, Stanley. *Duties Beyond Borders: On the Limits and Possibilities of Ethical International Politics.* Syracuse, NY: Syracuse University Press, 1981.

Kapstein, Ethan B. "Workers and the World Economy." *Foreign Affairs* 75 (May/June 1996): 16-37.

Kaufmann, Chaim. "Possible and Impossible Solutions to Ethnic Civil Wars." *International Security* 20 (Spring 1996): 136-175.

Lake, David A. and Donald Rothchild. "Containing Fear: The Origins and Management of Ethnic Conflict." *International Security* 21 (Fall 1996): 41-75.

Lewy, Guenter. "The Case for Humanitarian Intervention." *Orbis* 37 (Fall 1993): 621-32.

Maynes, Charles W. "Containing Ethnic Conflict." *Foreign Policy* No. 90 (Spring 1993): 3-21.

Minear, Larry and Thomas G. Weiss. *Mercy under Fire: War and the Global Humanitarian Community.* Boulder, CO: Westview, 1995.

Mosley, Paul, Turan Subasat and John Weeks. "Assessing Adjustment in Africa." *World Development* 23 (Sept. 1995): 1459-1473. Politics or the economic system?

Orwin, Clifford. "A Distant Compassion." *National Interest* No. 43 (Spring 1996): 42-50. Opposes humanitarian intervention based on CNN pictures

Posen, Barry R. "Military Responses to Refugee Disasters." *International Security* 21 (Summer 1996): 72-111,

Weiner, Myron; Alan Dowty and Gil Loescher; and Barry Posen. three articles on "Refugees and Intervention." *International Security* 21 (Summer 1996): 5-111.

PUBLIC OPINION & POST-COLD WAR INTERNATIONALISM

The public perceptions that influenced intervention decisions.

Holsti, Ole R. *Public Opinion and American Foreign Policy.* Ann Arbor, MI: University of Michigan Press, 1997.

Kelleher, Catherine M. "Soldiering On: U.S. Public Opinion on the Use of Force." *Brookings Review* 12 (Spring 1994): 26-29. Chicago Foreign Relations Council data

Kull, Steven and I.M. Destler. *An Emerging Consensus: A Study of American Public Attitudes on America's Policy in the World.* College Park, MD: Center for International and Security Studies, Maryland University, July 10, 1996

Mueller, John. "The Common Sense." *National Interest* No. 47 (Spring 1997): 81-88.

Richman, Alvin. "The Polls: Poll Trends: American Support for International Involvement." *Public Opinion Quarterly* 57 (Summer 1993): 264-276; and same title 60 (Summer 1996): 305-321. Americans favor cooperation in world affairs and U.S. keeping troops in Europe but less support for global altruism by 1996

Sharkey, Jacqueline. "When Pictures Drive Foreign Policy." *American Journalism Review* 15 (Dec. 1993): 14-19. TV's affect on policy toward Somalia

Snyder, Jack and Karen Ballentine. "Nationalism and the Marketplace of Ideas." *International Security* 21 (Fall 1996): 5-40. Media conveys nationalistic ideas better than democratic ones

Yankelovich, Daniel. "Foreign Policy after the Election." *Foreign Affairs* 71 (Fall 1992): 1-12.

Yankelovich, Daniel and I.M. Destler. *Beyond the Beltway.* New York: Norton, 1994.

U.S. POLICY AND SOMALIA

Afrah, Mohamoud. *Target: Villa Somalis.* 2d ed. Karachi, Pakistan: Naseen. 1992. On Barre's overthrow in 1991

Bacevich, A.J. "Learning from Aideed." *Commentary* 96 (Dec. 1993): 30-33.

Blumenthal, Sidney. "Why Are We in Somalia?" *New Yorker* 69 (Oct. 25, 1993): 48-71.

Bolton, John R. "Wrong Turn in Somalia." *Foreign Affairs* 73 (Jan./Feb.1994): 56-66.

Carr, Caleb. "The Consequences of Somalia." *World Policy Journal* 10 (Fall, 1993): 1-4.

Church, George J. "Anatomy of a Disaster." *Time* 142 (Oct. 18, 1993): 40-50.

Church, George J. "Mission Half Accomplished." *Time* 141 (May 17, 1993): 42-4.

Clark, Jeffrey. "Debacle in Somalia." *Foreign Affairs* 72 (Jan. 1993): 109-123.

Clark, Jeffrey. "Debacle in Somalia: Failure of a Collective Response," in Lori Fisler Damrosch, ed. *Enforcing Restraint.* New York: Council on Foreign Relations, 1993, pp. 205-240.

Clarke, Walter and John Herbst. "Somalia and the Future of Humanitarian Intervention." *Foreign Affairs* 75 (Mar./Apr. 1996): 70-85.

Clough, Michael. *Free at Last: U.S. Policy toward Africa and the End of the Cold War.* New York: Council of Foreign Relations, 1992. Emphasizes aid, including Somalia, from 1962-1988.

Crocker, Chester A. "The Lessons of Somalia: Not Everything Went Wrong." *Foreign Affairs* 74 (May/June 1995): 2-7.

DeLong, Kent and Steven Tuckey. *Mogadishu: Heroism and Tragedy*. Westport, CT: Prager, 1994.

Deng, Francis M. and I. Willian Zartman, eds. *Conflict Resolution in Africa*. Washington, D.C.: Brookings Institution, 1991. Somalian issue in the context of African affairs.

Deng, Francis M. *Protecting the Dispossessed: A Challenge for the International Community*. Washington, DC: Brookings Institution, 1993.

DeWall, Alex. "The Shadow Economy." *Africa Report* 38 (Mar./Apr.1993): 24-28.

―――― and Rakiya Omaar. "Doing Harm by Doing Good? The International Relief Effort in Somalia." *Current History* 92 (May 1993): 198-202.

Drysdale, John. *Whatever Happened to Somalia*. London: Haan, 1994.

Glynn, Patrick. "Why Africa?" *New Republic* 207 (Dec. 28, 1992) 20-22.

Hansh, Steven, et.al. *Excess Morality and the Impact of Health Intervention in the Somalian Humanitarian Emergency*. Washington, DC: Refugee Policy Group, 1994.

Herbst, Jeffrey. "Responding to State Failure in Africa." *International Security* 12 (Winter 1996/97): 120-144. Success of northern Somalia state.

Hershberg, James G. "New East Bloc Evidence on the Horn of Africa, 1977-78." *Cold War International History Project Bulletin* No. 8/9 (Winter 1996-1997): 38-102.

Laitin, David and Said Samartar. *Somalia: A Nation in Search of a State*. Boulder, CO: Westview. 1987.

Lefebvre, Jeffrey A. *Arms for the Horn: U.S. Policy in Ethiopia and Somalia, 1953-91*. Pittsburgh, PA: University of Pittsburgh Press, 1993.

Lewis, I.M. *Blood and Bone: The Call of Kinship in Somalia Society*. Lawrenceville, NJ: Red Sea Press, 1994.

――――. *A Modern History of Somalia: Nation and State in the Horn of Africa*. Boulder, CO: Westview Press, 1988.

――――. *A Pastoral Democracy: A Study of Pastoralism and Politics Among the Northern Somali of the Horn of Africa*. New York: Africana Publishing Company for the International Institute, 1982.

――――. *Peoples of the Horn of Africa: Somali, Afar, and Saho*. London: International African Institute, 1969.

――――. *Somali Culture, History, and Social Institutions: An Introductory Guide to the Somali Democratic Republic*. London: London School of Economics and Political Science, 1981.

Lyons, Terrence and Ahmed Y. Samatar. *Somalia: State Collapse, Multilateral Intervention, and Strategies for Political Reconstruction*. Washington, DC: Brookings Institution, 1995.

Makinda, Samuel. *Seeking Peace from Chaos: Humanitarian Intervention in Somalia*. Boulder, CO: Lynne Reinner, 1993.

Menkus, Ken. "Somalia: Political Order in a Stateless Society." *Current History* 97 (May 1998): 220-224.

Morrow, Lance. "The Trouble with Good Intentions." *Time* 142 (Oct. 18, 1993): 36-40.

Nelan, Bruce W. "Taking on the Thugs." *Time* 140 (Dec. 14, 1992): 26-35.

Oakley, Robert B. and.Hirsch, John L. *Somalia and Operation Restore Hope: Reflections on Peacemaking and Peacekeeping*. Washington, DC: U.S. Institute of Peace, 1995.

Omaar, Rakiya. "The Last Chance for Peace." *Africa Report* 38 (May/June, 1993): 44-45.

Omar, Mohamed Osman. *The Road to Zero: Somalia's Self-Destruction* London: Haan, 1992. A Pakistani's account of January 1991.

Porter, Bruce D. *The U.S.S.R. in Third World Conflicts: Soviet Arms and Diplomacy in Local Wars, 1945-1980*. London: Cambridge University Press, 1984.

Richburg, Keith B. *Out of America A Black Man Confronts Africa*. New York: New Republic Book, 1997.

Rothchild, Donald and John Ravenhill. "Subordinating African Issues to Global Logic," in Kenneth Oye, et.al. *Eagle Resurgent? The Reagan Era in American Foreign Policy.* (Boston: Little, Brown, 1987): 343-429.

Sahnoun, Mohamed. *Somalia: The Missed Opportunities.* Washington, DC: U.S. Institute for Peace, 1994.

Samatar, Abdi. *The State and Rural Transformation in Northern Somalia, 1884-1986.* Madison: University of Wisconsin Press, 1989

Samatar, Ahmed I., ed. *The Somalia Challenge: From Catastrophe to Renewal?* Boulder, CO: Lynne Rienner, 1994.

Schraeder, Peter J., *United States Foreign Policy toward Africa: Incrementalism, Crisis and Change.* New York: Cambridge University Press, 1994.

Shoumatoff, Alex. "The 'Warlord' Speaks." *Nation* 258 (Apr. 4, 1994): 442-50.

Smolowe, Jill. "Great Expectations." *Time* 140 (Dec. 21,1992): 32-35.

Stevenson, Jonathan. "Hope Restored in Somalia?" *Foreign Policy* No. 91 (Summer 1993): 138-154.

———. *Losing Mogadishu: Testing U.S. Policy in Somalia.* Annapolis, MD: Naval Institute Press, 1995.

United Nations Blue Book Series. *The United Nations and Somalia, 1992-1996.* New York: UN Department of Public Information, 1996

U.S. State Department. "Intervention in Somalia." *Foreign Policy Bulletin* 3 (Jan./April, 1993): 18-29.

———. "Walk, Don't Run, to the Nearest Exit." *Foreign Policy Bulletin* 4 (Nov./Dec.1993): 19-27.

Young, Crawford, Lual Deng, and Markus Kostner, eds. *Democratization and Structural Adjustment in Africa in the 1990s.* Madison, WI.: University of Wisconsin, 1991.

U.S. POLICY AND HAITI

Abrams, Elliott. "Policing the Caribbean." *National Interest* No. 43 (Spring 1996): 86-92. Needs order more than democracy

———. "Policy Confronts Reality." *National Review* 44 (Mar.30, 1992): 38-39.

Acevedo, Domingo E. "The Haitian Crisis and the OAS Response," in Lori Fisler Damrosch, ed. *Enforcing Restraint.* New York: Council on Foreign Relations, 1993, pp. 119-156.

Aristide, Jean-Bertrand with Christophe Wargny. *Aristide: An Autobiography.* Trans. by Linda M. Maloney. New York: Orbis Books, 1993.

Aristide, Jean-Bertrand. *In the Parish of the Poor: Writing from Haiti.* Trans. by Amy Wilentz. New York: Orbis Books, 1993.

Bethell, Leslie, ed. *Latin America since 1930: Mexico, Central America, and the Caribbean.* New York: Cambridge University Press, 1990.

Bryan, Anthony T. "Haiti: Kick Starting the Economy." *Current History* 94 (Feb. 1995): 65-70.

Chomsky, Noam. "Democracy Restored? Intervention in Haiti, its Meaning and Prospects." *Z Magazine* 7 (Nov.1994): 49-61.

Congressional Quarterly Almanac, 1993. "Attempts Fail to Reinstate Haiti's Aristide." Washington, DC: Congressional Quarterly Publications, 1994, pp. 499-501.

———, 1994. "Clinton's Haiti Gamble Pays Off." Washington, DC: Congressional Quarterly Publications, 1995, pp. 449-451.

Constable, Pamela. "A Fresh Start for Haiti." *Current History* 95 (Feb. 1996): 65-69.

———. "Haiti: A Nation in Despair (includes Aristide interview)." *Current History* 93 (Mar. 1994): 108-114.

Cottam, Martha L. *Images and Interventions: U.S. Policies in Latin America.* Pittsburgh, PA: University of Pittsburgh Press, 1994.

Council of Freely Elected Heads of Government. "Mission to Haiti #2" (President Carter, Senator Nunn, General Powell). Atlanta, GA: The Carter Center of Emory University, March 1995.

Cox, Ronald W. *Power and Profits: U.S. Policy in Central America.* Lexington, KY: University Press of Kentucky, 1994.

Damrosch, Lori Fisler, et. al. "Agora: The 1994 U.S. Action in Haiti." *American Journal of International Law* 89 (Jan. 1995): 58-87.

Danner, Mark. "The Prophet [Aristide]." *New York Review of Books* 40 (Nov. 4, 1993): 25-30 and (Nov. 18, 1993): 27-36.

Dayan, Joan. *Haiti, History, and the Gods.* Berkeley, CA: University of California Press, 1995.

Drummond, Tammerlin. "A Constabulary of Thugs." *Time* (Feb. 17, 1997): 62-63; and "Letters" (Mar.10, 1997): 12-13.

Farmer, Paul. "On Suffering and Structural Violence (Haiti)." *Daedalus* 125 (Winter, 1996): 261-283.

———. *The Uses of Haiti.* Monroe, ME: Common Courage Press, 1994.

Fass, Simon M. *Political Economy in Haiti: The Drama of Survival.* New Brunswick, NJ: Transaction Books, 1988.

Ferguson, James. *Papa Doc, Baby Doc: Haiti and the Duvaliers.* Oxford: Basil Blackwell, 1987.

Fick, Carolyn E. *The Making of Haiti: The Saint Domingue Revolution from Below.* Knoxville: University of Tennessee Press, 1990.

Foster, Charles R. and Albert Valdman, eds. *Haiti—Today and Tomorrow: An Interdisciplinary Study.* Lanham, MD: University Press of America, 1984.

Grugel, Jean. *Politics and Development in the Caribbean Basin.* Bloomington, IN: Indiana University Press, 1995.

Heinl, Robert Debs and Nancy Gordon Heinl. *Written in Blood: The Story of the Haitian People, 1492-1971,* Boston: Houghton Mifflin, 1978.

Knoll, Erwin. "Patrick Bellgarde Smith, an Interview." *Progressive* 58 (Nov. 1994): 28-33. Critic of Aristide's deal with the U.S.

Latin America and Caribbean Region Program. "Assessment Mission in Haiti, Dec. 11-14, 1994." Atlanta, GA: The Carter Center of Emory University, Jan. 5, 1995.

Leonard, Thomas. *Central America and the United States: The Search for Stability.* Athens, GA: University of Georgia Press, 1991

Logan, Rayford Whittingham. *The Diplomatic Relations of the United States with Haiti, 1776-1891.* New York: Kraus Reprint, 1969.

Lustig, Nora, ed. *Coping with Austerity: Poverty and Inequality in Latin America.* Washington, DC: Brookings Institution, 1995.

Maingot, Anthony P. "Haiti: The Political Rot Within." *Current History* 94 (Feb. 1995): 59-64.

———. "Haiti and Aristide: The Legacy of History." *Current History* 91 (Feb. 1992): 65-69.

———. *The United States and the Caribbean.* Boulder, CO: Westview, 1994.

McCrocklin, James H. *Garde d'Haiti, 1915-1934: Twenty Years of Organization and Training by the United States Marine Corps.* Annapolis, MD: United States Naval Institute, 1956.

McFayden, Deidre, et.al. eds. *Haiti: Dangerous Crossroads.* Boston, MA: South End Press, 1995.

Metraux, Alfred. *Voodoo in Haiti.* Trans. by Hugo Charteris. New York: Schocken Books, 1972.

Mintz, Sidney W. "Can Haiti Change?" *Foreign Affairs* 74 (Jan./Feb. 1995): 73-86.

Morici, Peter. "The United States, World Trade, and the Helms-Burton Act." *Current History* 96 (Feb. 1997): 87-88.

Narin, Allan. "Haiti Under Cloak." *Nation* 262 (Feb. 26, 1996): 4-5.

———. "Haiti Under the Gun: How U.S.-Backed Paramilitaries Rule." *Nation* 262 (Jan. 8/15, 1996): 11-15.

———. "He's Our S.O.B." *Nation* 259 (Oct. 31, 1994): 481-482.

———. "Our Man in FRAPH." *Nation* 259 (Oct. 24, 1996): 458-61.

———. "The Eagle is Landing." *Nation* 259 (Oct. 3, 1994): 344-348.

Nicholls, David. *From Dessalines to Duvalier: Race, Color and National Independence in Haiti*, rev. ed., New Brunswick, NJ: 1996; (Cambridge University Press, 1979).

Pastor, Robert. "Elections for Parliament and Municipalities, June 23-26, 1995." Atlanta, GA: The Carter Center of Emory University, July 17, 1995.

Rotberg, Robert I., ed. *Haiti Renewed: Political and Economic Prospects*. Washington, DC: Brookings Institution, 1997.

———. and Christopher K. Clague. *Haiti: The Politics of Squalor*. Boston: Houghton Mifflin, 1971.

———. and John Sweeney two articles under "Debate: The Haitian Intervention." *Foreign Policy* No.102 (Spring 1996): 134-151.

Rubin, Elizabeth. "Haiti Takes Policing 101." *New York Times Magazine* (May 25, 1997): 42-45.

Schmidt, Hans. *The United States' Occupation of Haiti, 1915-1934*. New Brunswick, NJ: Rutgers University Press, 1971.

Sciolino, Elaine. "Monroe's Doctrine Takes Another Knock." NYT (Aug. 7, 1994): E-6.

Serie Livres Bleu des Nationes Unies, Vol XI. *Les Nations Unies et Haiti, 1990-1996*. New York: Departement de l'information Nationes Unies, 1996.

Shacochis, Bob. "The Immaculate Invasion. " *Harper's* 289 (Feb. 1995): 44-62. Day by day from Sept. 17 to Oct. 15, 1994

———. "Letter from Haiti." *Columbia Journalism Review* 34 (July/Aug. 1995): 26-28.

Smith, Gaddis. "Haiti: From Intervention to Intervasion [sic]." *Current History* 94 (Feb. 1995): 54-58.

———. *The Last Years of the Monroe Doctrine*. New York: Hill & Wang, 1994.

Smolowe, Jill. "Haiti: With Friends Like These." *Time* 142 (Nov. 8, 1993): 44-45.

Stotsky, Irwin. *Silencing the Guns in Haiti: The Promise of Deliberative Democracy*. Chicago: University of Chicago Press, 1997.

Trouillot, Michel-Rolph. *Silencing the Past: Power and the Production of History*. Boston: Beacon Press, 1995. Interpreting Haiti's history

U.S. Army War College. *Success in Peacekeeping: U.N. Mission in Haiti*. Carlisle Barracks, PA: Army Peackeeping Institute, 1996.

U.S. State Department. "Governor's Island Agreement to Restore Aristide." *Foreign Policy Bulletin* 4 (Sept./Oct. 1993): 68-70; and "National Emergency Continues." Ibid. (Nov./Dec. 1993): 81-83.

———. "Refugees to 3rd Countries; Groundwork for Invasion." *Foreign Policy Bulletin* 5 (Sept./Oct. 1994): 10-23.

Weller, Marc and Ana MacLean, eds. *The Haitian Crisis in International Law*. New York: Cambridge University Press, 1995.

Wilentz, Amy. *The Rainy Season: Journals from Haiti, 1986-1989*. New York: Simon & Schuster, 1989.

THE DISINTEGRATION OF YUGOSLAVIA

Works about the early history and eventual break-up of Yugoslavia between 1987 and 1992.

Ajami, Fouad. "In Europe's Shadows," in Nader Mousavizadeh, ed.*The Black Book of Bosnia*. New York: Basic Books, 1996, pp. 37-54. Reprinted from *The New Republic* (Nov. 21, 1994)

Akhavan, Payam, ed. *Yugoslavia, The Former and Future: Reflections by Scholars from the Region*. Washington DC: Brookings Institution, 1995.

Banac, Ivo. *The National Question in Yugoslavia: Origins, History, Politics*. Ithaca, NY: Cornell University Press, 1984.

―――. "The Fearful Asymmetry of War: the Causes of Yugoslavia's Demise." *Daedalus* 121 (Spring 1992): 141-174.

Below, Nora. *Tito's Flawed Legacy: Yugoslavia and the West, 1939-1984*. London: Gollancz, 1995.

Benderly, Jill and Evan Kraft. *Independent Slovenia: Origins, Movements, Propects*. New York: St. Martin's Press, 1991.

Bennett, Christopher. *Yugoslavia's Bloody Collapse: Causes, Course, and Consequences*. New York: New York University Press, 1995.

Bookman, Milica Zarkopvic. "The Economic Basis of Regional Autarchy in Yugoslavia." *Soviet Studies* 42 (Jan. 1990): 93-109.

Burg, Steven L. "Elite Conflict in Post-Tito Yugoslavia." *Soviet Studies* 38 (Apr. 1986): 170-193.

Bugajski, Janusz. *Nations in Turmoil: Conflict and Cooperation in Eastern Europe*. 2d ed. Boulder, CO: Westview Press, 1995.

Cohen, Lenard J. *Broken Bonds: Yugoslavia's Disintegration and Balkan Politics in Transition*. 2d ed. Boulder, CO: Westview Press, 1995.

Communication in Eastern Europe: The Role of History, Culture, and Media in Contemporary Conflicts. Mahwah, NJ: Lawrence Erlbaum, 1995.

Cseres, Tibor. *Titoist Atrocities in Vojvodina, 1944-1945: Serbian Vendetta in Bacska*. Buffalo, NY: Hunyadi, 1993.

Danforth, Loring M. *The Macedonian Conflict: Ethnic Nationalism in a Transnational World*. Princeton: Princeton University Press, 1996.

Dedijer, Vladimir. *The Yugoslav Auschwitz and the Vatican: The Croatian Massacre of the Serbs during World War II*. Buffalo, NY: Prometheus, 1992. Selected documents on the Croatian UTASHE, Trans. by Harvey L. Kindall

―――. *The Road to Sarajevo [1914]*. New York: Simon & Schuster, 1966.

Dijlas, Aleksa. *The Contested Country: Yugoslav Unity and the Communist Revolution, 1919-1953*. Cambridge, MA: Harvard University Press, 1996.

―――. "A Profile of Slobodan Milosevic." *Foreign Affairs* 72 (Summer 1993): 81-96.

Dimitrijevic, Vojin. "The 1974 Constitution and Constitutional Process as a Factor in the Collapse of Yugoslavia," in Payam Akhavan, ed., *Yugoslavia: The Former and the Future*. Washington, DC: Brookings, Institution, 1995, pp. 45-74.

Donia, Robert and John Fine, Jr. *Bosnia and Hercegovina: A Tradition Betrayed*. New York: Columbia University Press, 1994.

Dragnich, Alex N. *Serbs and Croats: The Struggle in Yugoslavia*. New York: Harcourt Brace Jovanovich, 1992.

Friedman, Francine. *The Bosnian Muslims: Denial of a Nation*. Boulder, CO: Westview, 1996.

Gow, James. *Legitimacy and the Military: The Yugoslav Crisis*. London: Pinter and New York: St. Martin's, 1992.

Hall, Brian. "Rebecca West's War." New Yorker 72 (Apr. 15, 1996): 74-83.

Harris, Paul. *Somebody Else's War: Frontline Reports from the Balkan Wars 1991-92.* Stevenage, England: Spa, 1992.

Heuser, Beatric., *Western Containment Policies in the Cold War: The Yugoslav Case, 1948-53.* London: Routledge, 1989.

Hoptner, J.B. *Yugoslavia in Crisis, 1934-1941.* New York: Columbia University Press, 1962.

Irvine, Jill A. *The Croat Question and the Formation of the Yugoslavian Socialist State.* Boulder, CO: Westview, 1993.

Judah, Tim. *The Serbs, History, Myth and the Destruction of Yugoslavia.* New Haven, CT: Yale University Press, 1997.

Kaplan, Robert D. "A Reader's Guide to the Balkans." *New York Times Book Review* (Apr. 18, 1993): 1, 30-32.

———. *Balkan Ghosts: A Journey Through History.* New York: St. Martin's Press, 1993.

Kerner, Robert J. "The Yugoslav Movement" and "Yugoslavia and the Peace Conference [of 1919]," in Robert J. Kerner, ed. *Yugoslavia.* Berkeley: University of California for United Nations Series, 1949, pp. 33-41, 92-106.

Karlovic, N.L. "Croatia and Its Future: Internal Colonialism or Independence?" *Journal of Croatian Studies* 22 (1981): 49-115.

Lampe, John R.; Russell O. Prickett; and Ljubisa S. Adamovic. *Yugoslav-America Economic Relations since World War II.* Durham, NC: Duke University Press, 1990.

Lampe, John R. *Yugoslavia as History,* New York: Cambridge University Press, 1996.

Lockwood, Ivo L. *Yugoslavia at the Paris Peace Conference: A Study in Frontier Making.* New Haven, CT: Yale University Press, 1963.

Lockwood, William G. *European Moslems: Economy and Ethnicity in Western Bosnia.* New York: Academic Press, 1975.

Lydall, Harold. *Yugoslavia in Crisis.* New York: Oxford University Press, 1989.

Magas, Branko. *The Destruction of Yugoslavia: Tracing the Break-up, 1980-1992.* London: Verso, 1993.

Malcolm, Noel. *Bosnia: A Short History.* London: Macmillan and New York: New York University Press, 1994.

———. "Seeing Ghosts." National Interest No. 32 (Summer 1993): 83-88. Reviews Kaplan's *Balkan Ghosts.*

Mastnak, Tomaz. "Civil Society in Slovenia: From Opposition to Power," *Studies in Comparative Communism* 23 (Autumn 1991): 305-317.

Norris, H.T. *Islam in the Balkans.* Columbia: University of South Carolina Press, 1994.

Pavlowitch, Stevan K. *Tito: Yugoslavia's Great Dictator: A Reassessment.* London: C. Hurst, 1992.

Peirovich, Ruza. "The National Composition of Yugoslavia's Population." *Yugoslav Survey* 33:1 (1992): 3-24.

Pinson, Mark, ed. *The Muslims of Bosnia-Herzegovina: Their Historic Development from the Middle Ages to the Dissolution of Yugoslavia.* Cambridge, MA: Harvard University Press, 1993.

Poulton, Hugh. *Who Are the Macedonians?* Bloomington: Indiana University Press, 1994.

Ramet, Sabrina P. *Balkan Babel: The Disintegration of Yugoslavia from the Death of Tito to Ethnic War.* Boulder, CO: Westview, 1996.

———. *Nationalism and Federalism in Yugoslavia, 1962-1991.* 2d ed. Bloomington: Indiana University Press, 1992.

———, ed. *Yugoslavia in the 1980's.* Boulder, CO: Westview, 1985.

Rubinstein, Alvin Z. *Yugoslavia and the Nonaligned World.* Princeton, NJ: Princeton University Press, 1970.

Schmitt, Bernadotte E. *The Annexation of Bosnia, 1908-1909.* New York: H. Fertig, 1970.

Schopflin, George. *Politics in Eastern Europe, 1945-1992.* Cambridge, MA: Blackwell, 1993.

Serbian Academy of Arts and Sciences. "1986 Memorandum of the Serbian Academy of Sciences (SANU)", trans. by Denison Rusinov, in Peter H. Sugar, ed. *East European Nationalism in the Twentieth Century.* Washington, DC: American University Press, 1995, pp. 275-280.

Silber, Laura and Allan Little. *Yugoslavia: Death of a Nation.* New York: Penguin, TV Books, 1996. Published for BBC Documentary: "Yugoslavia: Death of a Nation"

Singleton, Frederick B. *A Short History of the Yugoslav Peoples.* New York: Cambridge University Press, 1985.

Tanner, Marcus. *Croatia, A Nation Forged in War.* New Haven, CT: Yale University Press, 1997.

Tritle, Lawrence A., ed. *Balkan Currents: Studies in the History, Culture and Society of a Divided Land.* Los Angeles: Loyola Marymount University, 1998.

Vasic, Milos. "The Federal Army and the Agony of Change," in Anthony Borden, et.al., eds. *Breakdown: War and Reconstruction in Yugoslavia.* London: Institute for War and Peace Reporting, 1992.

Vucinich, Wayne S. *Serbia Between East and West: The Events of 1903-1908.* New York: AMS Press, 1968.

West, Richard. *Tito and the Rise and Fall of Yugoslavia.* New York: Carroll & Graf, 1995.

Woodward, Susan L. *Balkan Tragedy: Chaos and Dissolution after the Cold War.* Washington, DC: Brookings Institution, 1995.

———. *Socialist Unemployment: The Political Economy of Yugoslavia, 1945-1990.* Princeton, NJ: Princeton University Press, 1995.

Zivojinovic, Dragan R. *America, Italy and the Birth of Yugoslavia: 1917-1919.* New York: Columbia University Press, 1972.

Zupanov, Josip; Dusko Sckulic; and Zeljka Sporer. "A Breakdown of the Civil Order: The Balkan Bloodbath." *International Journal of Politics, Culture and Society* 9:3 (1996): 401-420.

U.S. POLICY AND RELATIONS WITH EUROPE

The studies by Susan Woodward and Lenard Cohen, above, are especially useful on U.S., EU and UN policies until early 1994 and should be used in addition to those listed in the sections on U.S. policy in the Balkans.

Arnold, Hans. "Maastrict; The Beginning or End of a New Development?" *Aussen Politik* 44:3 (1993): 271-280.

Center for Defense Information. "What Next for NATO?" *Defense Monitor* 24:2 (1995): entire issue.

Feldstein, Martin. "Why Maastricht will Fail." *National Interest* No. 32 (Summer 1993): 12-19.

Freedman, Lawrence, ed. *Military Intervention in European Conflicts.* London: Blackwell, 1994.

Fuller, Graham E. and Ian O. Lesser. *Turkey's New Geopolitics: From the Balkans to Western China.* Boulder, CO: Westview, 1992.

Gow, James. *Triumph of the Lack of Will: International Diplomacy during the Yugoslav War.* New York: Columbia University Press, 1997.

Holbrooke, Richard. "America: A European Power." *Foreign Affairs* 74 (Mar./Apr. 1995): 38-51.

Hoppe, Hans-Joachim. "Moscow and the Conflict with Yugoslavia." *Assen Politik* 48:3 (1997): 267-277.

Howorth, Jolyon. "The Debate in France over Military Intervention in Europe." *Political Quarterly* 65 (Jan./Mar. 1994): 106-124.

Joffe, Josef. "The New Europe: Yesterday's Ghosts." *Foreign Affairs* 72 (Winter 1992/1993): 29-43.

Koslowski, Gerd. "Bosnia: Failure of the Institutions and of the Balance of Power in Europe." *Aussen Politik* 47:4 (1996): 359-367.

Lucas, Michael R. "The OSCE Code of Conduct and its Relevance in Contemporary Europe." *Aussen Politik* 47:3 (1996): 223-235.

Malcolm, Noel. "The Case Against 'Europe'." *Foreign Affairs* 74 (Mar./Apr. 1995): 52-69. British scholar's viewpoint

Mandlebaum, Michael. *The Dawn of Peace in Europe.* New York: 20th Century Fund Press, 1996.

Moisi, Dominique. "Chirac of France." *Foreign Affairs* 74 (Nov./Dec. 1995): 8-13.

Noetzold, Juergen. "The Eastern Part of Europe: Peripheral or Essential Component of Eurpean Integration?" *Aussen Politik* 44: 2 (1993): 326-334.

Reynolds, David, ed. *The Origins of the Cold War in Europe: International Perspectives.* New Haven: Yale University Press, 1994.

Rudolf, Peter. "The Strategic Debate in the United States: Implications for the American Role in Europe." *Aussen Politik* 44:2 (1993): 111-120.

Sharp, Jane M.O. "Dayton Report Card." *International Security* 22 (Winter 1997/98): 101-137.

Sobell, Vlad. "NATO, Russia and the Yugoslav War." *World Today* 51 (Nov. 1995): 210-215.

United Nations Blue Book Series. United Nations and the Former Yugoslavia. 3 vols. New York: UN Department of Public Information, 1998.

Van Evera, Stephen. "Why Europe Matters, Why the Third World Doesn't: American Grand Strategy after the Cold War." *Journal of Strategic Studies* 13 (June 1990): 1-51.

Weidenfeld, Werner and Josef Janning, eds. *Europe in Global Change.* Gurtersloh, Germany: Bertelsmann Stiftung Publications, 1993.

Zelikow, Philip and Condoleeza Rice. *Germany Unified and Europe Transformed: A Study in Statecraft.* Cambridge, MA: Harvard University Press, 1995.

U.S. POLICY AND THE BALKANS

Citations include materials on U.S. policy and developments in the Balkans from 1992 through 1996. Also see Powell, Cohen and Woodward.

Ajami, Fouad. "The Mark of Bosnia: Boutros-Ghali's Reign of Influence." *Foreign Affairs* 75 (May/June 1996): 162-164.

Ash, Timothy Garton. "Bosnia in Our Future." *New York Review of Books* 42 (Dec. 12, 1995): 27-31.

———. "In the Serbian Soup." *New York Review of Books* 44 (Apr. 14, 1997): 25-30.

Baker, James A., III. *The Politics of Diplomacy.* New York: Putnam's, 1996.

Best, Wayne. *The Reluctant Superpower.* New York: St. Martin's, 1997.

Block, Robert. "The Madness of General Mladic." *New York Review of Books* 42 (Oct. 5, 1995): 7-9.

Borden, Anthony, et.al. "Bosnia's Democratic Charade." *Nation* 259 (Sept. 23, 1996): 14-20.

Boyd, Charles G. "Making Peace with the Guilty." *Foreign Affairs* 74 (Sept./Oct. 1995): 22-38. Should let Russia and Europeans deal with the Balkans. For responses to Boyd see Ibid. (Nov./Dec. 1995): 148-155.

Calic, Marie-Janine, "Bosnia-Hercegovinia after Dayton: Opportunities and Risks for Peace." *Aussen Politik* 47:2 (1996): 127-135.

Carpenter, Ted and Amos Perlmutter. "Strategy Creep in the Balkans." *National Interest* No. 44 (Summer 1996): 53-59. Unwise U.S. commitment to the Balkans

Church, George. "Pity the Peacemakers." *Time* 45 (June 5, 1995): 38-40.

Cohen, Roger. "Taming the Bullies of Bosnia [On Holbrooke]." *New York Times Magazine* (Dec. 17, 1995): 58-63.

Danner, Mark. "The U.S. and the Yugoslavia Catastrophy." Series of articles in *New York Review of Books* (Nov. 20, 1997): 56-64; (Dec. 4, 1997): 5-65; (Feb. 5, 1998): 34-41; (Feb. 19, 1998): 41-45; (Mar. 26, 1998): 40-52; (Apr. 23, 1998): 59-65; (Sept. 24, 1998): 63-77; (Oct. 22, 1998): 73-79.

Feinberg, Richard E. "American Power and Third World Economics," in Kenneth A. Oye, et.al., eds. *Eagle Resurgent? The Reagan Era in American Foreign Policy.* Boston: Little Brown, 1987, pp. 145-166.

Gagnon, V.P., Jr. "Ethnic Nationalism and International Conflict: The Case of Serbia." *International Security* 19 (Winter 1994/95): 130-166.

Garthoff, Raymond. *The Great Transition: American-Soviet Relations and the End of the Cold War.* Washington, DC: Brookings Institution, 1994.

Glenny, Misha. "Heading Off the War in the Southern Balkans." *Foreign Affairs* 74 (May 1995): 98-108.

Gompert, David. "How to Defeat Serbia." *Foreign Affairs* 73 (July/Aug. 1994): 30-47.

Gutman, Roy. *A Witness to Genocide.* New York: Macmillan, 1993.

Hendrickson, David C. "The Recovery of Internationalism [Clinton]." *Foreign Affairs* 73 (Sept./Oct. 1994): 26-44.

Holbrooke, Richard. "Backsliding in Bosnia." *Time* 47 (May 20, 1996): 38.

————. "On Bosnia." *Foreign Affairs* 76 (Mar./Apr. 1997): 170-172. Response to Radha Kumar, see below.

————. "The Road to Sarajevo." *New Yorker* 72 (Oct. 21, 1996): 88-104. Negotiating in 1995.

————. *To End a War.* New York: Random House, 1998.

"House Shies Away from Conflict with Clinton over War Powers: Representative (Tom) Campbell's Effort to Make Test Case of Bosnia...." *Congressional Quarterly Weekly* 56 (Mar. 21, 1998): 760-761.

Human Rights Watch/ Helsinki Report. "The Fall of Srebrenica and the Future of UN Peacekeeping." 7 (Oct. 13, 1995): entire.

Ignatieff, Michael. "The Missed Chance in Bosnia." *New York Review of Books* 43 (Feb. 29, 1996): 8-10.

Kearns, Ian. "Croatian Politics: The New Authoritarianism." *Political Quarterly* 67 (Jan./Mar. 1996): 26-35.

Kenny, George. "No Exit in Bosnia." *Nation* 263 (Dec.9, 1996): 4-5.

Kumar, Radha. "The Troubled History of Partition." *Foreign Affairs* 76 (Jan./Feb. 1997): 22-34. See Holbrook, above.

Lane, Charles and Thomas Shanker. "What the CIA Didn't Tell Us." *New York Review of Books* 43 (May 9, 1996): 10-15.

McAllister, J.F.O. "Pity the Peacemakers." *Time* 141 (June 26, 1993): 46-48.

McConnell, Malcolm. "When NATO Went to War." *Reader's Digest* 148 (Sept. 1996): 91-96.

Mandlebaum, Michael. "The Bush Foreign Policy." *Foreign Affairs* 70 (Winter 1990-91): 5-22.

————. "The Reluctance to Intervene." *Foreign Policy* No.95 (Summer 1994): 3-18.

Mervin, David. *George Bush and the Guardianship Presidency.* New York: St. Martin's, 1996.

Mousavizadeh, Nader ed. *The Black Book of Appeasement.* New York: Basic Books, 1996. Articles from the *New Republic*

Neier, Aryeh. "Impasse in Kosovo." *New York Review of Books* (Sept. 25, 1997): 51-53.

Newhouse, John. "Dodging the Problem." *New Yorker* 68 (Aug. 24, 1992): 60-71.

O'Grady, Scott and Jeff Coplon. *Return With Honor.* New York: Doubleday, 1995. On being shot down in Bosnia.

Owen, David. *Balkan Odyssey.* New York: Harcourt Brace, 1995.

———. "The Future of the Balkans: An Interview with David Owens." *Foreign Affairs* 72 (Spring 1993): 1-9.

Rieff, David. *Slaughterhouse: Bosnia and the Failure of the West.* New York: Simon & Schuster, 1995.

Rohde, David. *Endgame: the Betrayal and Fall of Srebrenica.* New York: Farrar, Straus & Garoux, 1997.

Sadowski, Yaha. "Bosnia's Muslims: A Fundamentalist Threat?" *Brookings Review* 13 (Winter 1995): 10-15. There is no threat.

Schild, Georg. "The USA and Civil War in Bosnia." *Aussen Politik* 47:1 (1998): 22-32.

Smolowe, Jill; James Graff; and George Church. three articles under "Land of Slaughter." *Time* (June 8, 1992): 32-39.

Tindemans, Leo, et.al. *Unfinished Peace: Report of the   International Commission on the Balkans.* Washington, DC: Carniegie Endowment for International Peace, 1996.

Tucker, Robert W. and David Hendrickson. "America and Bosnia," *National Interest* No. 33 (Fall 1993): 14-27.

Unal, Hasan. "Trop de Zele." *National Interest* No. 43 (Spring 1996): 93-96. Turkish critic reviews David Owens' book.

Weller, Mark. "The International Response to the Dissolution of Yugoslavia." *American Journal of International Law* 86 (July 1992): 569-606.

Werner, Roy A. "The Burden of Global Defense," in William Snyder and James Brown. *Defense Policy in the Reagan Administration.* Washington, DC: National Defense University, 1988, pp. 143-168.

Woodward, Susan. "Bosnia After Dayton." *Current History* 96 (Mar.1997): 97-103.

Zimmermann, Warren. "The Choice in the Balkans." *New York Review of Books* 42 (Sept. 21, 1995): 4-7.

———. "The Demons of Kosovo." The National Interest No.52 (Summer 1998): 3-11.

———. "Last Chance for Bosnia." *New York Review of Books* 44 (Dec. 19, 1996): 10-13.

———. *Origins of a Catastrophe.* New York: Random House/Times, 1996.

BALKAN ATROCITIES, REFUGEES AND WAR CRIMES

Aldrich, George. "Jurisdiction on the International Crimes Tribunal for the Former Yugoslavia. " *American Journal of International Law* (AJIL) 90 (Jan. 1996): 64-68.

Allen, Beverly. *Rape Warfare: The Hidden Genocide in Bosnia-Herzgovinia and Croatia.* Minneapolis, MN: University of Minnesota, 1996.

Clark, Roger and Madeleine Sann, eds. *The Prosecution of International Crimes: A Critical Study of the International Tribunal for the Former Yugoslavia.* New Brunswick, NJ: Transaction Publications, Rutgers Univesity 1996. Essays from a special issue of *Criminal Law Journal: An International Journal.*

Cohen, Roger. *Hearts Grown Brutal, Sagas of Sarajevo.* New York: Random House, 1998.

Danner, Mark. "The Killing Fields." *New York Review of Books* (Sept. 24, 1998): 63-77.

Filipovic, Zlata. *Zlata's Diary: A Child's Life in Sarajevo.* New York: Viking, 1994.

Gjelten, Tom. *Sarajevo Daily: A City and Its Newspaper under Siege.* New York: Harper Perennial, 1993

Harris, Paul. *Cry Bosnia.* Northampton, MA: Interlink, 1996.

Honig, Jan Willem and Norbert Both. *Srebrenica: Record of a War Crime* New York: Penguin, 1997. The role of the Dutch as UNPROFOR troops at Srebrenica.

Hukanovic, Rezak. *The Tenth Circle of Hell: A Memoir of Life in the Death Camps on Bosnia.* Trans. by Colleen. New York: Basic Books/New Republic, 1996.

Human Rights Watch/Helsinki. *A Threat to Stability: Human Rights Violations in Macedonia.* New York: Human Rights Watch, June 1996.

———. "Cease-Fire and Peace Negotiations," (Feb. 1996); "Human Rights Violations in Bosnia-Hercegovina Post Dayton," (Mar. 1996); and "A Failure in the Making: Human Rights and the Dayton Agreement," (June 1996) reports from Human Rights Watch/New York.

Labon, Joanna, ed. *Balkan Blues: Writing out of Yugoslavia.* Evanston, IL: Northwestern University Press, 1996.

Lesic, Zdenko, ed. *Children of Atlantis: Voices from the Former Yugoslavia.* New York: Oxford University Press, 1996.

Licklider, Roy, ed. *Stopping the Killing.* New York: New York University Press, 1993.

Maass, Peter. *Love Thy Neighbor: A Story of War.* New York: Knopf, 1996.

Meron, Theodor. "The Case for War Crime Trials in Yugoslavia." *Foreign Affairs* 72 (Summer 1993): 122-135.

———. "Rape as a Crime under International Law." *American Journal of International Law* 87 (July 1993): 424-428.

———. "War Crimes in Yugoslavia and the Development of International Law." *American Journal of International Law* 88 (Jan. 1994): 78-87.

Monroe, Leigh. "The Yugoslav Tribunal's Use of Unnamed Witnesses Against Accused." *American Journal of International Law* 90 (Apr. 1996): 235-237.

Mertus, Julia, et.al. eds. *The Suitcase: Refugee Voices from Bosnia and Croatia.* Berkeley: University of California Press, 1997.

Neier, Aryeh. Brutality, *Genocide, Terror and the Struggle for Justice.* New York: Times Books, 1998.

O'Brien, James C. "The International Tribunal for Violations of Humanitarian Law in the Former Yugoslavia." *American Journal of International Law* 87 (Oct. 1993): 639-58.

Sells, Michael S. *The Bridge Betrayed: Religion and Genocide in Bosnia.* Berkeley: University of California Press, 1996.

Stiglmayer, Alexandra, ed. *Mass Rape: The War Against Women in Bosnia-Herzegovina.* Trans. by Marion Faber. Lincoln: University of Nebraska Press, 1994.

Sudetic, Chuck. *Blood and Vengeance: One Family's Story of the War in Bosnia.* New York: W.W. Norton, 1998. A personalized perspective on the fall of Srebrenica

Walsh, James. "Unearthing Evil." *Time* 47 (Jan. 22, 1996): 46-47.

Williams, Donald E. "Probing Cultural Implications of War-Related Victimization in Bosnia-Herzegovina, Croatia and Serbia," in Casmir, Fred L., ed. *Communication in Eastern Europe; The Role of History, Culture, and Media in Contemporary Conflict.* Mahwah, NJ: Lawrence Erlbaum, 1995.

THE UNITED NATIONS ROLE IN INTERVENTIONS

Bennis, Phyllis. *Calling the Shots: How Washington Dominates Today's U.N.* New York: Olive Branch Press, 1996.

Boutros-Ghali, Boutros. *An Agenda For Development, 1995.* New York: United Nations, 1995.

———. "Empowering the United Nations." *Foreign Affairs* 71 (Winter 1992/93): 89-102.

———. "Global Leadership after the Cold War." *Foreign Affairs* 75 (Mar./April 1996): 86-98.

Cohen, Ben and George Stankowski, eds. *With No Peace to Keep.* London: Grainpress, 1996.

Helms, Jesse. "Fixing the U.N." *Foreign Affairs* 75 (Sept./Oct. 1996): 2-7.

Hume, Cameron R. *The United Nations, Iran and Iraq: How Peacekeeping Changed.* Bloomington: Indiana University Press, 1994.

Lefever, Ernst W. "Reining in the U.N." *Foreign Affairs* 72 (Summer 1993): 17-21.

Mayall, James ed. *The New Interventionism: United Nations Experience in Cambodia, Former Yugoslavia and Somalia.* New York: Cambridge University Press, 1996.

Picco, Giandomenico. "The U.N. and the Use of Force." *Foreign Affairs* 73 (Sept./Oct. 1994): 14-18.

Righter, Rosemary. *Utopia Lost: The United Nations and World Order.* New York: 20th Century Fund Press, 1995.

Roberts, Adam. Marrach Goulding and Rosalyn Higgins. 3 articles under "Humanitarian War: The New U.N. and Peacekeeping." *International Affairs* 69 (July 1993): 429-84.

Shawcross, William."Tragedy in Cambodia." *New York Review of Books* 44 (Nov. 14, 1996): 41-49.

Touval, Saadia. "Why the U.N. Fails." *Foreign Affairs* 73 (Sept./Oct. 1994): 44-57.

Urquhart, Brian, "Who Can Police the World?" *New York Review of Books* 39 (May 12, 1994): 29- 33.

VanAtta, Dale. "The United Nations is Out of Control." *Reader's Digest* (Nov. 1995): 149-154.

REFERENCE WORKS ON SOMALIA, HAITI, YUGOSLAVIA

Carter, April. *Marshal Tito: A Bibliography.* Westport, CT: Meckler, 1990.

Chambers, Frances, ed. *Haiti: A Bibliography,* rev. ed. Santa Barbara, CA: ABC/Clio, 1994.

Delancy, Mark W., et.el. *Somalia: Bibliography.* Santa Barbara, CA: ABC-Clio, 1988.

Friedman, Francine, ed. *Yugoslavia: A Comprehensive English- Language Bibliography.* Wilmington, DE: Scholarly Resources, 1993.

Lawless, Robert, ed. *Haiti: A Research Handbook.* New York: Garland, 1990.

Marcus, Harold. *The Modern History of Ethiopia and the Horn of Africa: A Select and Annotated Bibliography.* Stanford, CA.: Hoover Institution Press, 1972.

Matulic, Rusko, ed. *Bibliography of Sources on Yugoslavia.* Palo Alto, CA: Ragousa Press, 1981.

Pratt, Frantz, ed. *Haiti: A Guide to the Periodical Literature in English, 1800-1990.* Westport, CT: Greenwood, 1991.

Statterts, Robert and Jeannine Laurens, eds. *Historical Dictionary of the Republic of Croatia.* Metuchen, NJ: Scarecrow, 1995.

INDEX